DATE DUE

MY 07 '02			
GAYLORD			PRINTED IN U.S.A.

BORN TO BATTLE

Born to Battle

THE SALVATION ARMY IN AMERICA

by
Sallie Chesham

RAND McNALLY & COMPANY
Chicago · New York · San Francisco

267.1

TO THE
UNNAMED

FOREWORD

FOUNDED A CENTURY AGO this year, The Salvation Army has symbolized around the world a deeply religious concern for the welfare of the human individual, whatever his race or creed or position in society.

The worth of the individual, made in the image of God and divine in his destiny, has everywhere been for its members a fundamental fact of life. In their commitment to it, they have become a world resource for the relief of the distressed and afflicted, for neighborly help to all in need.

Among Americans, The Salvation Army has long been a symbol of whole-hearted dedication to the cause of human brotherhood. In time of war, the men and women of this organization have brought to those serving their country far from home friendliness and warm concern. In the quieter days of peace, their work has been a constant reminder to us all that each of us is neighbor and kin to all Americans. Giving freely of themselves, the men and women of The Salvation Army have won the respect of us all.

To every American, I commend the reading of the History of The Salvation Army of the United States—a record of sacrifice by individuals for their fellowmen that should inspire all of us to a like faith in humanity and in God.

DWIGHT D. EISENHOWER
Gettysburg, Pennsylvania

April 6, 1965

PREFACE

ALTHOUGH 1965 is the centennial year of the international Salvation Army, BORN TO BATTLE is chiefly concerned with the beginning of The Army in the United States in 1879, and with tracing its growth against the background of secular history. Incidents and personalities from other countries do have importance in this story, but are treated largely as a backdrop for The Salvation Army in America.

Most people today are aware of The Salvation Army. Fewer, perhaps, are familiar with its beliefs, objectives, or the extent of its services. As an international religious and charitable movement organized on a semi-military pattern, The Army is unique. The motivation for this organization, as with all churches, is love for God and a practical concern for the needs of humanity, expressed by a spiritual ministry. But no other church seeks the particular outreach The Army does, judging every member a fighting soldier; no other church has such a variety of bastions, from homes for unmarried mothers to mobile canteens. The Army has been called a "church-plus," a "religious organization with a social aim and a social organization with a religious aim," and "a force for God," but possibly the "militant arm of the Christian Church" fits best.

From the first day of his evangelistic ministry, founder

9

William Booth was consumed by social concern. "You can't preach to a man on an empty stomach," he explained, and proceeded to open the first Army shelter home. As he observed the squalor of living conditions in London, the brutal treatment of children, and the growth of white slavery, programs and solutions evolved. Nevertheless, from the very first, he made this point: "Our primary responsibility is not to take man out of the slums, but to take the slums out of man." The Army has built on that premise for 100 years.

"No other man is General of an army of people that circles the globe," stated the *Chicago Interocean* of William Booth in 1903. "No other man is called commander by men and women of so many nationalities." This applies even more today, for The Army serves in 69 countries, and is heard in 162 languages and dialects. It has 16,767 corps and outposts, 25,418 officers and 117,227 local officers or lay leaders. It operates 490 homes for the homeless, 205 men's work centers, 29 general hospitals, 12 convalescent hospitals, 86 maternity homes for unwed mothers, 6 leprosaria, 72 dispensaries and clinics, 13 probation and training homes, and 121 fresh air camps. (1963 International Statistics.)

Additionally, it supplies leadership education, bible and music training to thousands of young people and adults, and operates children's homes, community centers, boys' and girls' clubs, golden-age centers, correctional services, and employment bureaus. Its family service departments supply both emergency and long-term aid, its members and friends visit various institutions regularly, operate emergency and disaster service mobile canteens and hospitality centers for service personnel.

William Booth never wanted nominal members. He wanted active soldiers. The Salvationist is a combatant against sin, deprivation, sorrow, and illness. He feels compelled by God to live for others. He declares his belief that The Army was raised up by God and is sustained by him, and he affirms his acceptance of Army rules and regulations and Army tenets of doctrine.

Who joins The Army? Salvationists are drawn from all walks of life. Contrary to belief by some, Army leadership, for the most part does not, nor ever did, come from the ranks of derelicts. Usually, the man who has reached bottom and has been reclaimed, returns to the church home of his family. More than 50 per cent of present-day American Salvationists are second and third generation Salvationists, and during the past 10 years 51 per cent of enlistees for officership were children of Salvationists. Most other soldiers are attracted to The Army in their youth through various Army programs or through friendship with Army personnel.

Recruits become soldiers (members) after a six-month period of probationary training. Lay soldiers are expected to participate in as many regular corps activities as strength and time will allow and they may also be appointed to certain local officer (lay-leadership) positions.

Candidates for full-time officership must be between the ages of 18 and 35, except under very unusual circumstances. The most important prerequisite for officership is the applicant's confidence that he is led by God. Viewing officership as a job means eventual tragedy both for him and for The Army. Army leaders say, "With the latter attitude a young person would find the sacrifices too great, the rewards too few."

If a candidate is accepted, he must first complete a six-month course of general study before entering as a cadet, one of four Schools for Officers' Training. These schools are not bible schools or accredited colleges. The two-year course offered is designed to give students intensive training to meet the spiritual and physical needs of the people they will serve. After being commissioned as an officer, the cadet must complete a five year plan of advanced studies. The Army also gives assistance to many officers for further study in specialized fields.

The Salvationist finds his church home in the local Army Corps, and a commissioned officer is legally accepted as an ordained minister. Thus, both men and women officers are qualified to officiate at marriages and funerals and to perform all other ministerial duties.

Both soldiers and officers wear uniforms, although for the former it is not compulsory except in certain positions of responsibility. The uniform has often been criticized. William Booth said of it: "The uniform has been objected to very frequently as savoring of formalism and the like. Its one object is to combine simplicity of dress with the testimony of separation from the world."

Internationally, the annual attrition rate of officers is between two and three per cent. Both officers and soldiers may be disciplined or removed from the ranks for unacceptable conduct by a court of inquiry in some cases and by a court martial in others, but annually, only a fraction of one per cent are asked to resign for such reasons.

A complete record of the dramatic, strife-ridden history of The Salvation Army would require a shelf of books. BORN TO BATTLE regrettably mentions but a few Army warriors, and regrettably fewer of the thousands of friends who, as "civilian soldiers," fought and still are fighting in response to the challenges and battles of our day.

Salvation Army leaders gave the author free access to all Army literature, including books, periodicals, pamphlets, and unpublished records of every kind, much of which quotes and requotes original sources, which (for early history) are the Booths. Secular books written about The Army were perused but supplied little material hitherto unrecorded, with the exception of St. John Irvine's *God's Soldier*. Where critical analysis or personal opinion has been quoted, credit is given in the book.

Special credit is due many officers, soldiers, and friends,

particularly retired Salvation Army officers and veterans of the United States armed forces, who gave valuable assistance; also Howy, David, Julie, and Petti, loyal soldiers in the struggle for facts; and Mr. Roy Porter, Miss Cynthia Smith, and Mrs. Shirley Warren of Rand McNally and Company. Credit is due Army veterans and their descendants for photographs. Most of the art used is from the *War Crys* of the four American territories, and from other Army publications, secular magazines, and newspapers. Newspapers throughout the country deserve commendation for having kept dependable records, and for their excellent co-operation.

For errors in BORN TO BATTLE, the author takes full responsibility; for any inspiration readers may receive, to God be the glory!

SALLIE CHESHAM

TABLE OF CONTENTS

15

ILLUSTRATIONS

BORN TO BATTLE

Chapter One
1829/1865

WHO IS THIS SOLDIER?

THE MOB numbered thousands. They hooted, screamed, spit, cursed, threw refuse and brickbats, and charged with what the press described as "savage ferocity."

The assaulted, marching to council in Sheffield, England, did not retaliate but continued to march forward, drums booming, flags flying, singing about the conquering Son of God. The troops were commanded by General William Booth who, despite taunts of "Kill 'em!" and "Down with The Salvation Army!" stood riding in an open carriage with Mrs. Booth beside him.

Bruised and bleeding, their uniforms muddied, torn and buttonless, the forces arrived at their fort shouting, "Hallelujah!" "Now's the time to have your photographs taken," their General said wryly, then led them in prayer for the mob. Yells could be heard all afternoon on that Monday in January, 1882.

Multiply this scene by thousands of similar scenes of abuse throughout the world and you have a glimpse of the treatment The Salvation Army withstood in the years of its militant beginnings.

Organized as a simple mission to reach the outcasts of London's East End, The Salvation Army today encircles the globe. It believes God is man's answer and that there can be no peace

21

on earth or in any man's heart until a proper relationship is effected for the whole man—body, mind, and spirit. It operates hundreds of worship centers, hospitals, community centers, nurseries, coffee-and-doughnut canteens, alcoholic centers, schools, golden-age clubs, bands, songster brigades, etc., adding preventive efforts to those of rescue, backed by Booth's words: "The work [social service operations] was started as an ambulance to pick up at the foot of the precipice of human failure those who had fallen, but the better method would be to erect a fence at the top. . . ." and appropriating the commission Jesus stated as His own:

"God hath anointed Me to preach the gospel to the poor; He hath sent Me to heal the brokenhearted, to preach deliverance to the captives, and recovering of sight to the blind, to set at liberty them that are bruised, to preach the acceptable year of the Lord." (Luke 4:18–19)

Where did early Salvationists get their courage to stubbornly embrace this ministry which has been variously called "crackpot," "a desecration," and "the militant arm of the Christian Church"? It is no secret. They were attracted, organized, and led by William Booth, who said he was commanded by God. The command came at an early age.

William Booth was born April 12, 1829, in Nottingham, England, to Samuel and Mary Moss Booth. Legend has made him the son of an upper-class, well-to-do merchant and builder who, after suffering heavy financial losses, lost heart and died. Obscure as Booth's beginnings are, it is probably more accurate to say that father Samuel was a taciturn, acquisitive nailmaker who set to work building artisans' houses when industry moved into Nottingham. Mary Moss was Samuel's second wife, and is believed to have been part Jewish. Samuel prospered for some time, then had grave reverses requiring a move to less commodious quarters.

William spoke little of his father throughout his life but

did admit, "My father was a grab, a get. He had been born in poverty. He determined to grow rich and he did. He grew very rich because he lived without God and simply worked for money; and when he lost it all, his heart broke with it, and he died miserably."

William had three sisters, Ann, Emma, and Mary. Although they adored "Willie," there was little gaiety in the Booth home in Sneinton, a Nottingham suburb. Mother Mary was reserved and burdened, "a somber, sad, silent, and tragic figure in the threatened home," according to biographer Harold Begbie. One of Ann's friends commented years later that mystery seemed to pervade the home. "They gave me the impression of a very proud, reserved family who felt their position acutely and wished to keep to themselves." That William was later affected by the joylessness in his home life is true, but that he was even more affected by the times in which he lived is strikingly apparent.

By the time of his birth, thousands of villagers had crowded into the big cities and smaller industrial towns. Life for the masses was brutish and short, neither quietly rural nor respectably urban. Factories had sprung up on the meadows, and about them clustered the drones' cottages. In the larger cities the pattern was the same, but instead of cottages, housing consisted of disreputable tenements. One of the sights William never forgot occurred in 1844: "The spectacle of children crying for bread in the streets of Nottingham."

William was sensitive, eager, concerned—and a natural leader. No wonder he rasped later, "Some children are not born into this world. They are damned into it!" A one-time neighbor, interviewed years later, chuckled, "Billy was always rather forward—not aggressive, not violent, but forward." A ringleader. Before he reached his adult height, he became known for his long legs and long nose. William at that time exhibited two talents, one for mischief and one for reading: "I have wondered I did not go straight to hell," he observed later. In his early teens he read anything he could find and especially enjoyed the poetry of Kirke White and the fiction of Sir Walter Scott and James Fenimore Cooper. In later life his reading was equally avid, partly as a release, and seemed to include almost everything but religious fiction, which he detested.

His high-spirited gamboling came to an end when, at 13, he was taken out of Mr. Biddulph's select academy and apprenticed to a pawnbroker. A mortgage foreclosure had completed his father's financial ruin. The apprenticeship, which William loathed, was chosen, according to William, because his father "knew no greater gain than to make money." Within a year, in September, 1843, Samuel Booth became gravely ill. An Anglican, he received the sacrament in dim candlelight. Mary and the children sang, "Rock of Ages," Samuel committed them into Omnipotent hands and died.

What impression his father's death made on young William is not known, but very soon thereafter he went to a Wesleyan Methodist chapel to hear evangelist Isaac Marsden preach and came away deeply disturbed. He wanted desperately to be right with God.

The family moved again, this time to a tiny shop in a poor quarter of Nottingham, where his mother sold small needs for the home. Conditions worsened but not life. After Samuel's death, Mary Booth seemed to escape her burden, and the family grew much closer together. William continued to attend the Wesleyan chapel, aching now for inner peace. He wanted, he said later, "in the place of the life of self-indulgence to which I was yielding myself, a happy, conscious sense that I was pleasing God, living right and spending all my powers to get others into such a life."

William lacked finesse and had little experience and knowledge, but he had a sense of destiny. After his conversion to God at 15, he and a friend, Will Sansom, held street meetings, preaching from a box or a chair, though for some time William was too shy to speak in public.

"Your timidity is a form of selfishness," counseled David Greenbury, a visiting evangelist. From then on William not only preached in public but also took over leadership of the youth group.

At 17, he was deeply impressed by the flaming Irish-born American evangelist, James Caughey. He was struck by Caughey's realism, conversational style, and open-air preaching; and Caughey, dark and theatrical, taught William many of the methods he was later to use. William's daughter Evangeline, who later commanded Salvation Army forces in the United States, said Caughey influenced her father more than any other person. British cries of "Un-English!" "Flashy!" and "American!" probably were well-founded. Booth's ministry from the first was American in enthusiasm and color.

William was always very much concerned for the underprivileged. As a youth he sought the boys of Nottingham slums and was so delighted with their response to his preaching that a visit to church seemed in order. One Sunday he marched the whole ragged, odorous crew into the best chapel seats and sat among them throughout the service, his long, pale face glowing. His delight was short-lived, for it was suggested to him in unmistakable terms that the urchins might honor the congregation with a second visit only if they used a back door and sat out of sight of the rest of the worshipers.

In his late teens he was urged by his pastor, the Reverend Samuel Dunn, to enter the ministry. However, William's fear of inadequacy, his sense of responsibility for his mother and sisters, and a doctor's report that twelve months of ministerial life would land him in the grave, seemed to stand in the way.

At the conclusion of his apprenticeship, William hunted work for a year and, finally, in 1849, left for London. Here he expected to live with his sister Ann and her husband, an old schoolmate of his, but found conditions deplorable. The brother-in-law, reputed to be "very wealthy," had become an aggressive as well as an agnostic drunkard and succeeded in dragging a protesting Ann along with him. Both had become alcoholics. Very soon he ordered William from the house, and though nothing is substantially recorded about Ann and her husband later, it is believed they died prematurely, their fortune completely dissipated.

Now William was homeless, jobless, and penniless. He had only his stubborn faith for company. He finally found a job with a Walworth pawnbroker, and began immediately to search for opportunities to preach.

During the 1840's there was a crisis in Methodism. Reformers in the church wanted to free it from "papal autocracy" and liberalize doctrine. Five ministers were expelled (among them, Samuel Dunn), taking with them a more democratic structure and many parishioners. They called themselves Reformers, stressed revivals and evangelism. Methodism had become somewhat conservative, even stiff, emphasizing methodical attention to religious duties. Evangelistic street services were rigidly controlled.

Although William was at heart not a revolutionist, desiring and respecting authority and order, so earnestly did he want to preach that he rushed from his work to conduct outdoor services, often without eating. Possibly believing he was a secret Reformer, church authorities withheld his ticket of membership. He continued preaching and was soon approached by Edward H. Rabbits, a wealthy boot manufacturer and Reformer, who had heard his first sermon in the Walworth Road Wesleyan chapel. He took William home to dinner, they became friends, and one day Rabbits offered to support him for three months if William would devote himself to preaching.

William quit his job on Good Friday, which was also his birthday. That night he accompanied Rabbits to a service in a schoolroom on Cowper Street, City Road, and there fell head over heels in love with Catherine Mumford, a cultured young lady he had met once before in the Rabbits' home. He escorted Catherine home in a carriage. She said later of the experience:

"It is true that nothing particular occurred, except that as William afterwards expressed it, it seemed as if God flashed simultaneously into our hearts that affection which afterwards ripened into what has proved at least to be an exceptional union of heart and purpose and life. . . . He impressed me . . . and then we struck in at once in such wonderful harmony of view and aim and feeling on varied matters that passed rapidly before us."

Thus began an amazing and satisfactory union of contrasting personalities: William, clumsy, impassioned, impulsive, dramatic; Catherine, cultured, reserved, logical, introspective, keenly intellectual.

Catherine was born on January 17, 1829, the only girl in a family of five. She was frail from birth, and a severe illness when she was 12, resulting in a spinal defect, made her a semi-invalid for years. Unable to attend school, she was taught at home, spending a great amount of time reading, especially history, geography, and contemporary theology. She became a lively participant at adult round tables while in her teens. Her puritanical likes and dislikes were equally strong; she hated worldliness, cruelty, and intoxicants; she loved animals, the truth, the downtrodden and troubled. Once she saw a man being dragged away by a constable with no one to protest. Rushing to his side, she walked to the jailhouse with him. Another time, while riding with a friend, she saw a boy beating a donkey with a hammer. She jumped out of the carriage, tripped and fell flat on her face. Undismayed, she rose and, gripping the reins, secured the hammer and fiercely reprimanded the boy. Then she fainted.

During the three years of their courtship, William was

absorbed in evangelism, fired with ambition and the desire to bring men to God. Now, added to his sense of commission, was Catherine's firm and discerning guidance, her devotion to God. While William was tossed by many an ill wind and often cried his dismay, Catherine refused to be an echo. Her advice was succinct, often intuitive:

"My dearest love, beware how you indulge that dangerous element of character, ambition. . . ."

"If you really see no prospect of studying, then, I think in the highest interest of the future, you ought not to stay. . . ."

After the promised three months preaching for the Reformers, William dissolved his connection with them. He felt they deprived the minister of too much authority; the organization seemed wanting. Under Catherine's prodding and with extreme hesitancy, he decided to study for the Congregational ministry. Not long before, Catherine, a Wesleyan, had spoken in favor of the Reform movement, as much against the lethargy and cool formality of the Wesleyans as for the rebellious evangelistic Reformers. But, like William, she found much lacking among the Reformers and now was enjoying the preaching of a Congregational minister. Congregational friends assured her that the church no longer clung to strict Calvanistic belief. She urged William to be interviewed by a Dr. Campbell, who told him: "Now you must go to college and study over your Bible and what you find there you must go out and preach, and that will be all that Independents will require from you."

Other leading ministers of the denomination supported this view. However, having passed the entrance examination, William was informed that he must conform doctrinally. He was staggered. He could not believe that God's love was not free to all. He left immediately and accepted a Reform invitation to become circuit minister of the Spalding, Lincolnshire, circuit which spread about thirty miles around the town.

Here he spent fifteen months. The distinctive manner and appearance that was to be known around the world in later years, developed rapidly now—a slight stoop in the great height, flowing black beard and piercing black eyes, bony restive hands, voice already rasping from abuse, and the aura of absorption which was to drive him past physical and mental dilemma, sorrow, even death itself.

Catherine, who had once declared she would never marry a seafaring man because he would be away too much, submitted to the separation without rancor, warming William with concern for his health and spiritual growth, admonishing him, and giving him advice and encouragement. When he protested that he had not had the "liberty" in preaching he desired, she answered, "God is not glorified so much by preaching or teaching or anything else as by holy living." When he mentioned that someone had suggested a little wine would settle his stomach, she told him heatedly, "I abominate that hackneyed but monstrously inconsistent tale—a teetotaler in principle but obliged to take a little for 'my stomach's sake,'" and when he wrote of excited listeners, she cautioned, "Watch against mere animal excitement. . . . I never did like noise and confusion. . . . I don't believe that the Gospel needs such roaring and foaming to make it effective—and to some minds it would make it appear ridiculous." Perhaps her stiffest counsel came in such warnings as this: "If you keep back anything from God, if you suffer self to share the glory, He will frustrate your designs and spoil your happiness." When he scolded her for chiding, she answered, "Scold me if you like; blame me if you like, but faithful as well as loving I must ever be. . . ."

The Reformers, gratified with William's energetic ministry, wanted him to settle in the circuit. They would provide him a home, a horse and a gig, and a good enough salary to support a wife. But Catherine, sensing restriction and eager for him to get an education, urged William to enter the Methodist New

Connexion seminary. At the time, this was a better organized, longer established splinter group of the Wesleyans, combining a liberal government with Wesleyan doctrine, and appeared to represent solid ground.

Instead of entering a seminary, William, with several other students, was taught by the Rev. Dr. William Cooke, revered and respected theologian and writer, in Dr. Cooke's home. William was no prize student. Often he knelt in agonized prayer when he should have been studying Greek declensions. Nonetheless, he had a thirst for knowledge and deplored his intellectual deficiencies. He worked hard and gave himself to communication as opposed to bombastics and rhetoric. He believed that if he wanted to reach the people, he must speak in language they could understand but also enjoy. He was often released for preaching engagements, and Cooke soon proposed to make him the next superintendent of the London circuit. Overwhelmed by a sense of inexperience and his youth, William declined but accepted the position of assistant, with permission to marry in one year instead of four. Catherine was elated. But William's enthusiasm cooled suddenly under the sanctimonious, stiff behavior of the superintendent, which helped form the opinion expressed later: "The want of heart is the great infidelity."

His preaching stabbed the spirit, then offered the healing of Divine love. He chose dramatic and fighting subjects which urged his hearers to stand against sin. He wrote Catherine hurriedly for outlines:

"I want a sermon on the flood, one on Jonah, and one on the Judgment. Send some bare thoughts, some clear, startling outlines. Nothing moves people like the terrific. They must have hellfire flashed before their face, or they will not move!"

The New Connexion conference resolved that "the Rev. W. Booth, whose labors have been so abundantly blessed in the conversion of sinners, be appointed to the work of an evangelist, to give the various circuits an opportunity of having his services during the coming year." After their marriage on June 16, 1855, the Reverend and Mrs. Booth honeymooned one week; then, beginning in Guernsey, they started a campaign which lasted two years.

Accompanied by Catherine, William conducted revivals with amazing success. In four months, 1,739 people sought salvation at nine separate centers. There was a realism about him that gripped his hearers. Perhaps they sensed that evil was as apparent to him as good, damnation as close as heaven. He talked as if he believed not only in a just and good God but also in a personal devil. The person of Jesus Christ was more important than the "package" of any creed. He talked and acted like a man who, mortally beset by evil, had overcome the aggressor through Divine power. His listeners, largely drawn from the middle classes, sometimes objected to his forth-rightness, his imagery, his persistent presentation of self-willed man born in sin, but they could not withstand his power. He appeared then, as throughout his life, as one having authority. He rarely sought to prove Christianity, and his preaching was not an examination of *what* to believe but in *whom* to believe.

During this period he was beset with difficulties, though spiritual results increased. Some ministers exhibited jealousy of him. He suffered from chronic dyspepsia so intensely that a self-imposed diet included only the simplest and most easily digested foods. He was as sensitive to self as to others, and agonized over his faults and inadequacies. His temptations were those peculiar to his passionate nature—discouragement and depression. "Many a time," he said later, "I have been tempted to say to myself, 'There is no one fixed so awkwardly for holy living and faithful fighting as I am.'"

Nevertheless, from the time of his conversion he had a conviction that he was God's man. In him, as Begbie states, "was a cry that somewhere, somehow, he would veritably strike an immortal blow for God and his fellow man. . . . He had a conviction of destiny."

Bramwell, their eldest child, who, at his father's death was to become General of The Salvation Army, was born March 8, 1856, while his father was directing an evangelistic campaign.

Catherine continued to follow along despite her frailness. She was analytic, intuitive, and honest. William never had to question where she stood on any issue.

During the next two years several seemingly inconsequential incidents had a bearing on the Booths' future and that of the Army-to-be. Near the end of the campaign in Sheffield, William was presented with a portrait of himself, a very good one, which he accepted. Afterward, he was conscience-stricken as he feared the meeting had been spoiled by his acceptance of the picture as a part payment for sacred duty. He vowed never to accept another gift related to his work, and when The Salvation Army came into being, this became part of the *Orders and Regulations*.

Besides the jealousy of other ministers, there was some dissatisfaction, even revulsion, concerning William's methods in New Connexion circles. He was considered sensational; he brought out emotion in people; he shocked the conservative, and he disturbed everybody. At Chester, the press attacked him, and for the first time in his life he was heckled and opposed by a mocking crowd. Actually, he disliked tasteless demonstration. In the Staffordshire potteries he stopped some women from clapping their hands when they had become overly excited. At St. Agnes one night, a woman ecstatically leaped to her feet and began to jump up and down to the singing. Every time she went up she shouted, "Glory!" Afraid of losing control, William ordered her subdued. The spirit of the meeting collapsed, and he vowed that in the future he would guide emotion, not suppress it.

Ballington, the second child, later to command Salvation

Army work in the United States, was born in 1857 in Brighouse, an industrial town.

The following year William was fully ordained. The conference voted to appoint him to a regular circuit. Disappointed that he was not allowed to continue as an evangelist, he commented in private correspondence:

"A year's rest will be very acceptable. By that time God will, I trust, make plain my way before me, either to abide as a circuit preacher or by opening me a door which no man or number of men shall be able to shut."

Their third child, Catherine, who when 22 years old, would begin work in France amid fierce persecution, was born in 1858, at Gateshead, a town nicknamed "the converting shop." Here, open-air ministry, a novelty, was conducted in earnest. Every Sunday, members paraded from 5:00 to 6:00 P.M., singing and speaking. On several occasions publicans organized bands of hecklers to sing them down, but William merely ordered his workers to sing even louder, putting religious words to the same tunes. It worked.

Despite her growing family and frailty, Catherine longed to throw herself into the ministry completely. She visited in homes, bathed sick mothers and babies, talked to drunkards on the streets and in their homes, and conducted small services in cottages for neighborhood people. But she felt compelled to speak in public, in an era when women writers often used pseudonyms and public speaking by women was unheard of. Previous to their marriage William had told Catherine:

"I would not stop a woman preaching on any account. I would not encourage one to begin. You should preach if you felt moved thereto; felt equal to the task. I would not stay *you* if I had the power to do so. Although, *I should not like it*. It is easy for you to say my views are the result of prejudice; perhaps they are. I am for the world's *salvation*. I will quarrel with no means that promises help."

In December of 1859, she read a pamphlet by the Rev. Arthur Augustus Rees who, on Scriptural grounds, condemned women who spoke in public. Although ill when she read it, she wrote 32 pages of refutation for publication. Her fourth child, Emma, was born a few days later.

On May 27, 1860, during a service conducted by William in Bethesda chapel, with 1,000 present, she felt compelled by God to speak.

She walked down the aisle, startling William, who was just concluding.

"What is the matter, my dear?"

"I want to say a word," said Catherine.

"My dear wife wants to say a word," said William and sat down.

Catherine made her confession, stating that she felt God had wanted to use her to speak for years, but she could not until that day. The congregation was profoundly stirred. It was said later that "God opened the windows of Heaven and poured out such a blessing that there was not room enough to contain it." Despite a large family, her writing, and her work with William, Catherine broadened her public ministry until, during her final public address, London's famed City Temple was crowded to the rafters.

William was working ceaselessly now, preaching the necessity for a Christ-centered life, making it hard for the sinner by promising not static "happiness" but dynamic fulfillment. Overwork broke his health as he tried to manage both evangelistic and administrative duties during 1860. He went to Matlock for hydropathic treatment, while Catherine substituted for him in the chapel. She wrote in her loneliness, "We lacked a General." Whooping cough infected the children. Catherine wrote her mother that if the conference had no place for an evangelist then they "must go out into the wilderness alone."

William asked for reappointment to evangelistic work,

knowing that this had been proposed at the Hull Conference in 1858.

The Liverpool Conference in 1861 was of such importance to the Booths that Catherine went along, stumping for an all-out break with the New Connexion, though William, thinking of the family, stood for compromise. He was called to read the letter he had addressed to the annual committee in March, asking for reappointment to evangelistic work. The ensuing debate became heated and long. Dr. Cooke, under whom he had studied and upon whom they counted for support, suggested a compromise, proposing that William take the Newcastle circuit but have time off for revival services. William refused. As Dr. Cooke turned to William in entreaty, Catherine called determinedly from the gallery, "Never!"

The vote was against William. He took his hat, walked quietly to the door where he met Catherine, and they "went out into the wilderness" together.

It has been said that the Booths were thrust out of the New Connexion, but such is not the case. Persistent efforts were made to draw him into the circle of conventional ministry, but service in the Newcastle circuit proved impossible and the Booths felt impelled to "go forth without a friend and without a farthing."

On August 26, 1862, the fifth child, Herbert, was born. He was to be the family's most talented musician and later became commander of Canada, and still later, Australia.

From 1861 until 1865 they threw themselves into revival work, enjoying outstanding success, since both of them now participated. Catherine often conducted separate campaigns when wider ministry was required. A severe setback came when, in 1862, the New Connexion Conference voted against the use of revivalists, a direct attack on the Booths. They were forced into what was to become a Salvation Army tradition—secular buildings used for religious services. One of the first such services was conducted in a circus building in Cardiff.

During the Booths' Cornish campaign, 7,000 persons were converted, yet they were troubled. Their ministry was successful, but they were not making enough money for traveling expenses. William's throat had become ulcerated. He suffered a severe ankle sprain and was tormented by a restlessness he could not explain. Furthermore, their six children needed a home. Marian, born May 4, 1864, and the only one not to become an evangelist of note, suffered convulsions soon after birth and was constitutionally frail. She was reared as a semi-invalid.

Early in 1865 Catherine was invited to Rotherhithe, in southeast London, for a brief campaign. She was overwhelmed by the incredible squalor. During a campaign a little later in Bermondsey, the work of the Midnight Movement for Fallen Women captured her interest. She preached to forsaken girls, many of whom were mere children. There was urgency in her oratory and a pressing sense of responsibility in her private conversation. Back home in Leeds, she now shared with William a growing awareness that they should make London their headquarters and work through existing agencies.

They moved to Hammersmith, a London suburb, in 1865, and both continued to campaign. Then a significant incident occurred. William was rebuked by the Messrs. R. C. Morgan and Samuel Chase, editors of *The Revival,* a nondenominational magazine. Morgan had been shocked to hear Catherine preach at Rotherhithe and had urged the censure. They remonstrated with their "beloved brother" Booth for allowing his wife to preach. They noted St. Paul's first Epistle to Timothy, in which he counsels women "to learn in silence with all subjection" and warns they must not usurp authority over men. However, the disturbed gentlemen were won over when they met Catherine and William and attended more of Catherine's meetings. Morgan even chaired some for her later.

The Booths characteristically made friends of their critics.

In June of that year, William Booth made his first contact with London's East End. After volunteering testimony with missioners in a Whitechapel open-air meeting, he was invited to direct an evangelistic tent campaign on an unused burial ground owned by the Society of Friends. One member of the deputation who waited on William Booth was Samuel Chase himself.

On July 2, 1865, William, oblivious to all but the paradoxical preachment of love sheathed in a sword case, strode into the steaming, vice-ridden East End.

"Booth, talk about peace!"

"No!" William replied, "the best preaching is damnation with the Cross in the middle!"

It was not a message calculated to appeal to denizens who knew much more about swords than saviors.

Chapter Two
1866 / 1878

PREACHER, GO HOME!

IT WAS the end of a sultry, sticky July day in 1865. Night at least would hide the lice-laced rags, the filth-crusted skins of Whitechapelans who filled the weathered tent. Smoking naphtha flares, hung on wires stretched between tent poles, flickered fingers of light and nauseated gin-soaked guests with their vapors.

The audience was composed not only of the reeling wretches and prostitutes from London's East End; children were present too, making steeples of their bony fingers, digging bare, callused feet in the dust, and shoving one another off the ends of benches. There were other groups—tradespeople from respectable East End thoroughfares, sober for the most part and better dressed, who had come either out of curiosity or because they too were uneasy about the jungle of distress all about them.

As the fierce-eyed, long-legged substitute preacher pulled off his top hat and strode to the platform, howls of laughter, coughing, mocking, and curses erupted.

"But Mr. Booth he shouted at them finely," recalled prize-fighter Peter Monk, a convert of one of the first meetings. "And then he gave out a hymn and led the singing till he just drowned their noise." He later commented of William's preaching: "It seemed as if he'd tear the soul out of your body.

38

And then in the midst of it all there'd be a bit that would make you want to cry, or a tale that would set you laughing fit to burst. But all the time you felt that he wanted to save your soul. There was no doubt about that."

The tent meetings continued. Hundreds attended the services, and a number were converted. Among them were respectable working people, who formed a vanguard of intelligent, knowledgeable fighters to improve the slum conditions. Some of the original group of missioners included Friends and Huguenots.

The work was precariously financed, however, and "S.C.," probably Samuel Chase, inserted the following notice in *The Revival,* the Morgan-Chase paper:

"Mr. Booth saw his way to give himself to the perishing thousands of the East of London; but this cannot be accomplished without increased funds for these East End services."

Late one night after a tent meeting William burst into his home. "Kate darling, I've found my destiny!" He flung himself into a chair. "Oh, Kate, as I passed by the door of the flaming gin-palaces tonight, I seemed to hear a voice sounding in my ears, 'Where can you go and find such heathen as these, and where is there so great a need for your labors?' And I felt as though I ought at every cost to stop and preach to those East End multitudes."

Catherine gazed into the fireplace. She knew this new sense of commission meant another departure, another start in life. What about support for the family? Now there wouldn't even be the collections to keep them going. It was impossible to suppose they could expect financial aid from among the East Enders.

She prayed, then turned to William.

"If you feel you ought to stay, stay. We have trusted the Lord once for our support, and we can trust Him again."

In the days that followed, William held two meetings a

day, one outside and one in the tent. On many days, four meetings were held. In between, he visited homes, roamed Mile End Waste, listened, watched, agonized. Of this experience he later said:

"I saw multitudes of my fellow creatures not only without God and hope, but sunk in the most desperate forms of wickedness and misery that can be conceived. I went out and looked on the wretched sons and daughters of debauchery and vice and crime who were all about me. The drunkenness and harlotry, and pauperism, and slumdom, and blasphemy, and infidelity of these crowds had a fascination for me. . . . I not only saw but compassionated the people sunk in the sin and wretchedness I beheld, and the everlasting woe that I knew must follow."

He did not look upon the wretched scene of his day as a social worker might today. Only and always he saw the salvation of the soul as the answer to man's need. If a man righted himself with God, all would be well. In William's mind, a man was empowered to grapple with the life situation and overcome it, or God had a purpose for his endurance. The believer, in William's mind, need not be crushed by outside influences of evil, whether spiritual or social. Only a man's self could effect his ruin. Only God could redeem.

Soon after, mention of the permanent character of his work began to appear in the press. *The Wesleyan Times,* August 20, 1865, reported:

"The Rev. William Booth has been engaged for the past seven weeks holding a series of special meetings in the East End of London. . . . Hundreds of working men and numbers of persons who never enter any place of worship have listened night after night to appeals of this devoted servant of God, and many conversions have taken place. The work is assuming a permanent character, and a large hall in the neighborhood is about to be engaged for the winter. . . ."

Finance was still a nettling problem when William received a letter from Samuel Morley, a wealthy manufacturer and philanthropist of Nottingham. He had heard of the tent meetings and wanted to see William. He discussed the matter of support for the Booth family, then wrote out a check for £100 as his first annual contribution and suggested other friends do likewise.* On the 1868 balance sheet for the East London Christian Mission, a footnote states: "The support of Mr. Booth is not included in the above sheet, that having been provided expressly for by a few Christian friends. . . ."

Crowds grew but not accommodations. The tent was cut down and slashed by the "blackguards" of Whitechapel. Sunday services were then held in Professor Orson's Dancing Academy, but the out-of-doors, as William often stated, was the missioners' cathedral. Harold Begbie said the Whitechapel experience was like "preaching in hell, for the atheism of East London in those days was a fierce and oppugnant atheism, an atheism which hated the very name of God, and to which Jesus appeared as the archdeceiver of the human race."

The Mission moved many times in the next few years; to a stable from which they were ejected for disturbing a gym on the other side of the wall; a penny gaff (cheap amusement house) at Limehouse; an old beer house; and in June of 1866, a decrepit wool warehouse in Three Colts Lane, in which 120 people could be seated.

"Unfortunately," said William, "the windows opened on the street. When crowded . . . it became oppressively hot, especially in summer. If we opened the windows the boys threw stones and mud and fireworks through, and fired trains of gun-

---

* It was in this manner that the Booths were supported throughout their lives, and such contributions meant they took nothing from Army funds. However, during times of slanderous attack on The Army, the cry went up: "Rich man! He'll soon settle in America on English money."

powder, laid from the doors inwards. But our people got used to this, shouting, 'Hallelujah!' when the crackers exploded and the powder flashed. . . . It was an admirable training ground for the development of The Salvation Army."

Until the Mission was two years old, Catherine Booth conducted her ministry in the West End exclusively, following a two-fold purpose: to bring the upper classes to God and to raise money for the Mission. Catherine rightfully is acknowledged as co-founder of The Salvation Army.

Two more children had joined the family—Eveline, later to be called Evangeline, born on Christmas Day, 1865; and Lucy, the last of their eight children, born in 1868.

Family did not come first with Catherine; her passion to win others to God did. With infinite care, the children were fitted to life not *with* the ministry but *into* it. Each felt himself an integral part of the "great commission," the success of the Mission work. Later, one of them spoke of their home as Grand Central station, with everyone in a whirl of coming and going about God's business. This involvement from babyhood compensated for the time Catherine did not spend with them. Their attitude was reflected even in their desires and games.

Catherine dressed them plainly, and Katie once cautioned her mother about a proposed shopping trip, "Do not buy us something pretty. Mind you, get something Christian." All the Booths, however, did possess taste and a sense of style. Their favorite game was prayer-meeting, with "mothers" struggling to quiet howling doll children and "preachers," Bramwell and Ballington, shouting, "Take out that baby!" Ballington often posed a pillow at the "penitent-form," * pounded it as he knelt

---

* The penitent-form is usually a low altar or "form" placed just below the pulpit though it may be a row of straight-backed chairs, a box, or a drumhead. Meaningless in itself, it becomes the doorstep of God when used as a place of public confession, dedication, entreaty, or meditative communion.

beside it and said, "Ah, this is a good case, bless him. Give up the drink, brother." Once he came home with a toy store ring on his finger, and the others shouted, "Ballington's a backslider! Ballington's a backslider!" William hushed them, and Catherine removed him to another room. Ten minutes later Ballington emerged with red eyes and no ring. William once took small Ballington with him to call on a nonteetotaling friend. While the gentlemen conferred, Ballington, unobserved, drank up almost all of the gin and water. On reaching home, he broke out in a frenzy, "Papa, Papa, I've broken my pledge!"

Much of the time, of course, the little Booths behaved like ordinary children. William frequently inspected the backyard menagerie of rabbits, guinea pigs, mice, rats, fowl, and silk worms. He often frolicked with the children on the floor, with the entire company clambering over his extraordinary length. One time, Emma, when she was six years old, tied his long hair into curl papers. A visitor was announced and William sprang to his feet, with the children dragging him back by the coattails, shrieking with laughter.

William's presence always stirred up the household.

"The General was a force," declared Jane Short, a woman who lived with the Booths for some time. "We used to call him General long before there was a Salvation Army. He couldn't bear beating about the bush. Prevarication, like stupidity, exasperated him. Everything had to go like clockwork, but much faster than time. I always say he got 48 hours out of 24." Besides this, he delighted in neatness and personal cleanliness. But he was often despondent. Miss Short recorded, "You could not meet a man whose nerves were more tortured by the spectacle of suffering. Pain in others made him wretched."

The Booth home never was a sanctuary of quiet; it was stimulating and lively. William encouraged discussion of all kinds, at practically all times. Though he could be abrupt and harsh, no one in his household feared him. Of necessity, for two overworked people, order was demanded. Meals were always on time and woe betide any child who was late. Occasionally, Catherine's physical difficulties made her overconscious of noise. She was a severe disciplinarian and sometimes irritable, yet the children seemed only to profit. In later years, Emma, explaining her absences from her own children to the American press, said of her mother:

"When we were little there were those who condoled with us because we saw so little of our mother. It was then so unusual for a woman to go upon the public platform that her work was not understood. We really saw more of our mother than did those children whose mothers were society women who went on rounds of endless calls, attended balls and receptions and other social functions. We were impressed by her example and tried to be like her."

In 1867 William was determined that his brood should have a fine Christmas—a happy, old-fashioned celebration. Preparations stretched throughout the week preceding Christmas. But when he returned from preaching at Whitechapel Christmas morning, he was white-faced and grim. Jane Short said, "He tried hard to enter into the fun but kept relapsing into silence and gloom. He looked ill with some grievous worry. Suddenly he burst out, 'I'll never have a Christmas Day like this again!'" Then stalking the room like a lion, he told of the sights he had seen that morning. "The poor have nothing but the public house—nothing but the public house." That was the last Christmas the Booths ever spent together.

The next year they were in the slums distributing plum puddings, 150 of them, many having been made in the Booth kitchen. It was a foreshadowing of the millions of Christmas dinners The Army was later to distribute in the Whitechapels of the world.

Not yet thinking in terms of an organized body, William

sent his converts to existing churches. Of this he commented later:

"From the first I was strongly opposed to forming any separate organization. . . . My first idea was simply to get the people saved and send them to the churches. This proved at the outset impracticable. First, they would not go when sent. Second, they were not wanted; and third, we wanted some of them at least ourselves to help us in the business of saving others. We were thus driven to providing for the converts ourselves."

Saving others was hard work and demanded help. William, in enlisting converts as seekers and saviors of the lost from whatever station in life, struck upon the key to a problem that ten years earlier had distressed him. His converts seemed to live much the same as they previously had. He thought new life should bring revolution. Now came the answer. Faith was not enough for the converts. They *must get to work*. This and public confession of Christ proved to be his two greatest aids for strengthening converts. He believed he had now struck on the kernel of his Master's teaching: "He that findeth his life shall lose it, but he that loseth his life for My sake shall find it."

What was meant by "for My sake"? No more, no less, thought William than "Love ye one another as I have loved you."

In 1867 the balance sheet of William's group, now called the East London Christian Mission, showed that the Mission employed the following means," together with 13 preaching stations:

> Preaching in the open air and in theaters, concert halls and shops and rooms, in prominent situations or very dark neighborhoods; visiting from house to house; Bible carriage for the sale of Bibles, tracts and soul-saving literature; Mothers' meetings; Bible

classes; Believers' meetings; Temperance meetings; Bands of love for children; Tract societies; Evening classes for reading, writing and arithmetic; Sunday, day and ragged schools; Reading rooms; Penny banks; Relief of the destitute, the sick and the poor by the distribution of bread, meat, small sums of money and through soup kitchens.

The ministry spread despite persecution by those who wished to suppress it and by those to whom it was addressed. In less than two years, social work efforts of an amazing variety had forced themselves into the evangelism of the "fanatical" Booth because he abhorred suffering.

Antidrink programs were conducted among adults and children. The *East London Evangelist,* forerunner of the *War Cry,* reported that on October 6, 1868, Sister Jermy single-handedly commenced a Band of Hope, enlisting about fifty children to sign the pledge and take as their theme song, to the consternation of many saloonkeepers and guzzling parents:

> We'll throw down the bottle,
> And never drink again.

There were many innovations now. Daytime meetings were begun because, William said, "The gin palaces are always open. The emissaries of evil are always at work; why should the ambassadors of Christ wait for the evening?" Missioners wanted a rescue home for fallen girls and women. Many had, for years, taken girls into their own homes. But the funds could not be raised, and the project was dropped. "All Nights of Prayer" were instituted. Musical "Free and Easy" meetings were begun, as a counterattraction to the saloon singsong. Free breakfasts for the poor were frequently served on Sundays.

To the old tune, "Men of Harlech," Christian Missioners sang:

Spread the Mission through the nation,
Planting everywhere a station;
Preach the Gospel of salvation
    To uncared-for men.
Point the drinking and blaspheming,
Careless, prayerless, idly dreaming,
To the blood so freely streaming
    There on Calvary.
Christ will ne-er deceive them,
He's ready to receive them,
And has power, at any hour,
    For all who will believe Him.
Onward press, Christ's love impelling—
Warning men—their danger telling—
And the ranks of Jesus swelling,
    Forward, Christian men!

As stations flourished and multiplied, more organization was required. In the beginning, William had guided paternally. "The Salvation Army started under one hat, and that hat was on my head," he had said. Due to his Methodist cleric training, he chose the conference method of leadership. In 1870, the first Christian Mission conference was held, structured almost identically with that of the Wesleyans.

Another matter of grave importance commanded his attention by 1872. It concerned religious experience. William realized that the preaching of conversion, turning from self to God by faith in Christ, while repenting of and confessing sins of the body, was not enough. As his biographer Begbie comments:

"To convert a thief, a drunkard, a swindler, an atheist, was only a first step to making these poor sinners the children of light. A thief might give up stealing and a drunkard abandon alcohol, yet remain for the rest of their lives only respectable and law-abiding or, at best, only formal disciples of that mystical religion which obviously has holiness for its supreme end."

There were so many godless people to reach. How could he do it? Should the Mission concentrate on personal holiness, on prayer, faith, self-abasement, and meditation? Should it form itself into a small, exclusive body whose radiant being would have profound influence on the relatively few it touched due to time necessarily spent on self, or should the Mission march into the wilderness, crying, "Behold, now is the day of salvation!" exhausting and denying self for others?

Catherine and young Bramwell advocated the first. Desperately, William struggled with the alternatives. Nobody knew better than he that the "Higher up Religion," as he characteristically called holy living, was imperative for spiritual power and constancy. His had always been a religion of experience and experiment, of the crises of conversion and consecration, but it was also a spiritual journey where failure to advance meant retreat, where light had to be followed or it was extinguished. And he had a commission to seek the lost.

That he was tending toward a holiness group is evident in correspondence in which he mentioned Wesley as establishing Methodism not only "by converting sinners but by making well-instructed saints. We must follow in his track or we are a rope of sand." Yet the plight of sick, sorrowing, sinful millions rose before him in ghastly reality. Holiness or salvation? On his knees he begged Divine help. Holiness or salvation? Could they not preach both? They could. They would. And they did.

William was urgently in need of intelligent, educated, and perceptive assistance. Until now, he had done most of the directing, recording, and bookkeeping, with Bramwell as his aid. The burden was becoming ponderous.

In 1873, 24-year-old George Scott Railton, keen-minded, wiry and quick, joined the Christian Mission as secretary. The work he did was so extraordinary that his name must be listed only beneath those of the founders and that of Bramwell. Besides secretarial work, his duties included the editing of the Mission magazine, evangelism and, later, acting as international troubleshooter for William. He was a spiritual world explorer, caring little for personal needs and unable to comprehend the word sacrifice. It was said that he believed in preaching until he was hoarse and praying until his knees were petrified. He considered sleep and food necessary evils. Dedicated people should eat only when nobody would listen and sleep when they couldn't keep themselves awake. He was a worthy addition to a band of people about whom the populace cried:

> Oh, what a noisy lot they are!
> I cannot make these people out,
> They're here and there and everywhere,
> And no one knows what they're about.
> Pray, kindly tell me if you can,
> What is this Christian Mission clan?

The conference system of leadership for the Mission did not work out. Committees met weekly to consider minutia and often months passed before converts were granted permission to evangelize or even distribute tracts. Older, less daring men often filled committee positions rather than the more active younger ones. Some stations were sadly in debt and exhibited little initiative in trying to pull themselves out.

Late in 1876, William's two valiants, Bramwell and Railton, approached him, supported by a group of the most faithful and efficient Missioners. They protested, "We gave up our lives to work under you and those you should appoint, rather than under one another."

A meeting of the Conference Committee was called and "government by committee" was abolished as too slow and too circuitous a process. This was no leisurely theoretical concern. They were in a war against sin. The annual conference, confirming the proposal, was changed from a legislative body to a briefing and inspirational "council of war"; and in June, 1877, complete power was vested in William.

The Christian Mission was a spiritual and spirited conglomeration by this time. It combined new methods with old, educated men with illiterates, conservatives with sensationally daring. William blazed away in the East End, Catherine persuaded West Enders, and the Missioners marched behind according to their light.

That some methods were ill-considered and extreme, some preaching too boisterous, William readily acknowledged. Commenting on his polyglot band, he said, "I wish we did not do so many silly things. I think I see a great difference between manly, natural, bold, daring action, and weak, frivolous, childish comicality." However, Catherine soon after allowed herself to be pulled in a wheelchair at the head of a procession because someone felt it would draw a crowd; and Bramwell, in defense of "peculiar methods," said of his fellow campaigners:

"We in The Army have learned to thank God for eccentricity and extravagance, and to consecrate them to His service. We have men in our ranks who can frolic for God. Often they have blundered and occasionally they land us in awkward places. . . . Thank God for the daredevils!"

Some early converts could not write their names. Elijah Cadman, an ex-chimney sweep who later became a Commissioner, was illiterate when he joined the Mission. Told one time that he'd read the Scripture from an upside-down Bible, he replied, "Were there any mistakes?" "No," said the accuser. "Then," said Elijah, "what are you criticizing? It's not every man that can read upside down." Many were uneducated, rough, and mannerless, but they shared in common the joy in deliverance, compassion for the outcast, and a singing spirit. They sang constantly. Regardless of tonal quality or pitch or sense of rhythm, they sang—in their homes, in the street, on their knees and, soon, in prison.

A sense of holy war gripped the Mission. The Christian Mission song book contained 25 songs with war overtones. On Good Friday, 1878, Elijah Cadman, one of the Mission's most audacious members, displayed at the head of his procession a banner which read: "WAR IS DECLARED: RECRUITS ARE WANTED" and a second: "THE HALLELUJAH ARMY! FIGHTING FOR GOD!" He also referred to William as General Booth but hid the poster for fear he had overstepped his prerogative.

When the proof of the Christian Mission report of 1878 was brought to William by Bramwell and Railton, he had it read to him, correcting as he strode back and forth. Railton sat at a table, writing. Bramwell sat by his side.

"The Christian Mission, under the superintendence of the Rev. William Booth, is a volunteer army," read Railton.

Bramwell exclaimed, "Volunteer! Here, I'm not a volunteer. I'm a regular or nothing!"

William stopped, studied Bramwell a moment.

"No, we are not volunteers for we feel we *must* do what we do, and we are always on duty," he said. British volunteers of that period were derided as lazy louts, "city soldiers." He took the pen from Railton, scratched out the word "volunteer" and wrote in its place "salvation."

The effect of that one word upon Railton and Bramwell was extraordinary. They sprang from their chairs as Bramwell exclaimed, "Thank God for that." Railton was "equally enthusiastic."

Thus the destiny of an unknown Nottingham boy named William Booth was sealed, as well as the lives of a multitude of Salvationists with it. With the naming of The Salvation Army, everything fell into place. At Bramwell's bidding a huge sign was placed over the platform during the August

War Congress reading: THE SALVATION ARMY. William talked of the new name, stating that they were now "a Salvation Army to carry the blood of Christ and the fire of the Holy Ghost into every corner of the world." At that time, The Salvation Army consisted of 50 stations and 86 evangelists.

The entire organization was immediately dominated by the name. A month after the congress William exulted, "We've never moved so quickly before." Militant terms were employed. Members became soldiers; soldiers fired cartridges (weekly contributions); prayer meetings were kneedrills; evangelists were captains and majors; lay leaders were sergeant-majors, sergeants, and corporals. William was now called General, an abbreviation of General Superintendent. At first he disliked the title, feeling it was pompous. He wanted it put after his name in lower case. The first edition of *Orders and Regulations for The Salvation Army* was printed, detailing "how to attack, capture, and hold towns."

There was no attempt made to regulate the display of uniforms so long as they were dark and modest. The first women officers were put in charge of a station in 1878, and the stations were renamed corps. As the red, yellow, and blue flag waved in the breeze, 5,000 Salvationists sang lustily at Coventry, "We'll roll the old chariot along, and we won't drag on behind!" Captain William Pearson, formerly a Christian Mission evangelist, composed what is thought to be the first Salvation Army song:

> Come, join our Army, to battle we go;
> Jesus will help us to conquer the foe;
> Fighting for right and opposing the wrong,
> The Salvation Army is marching along.

In Salisbury, an incident occurred that was later responsible for fierce and prolonged criticism of The Army. It also set a precedent for worship and was to become one of the most effective weapons of Army warfare. When Captain Arthur Watts was appointed to Salisbury in August of 1878, he had a hard time with hooligans and was protected one time by passersby, Charles Fry and his three grown sons. Captain Watts visited the Frys and discovered that they were expert musicians. Charles was choir and orchestra conductor at the Methodist church and had been solo cornet player in the Rifle Brigade band. The Captain hoped music might subdue the crowd. Charles Fry and his sons were invited to play at the next open-air meeting. They played loudly but sweetly and the jeering stopped. Ruffians who could not or would not find God in words found him in melody, and the Frys, elated with their musical ministry, joined The Army.

William, who was always ready to appropriate any device that would win men to God, used the brass instruments widely. Though he disliked ornamentation, in music or in anything else, and would not often permit any music other than hymns in his own meetings, he gave his blessing to Army musicians, both vocal and instrumental. Later, when attacked on the point, he replied, "If standing on my head and beating a tambourine with my toes will win a soul for Jesus, I will do it."

Now, this strange new army, this *salvation* army, marched with horns playing, drums booming, flags waving, soldiers in step, at least for the most part, attracting high and low, who either clapped or shook fists, emptying saloons and parlors alike. Drunks, harlots, and street waifs often trotted along with processions, while troubled members of the gentry visited Army stations more secretly and discreetly. "England for God!" was the Salvationists' cry.

But General William Booth had not counted on the prophetic truth of a phrase he had spoken at the War Congress becoming a reality so soon. The Salvation Army, he had said, would proceed to march "into every corner of the world."

Chapter Three
1879/1889

THE UNITED STATES INVADED

"SO YOU want to rent the chair factory," said the Philadelphia businessman, scrutinizing two severely dressed females. "Have you seen it yet?"

"We were out there yesterday afternoon," replied the younger, a diminuitive, shiny-faced teen-ager. "It will need a lot of cleaning up before we can use it, but I think it will answer our purpose."

"What do you want it for?"

The girl looked at the older woman. She hesitated.

"We want it for The Salvation Army."

"My God!" said the man, "what is The Salvation Army?"

"We are The Salvation Army."

Eliza Shirley and her mother Annie were then called upon to explain The Army's principles, methods, and ability to pay rent, after which, apparently convinced, the businessman said, "And who is going to preach?"

"Oh, we do the preaching, sir," said Eliza.

"You mean a woman preacher?" He choked. "Why, we don't have women preachers in America. The people here will never stand for that sort of thing. It would be sacrilege."

The Salvationists stood up.

"We don't want to rush you now for an answer, sir," said Eliza, backing toward the door as he yelled after them, "Never mind coming back. I wouldn't think of renting the place for that purpose."

Eliza and Annie left, wondering just how long it would take to put the place in order. They were convinced the dilapidated factory was to become the first Salvation Army citadel in the new world. It wasn't much of an edifice but, for what they could pay, it was the best they could find. Four walls and a roof described it—shattered windows, roof shot full of holes, earthen floor strewn with bits of machinery, and a bony horse stabled in one corner. They were sure the landlord's heart would be miraculously softened and, by the next morning, it was. He agreed to the factory's use.

The Shirley women had not come by their courage in an explosion of fervor. They had belonged to The Army in England in Christian Mission days. Eliza, interviewed personally by William Booth as "Little Shirley," a girl who'd already made her mark as songstress and soul-winner, was appointed at 16 to help start Mission operations in Bishop Auckland just preceding the time of the naming of The Army. Soon after, Amos, her father, accepted a position as foreman in a Philadelphia silk mill. His letters were enthusiastic:

"You have no idea of the great numbers of people here who never go to church. . . . Far be it from me to ask you to abandon your work there, but if it should happen that the two of you might be able to come here we might easily start a work similar to that of the Mission and help to save these people who need salvation so badly."

Eliza believed this was God's call. She wrote her General. His reply by return mail bluntly advised that he was not prepared to release her. She waited one day while she prayed, then sent another letter. The reply this time was not so adamant, but made it clear that The Army was not prepared to assume jurisdiction in a land so far removed from its center of operation.

"But," concluded William, "if you are determined to go to America and you are determined to begin religious work there, you will do well to organize it along the line of The Army at home. If you do this, you have my permission to call it The Salvation Army; if it succeeds, and I believe it will, we may later see fit to take over the work you have started and continue it."

The Shirleys put their citadel in shape. A Negro convert whitewashed the ugly walls. Amos bought as much lumber as he could afford and nailed it in place to make a platform at one end. Seats on the platform would accommodate about 50 people. The remainder of the hall was without seats until a prosperous looking man came to the Shirley home and handed Amos a fat roll of bills, saying, "I don't know why I'm giving you this money, but on four successive nights God has told me to bring it to this address and I'm doing His will." The Shirleys bought 100 folding chairs.

Failing to attract a crowd near their home, the Shirleys marched to the slum section where crowds were as plentiful as abuse, but the scoffers wouldn't follow. Then one night a slobbering old drunkard decided he "wanted salvation," and they marched him to the chair factory. Hundreds shouldered their way along behind them. What hokus-pokus would these magicians work? Couldn't they see the penitent was dull as Monday and soaked to the gills? Suddenly the factory was jammed, with people hanging on windows and peering in through every crack. The Shirleys astounded their worshipers by putting their applicant to sleep behind the platform.

The people outside got an eyewitness account from a window watcher. "They're putting him to bed." "The girl says she's saved—by the grace of God." "Now, they're taking up a collection." The outdoor congregation took up their own collection and passed it in through the window. Word went around: "They're bringing him out from behind. See, they're making him kneel down in front and two of them are praying with him. Look at him shake. He's crying right out loud and praying fit to kill."

Excitement, amazement, incredulity, froze them as the drunk got to his feet—shaky but cold sober.

That was the beginning. After that night, the old factory burst its heaving two-by-fours and soon Eliza opened a second corps while her parents directed the first. With two corps in operation, Eliza reported to her General, who replied that he had read of the warfare and was sending George Scott Railton and some lassies to strengthen the work.

The American party had a great send-off on February 14, 1880. Railton had asked for women soldiers for his American detachment, partly because he wanted to show what they could do and partly because he desired that future officers in the United States be Americans. "America must be maintained by Americans and make its own officers if there is to be anything like progress," he said.

At a previous corps farewell for the girls, the eccentric Captain Elijah Cadman had advertised: "The Yankees Will Farewell Tonight!" and prayed at the end of the service, "Lord, these ladies are going to America to preach the Gospel. If they are fully given up to Thee, be with them and bless them, and grant them success. But if they are not faithful, drown 'em, Lord! Drown 'em!"

At a farewell tea with 500 present, William Booth announced that a request had come to invade France and another from Sweden. He continued that he hoped for penetration of Germany and Russia and, "last but not least there are the blessed Negroes." At this point, a converted Negro was pulled to his feet amid Hosannas to take up a special collection for the United States and "give Brother Railton £200 for the work."

Catherine eloquently presented the farewell party with

two flags, one for the first Pennsylvania corps and the other for the first New York corps. Remarking on the youth of the girls, she said, "You look young, and some people will think, insignificant, but so are we all. So did those women who stood grouped round the cross of Christ to the proud Pharisees who walked, mocking, past." She handed them the flags in the name of God and the General of The Salvation Army, praying that "God may give you, young as you are, strength to fight heroically under His banner, and to lead tens of thousands to the Cross."

The invading force sang all the way to the ship, then formed a ring and held a meeting. When they embarked, their comrades on shore sang, "Soldiers of Jesus be valiant and strong; The Salvation Army is marching along," and waved handkerchiefs. A *War Cry* report commented: "The Stars and Stripes and our Union Jack have gone together. The Salvation Army has married them, and our prayer is that the flags of all nations may soon be gloriously incorporated with the Blood and Fire."

Railton, togged in the first official uniform, hardy, cheerful, and excited, had only one thought during the three weeks of ocean swells and steerage accommodation: "We must go!" The voyage was not uneventful. An engine broke down and the ship had to complete the trip with just one against heavy backwinds and rough seas. Feminine fighters were laid low by seasickness. Finally, one blustery day in March, many days late, they entered Castle Garden, the immigrant station at the Battery, New York City, and, kneeling, claimed America for God. They were supported by documents which stated that Railton had been appointed "to extend to America the operations carried on by The Salvation Army in England" and to represent the General as his commissioner. This was the first official use of the title, "Commissioner," at present second in importance only to that of "General."

The press gave unusually vivid coverage to their arrival. The *New York Times* said on March 11, 1880:

". . . They [the Salvationists] created quite a sensation in the Garden and subsequently in the streets as they proceeded to the lodging house that had been provided for them. They were all attired in a uniform of dark blue cloth, edged with bright yellow binding and around their hats were broad bands of scarlet ribbon inscribed with the words: 'The Salvation Army' in gilt letters. . . . The band [group] gave a service of song in the Garden yesterday. It was noticeable that some of their hymns were set to American tunes such as 'Way down upon the Swanee River' and 'My Old Kentucky Home'. . . . They intend to spread themselves throughout the principal cities of the Union. . . ."

The contingent spent their first Sunday in America in an open-air attack. They entered barber shops and saloons, pricking at the conscience of everyone. A German saloon proprietress exclaimed, "Salvation Army, my God! Hans, lock the door." The first indoor meetings were held in a mission house, directed by a Mrs. Doolittle. Of one of these meetings, the *New York Herald* reported:

"A more motley, vice-smitten, pestilence-breeding, congregation could seldom be found in a house of worship. There were Negroes, dancing girls, prostitutes and station-house tramps sandwiched between well-dressed visitors who had sauntered in out of curiosity. . . . The floors were as clean as the deck of a man-of-war, but in a few minutes they were frescoed with tobacco juice, the stench became overpowering, and a yellow-fever pest house could not have been less attractive. . . . But The Salvation Army did not seem to mind the air, and the ladies knelt on the floor and took turns in praying. A 170-pound drayman-looking Negro came in and posed himself forward in prayer as unctuous as would a young lady in a 300,000 dollar Episcopal Church."

On the next Friday, the American invasion force was still without a suitable hall. Harry Hill, the vigorous and cagey proprietor of a Bowery theater, had been at Castle Garden the day they arrived. He undoubtedly saw in them a good comedy act for his patrons. How would the Salvationists like a spot on Sunday night's program? Railton visited the theater and "found a houseful of splendid young men and women drinking and dancing 'to hell.'" He accepted the offer but no remuneration personally. Harry Hill was amazed, "You're the greatest fools I've ever known!" A pastor heard of the invitation and fumed, "That is the most disreputable den in the United States. Go there and you will lose your reputation."

"Then that's the place for us," answered Railton.

The Harry Hill theater announced:

> The Salvation Army will attract [misspelling for attack] the Kingdom of the Devil in Harry Hill's Variety The-ater on Sunday, March 14, 1880, commencing at 6:30 p.m. sharp, after which the panorama of "Uncle Tom's Cabin." Admission 25c.

The meeting was conducted and Railton begged the audi-ence, "If you've never prayed in your lives before, pray now." He knelt in the middle of the stage. The group sang another hymn to the tune, "Rosalie, the Prairie Flower." A row of seekers knelt, and the theater band struck up "There's a Land that is Fairer than Day." Railton marched to the door, saying to Harry Hill, "Ah, Mr. Hill, we must have you. You're the sort of man we want in the army of the Lord."

It was in Harry Hill's theater that "Ashbarrel Jimmy," one of The Army's earliest American "trophies of grace" was converted. Jimmy was a well-known and typical Bowery drunk. One windy night his cap blew off in an empty wooden ash barrel. Trying to retrieve it, he toppled in head first and couldn't extricate himself. Eventually, a policeman came along and rapped the soles of Jimmy's feet with his night stick.

"Who is it?" he said.

"It's me," said Jimmy.

"And who are you?"

"Jimmy Kemp."

The policeman knew Jimmy well, having arrested him many times. He yanked hard but the nails in the rim of the barrel caught Jimmy's clothes, so he picked up Jimmy, barrel and all, and hustled him off to the stationhouse. The next morning the judge said, "Jimmy, I'm tired of sending you to jail so here's a new sentence. The Salvation Army is holding meetings in Harry Hill's theater, and I'm ordering you to attend their meetings."

That was the last time Jimmy ever showed up in a police court. His sensational conversion attracted huge crowds, crowds which gave enough in subsequent collections to "rent a hall on Seventh Avenue, and the real work of The Salvation Army began." This was New York's first corps, commanded by Captain Emma Westbrook.

Local ministers were, for the most part, unfriendly after the Bowery theater episode. Christianity had been scandalized. The religious press was aghast, though the secular press was more objective and from some quarters came appreciation. *Harper's Weekly* reported:

"Energy and perseverance in any undertaking are apt to bring their reward, and there can be no question that the labors of The Salvation Army have met with great apparent success. They seem to seek out and take into their organization persons from the very worst classes, and yet the work does not fall to pieces. That the labors of The Army will meet with as much success on our shores, as on the other side of the ocean, if not more, there can be little doubt. It scarcely behooves those who are doing little or nothing to help and regenerate their fellowmen to be too critical regarding the methods of conscientious persons who are devoting their lives to such work."

In addition to distress over lack of co-operation from the churches, Railton was having difficulty with the mayor of New York. He had wanted to hold an open-air service in Union Square the first Sunday, but had been refused permission since only ordained ministers could be accorded such courtesy. He would have defied local law in the name of liberty except that he felt without police protection open-air meetings were impossible, "ruffianism being what it was." The situation was intolerable to Railton. He asked to see the mayor, and on March 16, "to his Honor the Mayor and the Corporation of the City of New York, G. S. Railton by the grace of God and by the appointment of William Booth, General of The Salvation Army" set forth his position. He stated that if permission was not forthcoming, "I shall forthwith remove the headquarters of this Army in America to some city where equal privileges are enjoyed by all citizens ordained or not ordained in the matter of serving the Lord and saving souls. . . ."

When permission was not granted, Railton moved his entire force to Philadelphia and on March 24, preached to 1,500 people in his first service in the Athletic Hall on 13th Street. In May, 1880, two months after his arrival, he cabled his General that the American forces now consisted of 8 batteries, 16 officers, 40 cadets, 412 privates and that stations had been started in Philadelphia, New York, and Newark. He grieved that Negro response was less than he had expected, but noted. "We have the honor today to be the only white people to whose company, to whose platforms, to whose operations colored people have had the same welcome as others. . . . If they will not join themselves with other races, we will go farther still, and there will be found officers ready to leave off association with their own race in order to rescue those of another."

This gay glory preacher would not be depressed, even by lack of funds. London headquarters, which by this time subsidized the American venture, was worried about expense. Railton replied: "How could we appeal, either to God or man, if we stopped in our trenches all the time? To advance is one of the necessaries of life—to me anyhow—and advancing where nobody has been means getting into a desert where there is sure to be famine coming now and then, and lots worse than that. . . ."

He was elated over the opening of a German-American corps: "The first German corps has had a most promising start in one of the worst neighborhoods outside hell. A drunkard was saved and a brother had his eyes almost knocked out at the first service. Now, it is impossible for us to fight our way without winning, and therefore, how grand must be the future before us."

Fighting, to Railton, meant eventual victory.

In the fall, Railton decided to move "National" headquarters, a few papers, a table, chair and a bedstead in a basement room, to St. Louis, Missouri. Why, can only be conjectured. It was centrally located and possibly earlier reports of successful open-air evangelism influenced him. He went alone. Unfortunately, St. Louis was not waiting to welcome him.

Hall after hall was engaged, but owners threw out the international Salvation Army when they discovered what manner of people this unprepossessing Englishman magnetized: "Congregations that broke seats and chairs—hooted, catcalled, ate peanuts and spit on the floor." The city authorities again would not allow him the freedom of the streets. Railton, as always, had an idea:

"It struck me that the authorities of the city would have no power over the iced Mississippi, especially on the Illinois side. So after distributing handbills to the host of men hard at work on Sunday sawing and hauling ice to the storehouse, I went to the part where the skaters were, and began to sing, 'Sinners, whither would you wander?' It was quite a novelty to have a congregation come skating round one at a speed that made it seem certain to me would overturn the others, but they were too skillful for that. I felt blessedly at home, whilst urging them to seek God."

In St. Louis, Railton issued the first American *War Cry* although a paper called *The Salvation News* had been published previously. The *Cry* was dated January, 1881.

He was dismayed at the intolerance shown his American women converts and wrote Catherine Booth: "Those English may stick to their men as hard as they like, but I am certain it is the women who are going to burst up the world generally, especially American women. . . . American ladies are rapidly getting the first front places in the world. Yet no person has the wit or the diligence to make more of them. . . .

On January 22, 1881, in the midst of the battle, the General ordered Railton to return to London. His journalistic ability and his presence were needed. Ireland, France, and Australia had been invaded, and there were damaging riots by hoodlums in Whitechapel. Railton protested, but he finally went. He was a soldier and obeyed orders, a paradoxical element of his strange, tempestuous nature. When he presented a proposal to William which was turned down, he would say, "Well, all hands to the oars then," and the subject was closed.

Railton was indeed needed. The Booth children were increasingly helpful. Bramwell, 24, was Chief-of-Staff; Ballington, 23, and Catherine, 22, were eloquent evangelists. But the expansion of the Army had placed an unbearable burden on Bramwell. Riotous attacks were growing in number and brutality, and the elder Catherine was often too ill to be of any help. At Glasgow, in 1880, she was suddenly stricken, her leg swelling grotesquely. Urged by William not to disappoint the waiting throng, she was half carried to the meeting, but spoke with apparent ease and great "liberty": "I rose to speak in the strength of the Lord," she said later, "and from the moment I opened my mouth until I ceased I never felt my knee, except once or twice when I moved it."

Railton's successor to the American command, Major Thomas E. Moore, was appointed and dispatched to the United States immediately. Soon after assuming command, he struck out for a more independent American force. Undoubtedly he was influenced by American nationalism and believed independence from London to be the only answer. The idea of incorporation had firmly jelled in his head soon after his arrival, and was intensified when the Fifth New Jersey Corps of The Salvation Army rebelled against his authority and that of international headquarters and incorporated itself under state laws, legally demanding funds it had contributed to national headquarters. Moore would not agree, and he was embarrassingly arrested for his unlawful action. He was now convinced that The Salvation Army must be incorporated as a "religious and charitable organization under the laws of the various states."

Until property was acquired, no problem had developed regarding control and ownership. After property was owned, questions of title and property deeds had to be faced. In England, all "was under the General's hat," but for an alien to purchase and hold property in the United States at that time was difficult, if not impossible. Moore declared his intention of becoming a naturalized citizen, and therefore able to own real estate. The Salvation Army property was deeded in his name. He was now responsible morally to William Booth and legally to the United States government. To him this was an untenable position. In July, 1883, when he and two pioneers, Captains Emma Westbrook and Jonas Inman, presented the case personally to William, their General was against the move. William felt it would limit the authority of International Headquarters (IHQ). There must be unity, and there must be obedience. Distressed, Moore continued his plea for incorporation.

During these years, the salvation war in the United States was opposed with massive vigor. In March, 1880, the Salvationists used the old Odeon theater to bombard Newark, New Jersey. Citizens soon became vocal against the "fire hazard," and a Newark *Daily Advertiser* report said:

"There is not the least objection to The Salvation Army saving all the souls possible, but there are not many positive Christians who would care to go to heaven through a broken neck, or in a chariot of fire."

In 1882, meetings were conducted by Captain Westbrook in Brooklyn's Lyceum theater. There were disturbances from the beginning. During an open-air meeting in 1885, there was a sudden lunge by a drunkard who, swinging a brick, struck Captain Mary Powell a smashing blow across the forehead She crumpled to the street and that was the signal for a full-scale attack. Several Salvationists suffered broken arms and legs, and the Captain was unconscious for 24 hours. A few weeks later, at the same corps, Captain Richard Holz was hit by a brick and left for dead. Soldiers were then forbidden to hold open-air meetings. As an alternative, they marched very slowly through the streets, singing and testifying.

During the spring of 1883, Irish-born Alfred Wells was farewelled* from his appointment in northern Ireland to open

---

*Farewell: (From Orders and Regulations) When his superiors decide that an officer should have a change of appointment, he is sent Farewell Orders and is usually allowed two weeks to make preparations for departure. Marching Orders for the officer's new appointment usually follow Farewell Orders after an interval of a week. "Farewell" also refers informally to the entire procedure of an officer's leavetaking of an appointment, and to his final public and private services.

fire in San Francisco. Selected personally by General Booth, the 24-year-old Captain was commissioned a Major and told, "You are the man I've been looking for for 14 months. Are you willing to go as pioneer of the Army to California? They have been writing and rewriting for over a year . . . and the minute my eyes caught yours something said, 'That is the man you are looking for for California.'"

"I'm yours for China or anywhere else," said the dauntless Wells.

Two years earlier, a remarkable awakening had taken place on the Pacific Coast, especially in California. It was known as the Holiness Revival. It became the Holiness Association, which met annually at Beulah Park in Oakland. After studying a London *War Cry,* the evangelists decided they wanted to join The Army. They requested officers but none could be spared. They then fashioned themselves into The Army in the best way they could, wearing uniforms and publishing a *War Cry*.

Major Alfred Wells and his assistant, 22-year-old Captain Henry Stillwell, landed in New York on May 16, 1883. For six weeks they were entertained graciously by Major Moore while awaiting word from the Holiness Association, and both were active in meetings and conferences. Wells later commented that "the Major [Moore] was not at all himself physically and was crowded with the most important engagements both here and in Canada." After an official "send-off" from Brooklyn's Lyceum theater on June 7, Wells traveled alone to San Francisco, arrived on July 21, 1883, and began West Coast operations at 815 Montgomery Street. He was not joined by Captain Stillwell until later.

Not all of the Holiness Association members found Salvation Army methods as appealing as they had anticipated, and about half of the 30 members soon left the ranks. Wells reported:

"Some of these dear friends met me in a reception meeting at which we tried to make ourselves understood. Religion without the Cross is no part of a Salvationist's belief. . . . Very few of my new friends felt called to adorn themselves with our uniform or doctrine as a whole. Those who did proved to be friends indeed. In this world and the next I shall gratefully remember them."

By the time Stillwell arrived, Wells had set up headquarters at 142½ Fourth Street, near the docks, and had three corps under his command—San Francisco, Oakland, and San Jose. A year later, he and Captain Stillwell were joined by their fiancées from England, Captain Polly Medford and Captain Mary Matthews, and there was a double wedding. Afterward, Polly demanded a brass band, insisting that every decent Army corps must have one. Wells explained the necessity to the soldiery, who soon raised $600 to pay Sherman, Clay and Company for a complete set of instruments. A teacher was engaged, and seven lessons were given to each of 12 soldiers, who knew nothing about music. "Horrible faces they made," said Wells later. "I told them they blew their cheeks out and grew red in the face. After seven lessons, with new uniforms and instruments, we were out in Frisco's streets, more than ever a terror to the devil and all evildoers."

While Major Wells was training his first troops against tremendous opposition, help came in the person of one of the most picturesque and indomitable pioneers The Army ever had: Neshan (Joseph) Garabedean, an Armenian born in Turkey, who was converted in Los Angeles. A shoemaker by trade, he was referred to as "Joe the Turk." Six-feet-two, with the build of a prizefighter, flashing, mesmeric black eyes and fierce looking mustache, Joe appointed himself unofficial guard of the Salvationists. Nobody trifled with Joe. He was known as the "Walking Terror," and it was said that when he got into a vicious mood he would clean out a crowded barroom. He went out "every night looking for a fight," and there were plenty to be had. Burly Joe was so effective that the harassed Salvationists used to say, "If that fellow Joe is there tonight we'll have a good meeting."

Joe soon gave himself to God, becoming in turn, door-keeper, soldier, and officer, and was often appointed a roving evangelist wherever the fight was hottest. He became expert in court appeals and probably did more to win the right of free speech for Salvationists than any other person of his era. He soon adopted a uniform that would attract attention: shimmering crimson pantaloons, an Army tunic with his personally chosen decorations, and a Turkish fez.

He carried an ink pad and stamp, with the words "Jesus Saves," and wherever he marched, he stamped. A red-yellow-and-blue umbrella was also a characteristic of Joe, described in a *War Cry* report as "the only illuminated umbrella in the world . . . of great size, and illuminated by nine electric lights of different hues." Booth pictures decorated the sections, along with mottoes such as BE JUST AND FEAR NOT, JESUS IS MIGHT TO SAVE, GET RIGHT WITH GOD, and GOD BLESS OUR GENERAL. At the top was a novel design of the Statue of Liberty enlightening the world. He also played a shiny brass cornet "loud enough to wake up the old devil."

He painted his shoe shop red, yellow, and blue, decorated it with mottoes and Bible verses, and pounded brass nails on the sidewalk to read: "Are you saved?"

He put a flag over the building with SAN FRANCISCO FOR JESUS! embroidered on it, and pounded S's on the bottoms of all the shoes he repaired. It was said that "what used to be a hell-hole became a glory hole," with Joe exuberantly introducing people to God in his prayer room that had once been a gambling den.

During a Los Angeles campaign, in his guernsey (sweater) of red, with PREPARE TO MEET YOUR GOD on the front and SALVATION OR DAMNATION on the back, Joe was arrested and jailed. In seven days, he converted most of the 30 drunks locked up with him, cleaned up the "pig pen" with a hose and broom, and was finally defended by a lawyer who came to his cell, gasping, "Please let me defend you. I'm dying on my feet. I haven't slept since you have been in jail. Every time I close my eyes I see you marching through my house; and when I try to work I hear a voice demanding 'Get that man out of jail!' "

The judge was chagrined to hear that Joe had been in jail seven days without a trial.

"What was he arrested for?"

"For blowing a horn."

"Is blowing a horn a crime?" said the judge. "Every show and circus that comes to town blows horns whenever they want to." He dismissed the case, and Joe got on his big knees and prayed fervently for the court. During his career Joe was imprisoned 53 times and often was stoned and beaten by mobs.

In February, 1884, Captain William Evans invaded Buffalo, New York, and wired headquarters: "Tremendous opening at Buffalo; terrible engagement; the power of hell driven back; two prisoners," but the *Buffalo Express* had a somewhat different attitude, declaring:

"The 'Grand Salvation Free-and-Easy Meeting' in the afternoon was attended by a large and noisy crowd which, until a police officer arrived, ran things about as they liked. . . . Four converts were drummed in at this meeting."

In September, Boston was invaded by Captain Annie Shirley, mother of pioneer Eliza. Phillips Brooks wrote: "With the purpose you have in mind, you will not doubt my deepest sympathy. . . . I wish you the best guidance and blessing in all your work."

———————

During the summer of 1884, two International Headquarters representatives had been sent to study the need for incorporation and other aspects of Moore's administration, and after investigation had recommended that the property be kept in the name of Major Moore but mortgaged to General Booth. In addition, they reported unfavorably upon Moore's bookkeeping procedures, and relayed to IHQ the dissatisfaction of many of the country's divisional leaders. Moore was ordered to farewell and take command of Salvation Army forces in South Africa. Instead, on October 21, 1884, he seceded.

This almost lethal blow was struck at United States Salvation Army forces now numbering about 300 officers and 5,000 converts. Articles of incorporation of "The Salvation Army" were signed by Moore and five other men in defiance of the General's order not to incorporate. In seceding, Moore took with him 80 per cent of officers and soldiers, all properties, including land, barracks, musical instruments, books, hymnals, uniforms, and insignia. He also copyrighted the *War Cry* title. Many Salvationists followed him, some from insufficient knowledge, some in disquiet over what seemed to be lack of interest in London.

For one thing, the fourth anniversary congress, held in May, had been attended neither by William Booth nor Bramwell, though announcements of the appearance of one or both had been widely circulated. The Congress, of course, "was an important affair, attended by 2,000 Salvationists." It would have been an opportune time for the General to invigorate his American forces. Many of them had never seen him or heard his thunderous proclamations, nor had they felt the magnificence of his overpowering bearing, which far outweighed his seemingly autocratic and sometimes implacable nature.

Thirty-year-old Commissioner Frank Smith, from International Headquarters, took command of the American forces. He was a stiff-looking officer, with a long face, a mass of curly dark hair, and an intense expression. He commented on the situation: "Many of the officers, accustomed to implicit obedience, handed over to Moore the funds, etc., on hand, and the original Army was thus, as far as man could do it, ruined—a few corps only remaining. . . ."

However, Smith was a shrewd businessman. He grappled with the situation expertly and in two weeks the *War Cry* was again published, though only 17 posts remained. Said Smith in retrospect: ". . . Moore left behind him that which he had no power to take or to make, the enthusiasm, energy, and zeal of a band of men and women who, smarting under the desertion of their leader, were thereby drawn to lean more than ever upon God. . . ."

Smith was a harsh and unrelenting judge of all dissenters and tagged them "rebels unworthy of further trust." Among those who quickly saw their mistake was a man later to become a dynamic leader, Richard Holz. He could not get a hearing until Smith's successor arrived and publicly welcomed him and 31 others back at the town hall in Saratoga, New York, on October 16, 1889. By then, Moore's group had dissipated.

During Smith's command The Army fought forward, despite public disaffection, and in two years, it had doubled its numbers.

Canada, which had been under Moore, was now made a separate command under Major Thomas B. Coombs.

The West was opened and constituted Chicago and everything to the Coast except for San Francisco operations, which were directed from London until 1887.

On Washington's Birthday, 1885, Major William Evans, together with his wife Hannah and assistant, Captain Edwin

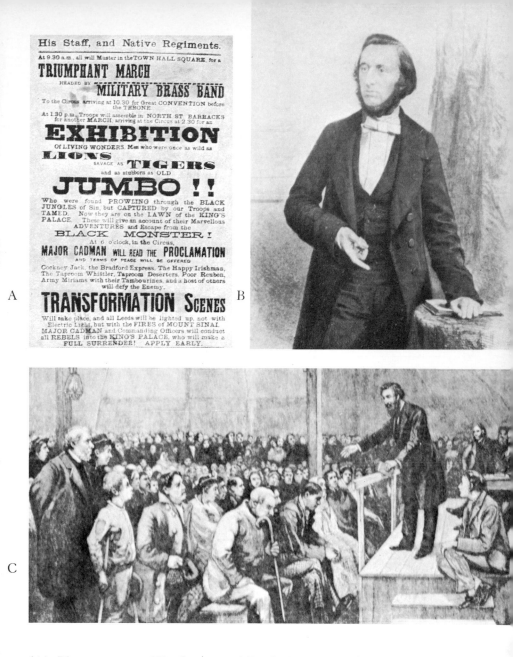

(A) *Pioneer poster;* (B) *Controversial painting presented to William Booth in 1856;* (C) *William Booth preaching at the Quaker Burial Ground, Whitechapel, 1865.*

A

(A) *Drawing of William Booth's ministry in East End of London;* (B) *Historic Christian Mission report of 1878 in which Salvation Army was named for the first time;* (C) *The Reverend William and Catherine Booth, 1860;* (D) *The Sheffield Riot.*

D

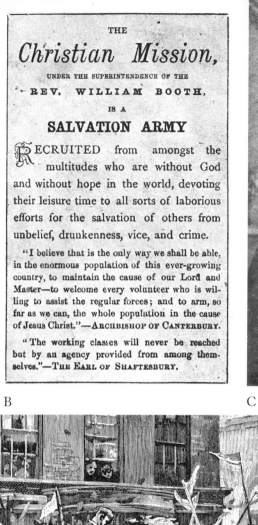

THE

Christian Mission,

UNDER THE SUPERINTENDENCE OF THE

REV. WILLIAM BOOTH,

IS A

SALVATION ARMY

RECRUITED from amongst the
multitudes who are without God
and without hope in the world, devoting
their leisure time to all sorts of laborious
efforts for the salvation of others from
unbelief, drunkenness, vice, and crime.

"I believe that is the only way we shall be able,
in the enormous population of this ever-growing
country, to maintain the cause of our Lord and
Master—to welcome every volunteer who is willing to assist the regular forces; and to arm, so
far as we can, the whole population in the cause
of Jesus Christ."—ARCHBISHOP OF CANTERBURY.

"The working classes will never be reached
but by an agency provided from among themselves."—THE EARL OF SHAFTESBURY.

B

C

A   B

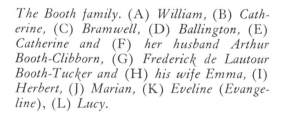

The Booth family. (A) *William,* (B) *Catherine,* (C) *Bramwell,* (D) *Ballington,* (E) *Catherine and* (F) *her husband Arthur Booth-Clibborn,* (G) *Frederick de Lautour Booth-Tucker and* (H) *his wife Emma,* (I) *Herbert,* (J) *Marian,* (K) *Eveline (Evangeline),* (L) *Lucy.*

C

D   E   F

G   H   I

J   K   L

A

B

C

D

(A) *Pioneer campaign brigade, U.S.A., 1890;* (B) *Ballington Booth and national headquarters staff, 1892;* (C) *Army bride and groom, 1890's;* (D) *New York and Brooklyn slum officers;* (E) *Preparing for open-air service, 1890's.*

E

A   B

C

D

(A) and (B) Salvation Army quarters at the Klondike, 1898; (C) Soapy Smith and bodyguards at bar in Skagway, Alaska, 1898; (D) The Yukon Field Force of the Salvation Army, 1898.

A   B

THE SALVATION ARMY AS EVANSTON SEES IT

EVANSTON MUST BE SAVED

C

SOMEBODY'S GIRL.

OUT in the darkness, out in the sleet,
 Outcast and homeless, walking the street,
  Sinful and wretched, friendless and poor,
Somebody's girl we find close to our door.

Chorus.—" Throw out the life-line."

Yes, they are wicked, degraded, and vile,
Seldom, if ever, does one of them smile;
Call it not laughter, the sound that they make,
Only to hide the heart ready to break.

Yet, they are sisters, yes, every one,
Reaping in sorrow the deeds they have done
And whilst the world its anathema hurls,
We mean to help them—somebody's girls.

We have the Shelter, the Home, and the light,
We long to bring to their lives something bright!
We will find shelter, if you will give gold,
Can you a little to help us withhold ?

Mothers, whose daughters are all that you would,
All that is virtuous, noble, and good,
Whilst at our efforts so many lips curl,
Help us to rescue some mother's lost girl!—L. F.

D

(A) *Samuel Logan Brengle, drawing by R. L. Keeler;* (B) *Cartoon depicting Salvation Army efforts in Evanston, Illinois, 1890's;* (C) *National Staff Band, 1899;* (D) *Poem appearing in the Salvation Army* War Cry, *1898.*

A

B

C

(A) *Contemporary drawing depicting arrival in the U.S. of the Railton party;* (B) *Poster announcing special service;* (C) *Blanche Cox, pioneer of the Cellar, Gutter, and Garret Brigade;* (D) *War Cry art, 1890's;* (E) *Lassies of the Railton party.*

D

YOU CAN HELP

E

A

B

(A) *Joe the Turk in 1928;* (B) *An early day picture of Joe the Turk;* (C) *Joe's trademark when he made shoes;* (D) *Captain and Mrs. Amos Shirley;* (E) *Embroidered bookmark sold by The Salvation Army;* (F) *Eliza Shirley;* (G) *Emma Westbrook.*

C

D

E

F

G

NOW, MR. BOOTH, LET US KNOW WHAT YOU ARE GOING TO DO WITH ALL
THIS MONEY!

. . . and became a fool for
Christ's sake . . .

While many scoffed at his
methods . . .

. . . he traveled around the earth . . .

Gay, arrived in Chicago in a snowstorm. Captain Gay was rarely separated from his concertina and played it vigorously whether encouraged or disdained. Although the *Chicago Tribune* dubbed them a "circus" and some rowdy Chicagoans tried to discourage their efforts, they readied the old Bush Temple in seven days for a meeting of 1,500 listeners in a building meant for 1,000. A *Chicago Tribune* reporter noted that many converts "looked as if they needed a change of linen as much as a change of heart."

The red-jerseyed evangelists made many immediate converts. As soon as they were suitably enrolled, they were instructed and sent to other parts of the city to establish new strongholds. Captain Gay was then left in charge, and the Evans moved on to other areas of challenge. Often, Mrs. Evans, carrying a new baby, conducted her own campaigns while her husband was busy in another town. Within four years, 76 corps, including eight in Chicago, had been opened under their leadership in the Midwest.

Times were difficult and persecution rife, but late in 1885, Evans reported happily: "Things are settling down." The first convert in Elgin, Illinois, was a ruddy-faced boy named Eddie Parker, who later became National Commander of American forces.

Things were hardly settling down in other parts of the country. The barracks in Dover, New Hampshire, were twice burned down by arsonists. But more than 1,000 converts were won in Augusta, Maine.

The Marshalltown, Iowa, *Herald* said that The Army had so revolutionized the morals that "saloon-keepers bewail the loss of their customers and talk of abandoning their businesses." An Ohio reporter got mixed up with Salvationists and with them was shoved in jail where he was converted during an all-night meeting.

In New Bedford, Massachusetts, The Army was invited to

hold services in a saloon on Acushnet Avenue. A man knelt, rough, shaggy, and forbidding. Pressed to decide for God, he said, "No, I'm too bad." "No," replied the officer, "God can save even a murderer." "Can he?" The strained face relaxed. "Then he can save me because I'm one."

William Booth visited the United States for the first time in 1886. He was 57 at the time. There were "238 corps in the Union, under the leadership of 569 officers, mostly Americans." His enthusiasm was unbounded. He wrote Bramwell from Columbus, Ohio:

"I shall soon love this country. I am not sure that if there were to be a quarrel between your herdmen and my herdmen, as with Abraham and Lot, and you were to have the choice of countries and you chose the Old One—I am not sure— whether I should not *very thankfully* take this, but we must have them both   "

In his correspondence during the journey there were repeated references to his son, Ballington. Obviously he believed Ballington was the man for the commandership of the States, but cautioned, "You know his danger. I don't want him to suppose that I am driven up to this. The temptation to linger will be awful. . . . It must be an appointment for a time, say five years. . . ."

During William's visit, he preached in a minor hall of Tremont Temple, Boston. The afternoon meeting "was crowded with preachers, several hundred strong." One engrossed Boston Theological Seminary student, Samuel Logan Brengle, cried emphathetically as William spoke. During the evening meeting, a young student named Charles R. Brown was converted with a number of others.*

---

*Charles Reynolds Brown later became a noted Congregational clergyman, lecturer, and author of religious books. In 1911 he became Dean of the Yale Divinity School.

Self Denial, an annual effort involving personal sacrificial giving for missionary work, was instituted. This was suggested when Irish-born Major John Carleton, a prominent officer who had been a successful businesman, sent a note to William during a meeting. A request had been made for desperately needed funds. The note said: "By going without my pudding [dessert] every day for a year, I calculate I shall save 50 shillings. This I will do and will remit the amount named as quickly as possible." William saw in this act a sound idea, but he felt a puddingless year too great a sacrifice so shortened the time to one week.*

The new commander of the United States, Ballington Booth, and his wife Maud, arrived in 1887 to succeed Smith, who was in poor health. The tall, handsome, eloquent Ballington, in so many respects like his father, was an intuitive and astute commander, possessing more suavity and gentility than William but almost as much "bullheadedness." Maud Charlesworth Booth, daughter of an Anglican minister and assistant to young Catherine Booth in her perilous invasion of France, was cultured, energetic, and winsome. She led in instituting prison work and pressing Auxiliary League membership for New York's leading citizens. She became New York society's delightful conversation piece.

The *War Cry* was playing an important role in conversions in America in 1887.

A woman wrapped her husband's dinner in a *War Cry* and after he'd eaten, when no one was near, he read it. He was convinced and converted. A Chinese laundryman sent collars and cuffs home in a leaf of the *Cry*. A woman who had never

---

* What was started to help meet general expenses became the present-day annual worldwide effort to aid missionary work. It is still traditional and, in the United States, falls each year on the week preceding Easter.

seen the paper read it, decided to go to a meeting and gave herself to God.*

During 1887 a most unpromising recruit joined the American ranks—Samuel Logan Brengle, the young Methodist minister who had been so impressed by General Booth during seminary days that he had cried. He volunteered for officership, despite the offer by millionaire wagon-maker, Clement Studebaker, that he become pastor of a new church Studebaker had built in South Bend, Indiana.

"Brengle," said William Booth, "you belong to the dangerous classes. You have been your own boss for so long that I don't think you will want to submit to Salvation Army discipline. We are an army, and we demand obedience."

Brengle was given several New England corps. High principled, disciplined, with a literary talent, Brengle had an aesthetic nature that mirrored the "Higher Religion" William taught his people to live. "He surrounded the victims of satan with the presence of the Savior," wrote Clarence Hall in Brengle's biography.

In November, 1888, orders came: "You are appointed as officer in charge of Boston #1 Corps." The city of his friends! Shortly after, a ruffian hurled a paving brick and hit Brengle full force in the head. For some time he was not expected to live. Determined not to waste time during his long convales-

---

* The *War Cry* is as powerful today as in the 1880's. A weekly magazine, uniquely slanted both to Christians and non-Christians, it has a distribution of well over 20 million copies yearly in the United States. It is published around the world in 51 editions and has been distributed door to door, to business and professional offices and to factories since the first copy rolled from The Army's creaking press in 1879. The local *War Cry* sergeant (seller) is often the most important Salvationist in town. He is The Army's contact man, the buffer, and daily gospel messenger. William Booth believed that the *Cry* was a good means of telling contributors what The Army was doing with the money entrusted to it. More important, it was needed to help make the world aware of both good and evil.

cence, he wrote a series of articles for the *War Cry,* titled, "Helps to Holiness." These were later translated into more than a dozen languages. Today they still are widely read. Brengle used to smilingly say, "Well, if there had been no little brick there would have been no little book."

Instrumental music was being used increasingly in the fray. The *War Cry* of June 25, 1887, reported:

"A large staff band has been started at our center in New York with a sure prospect of success. All the bandsmen are saved. They are all commissioned and will wear a special white uniform helmet. Cheer up, you silent corps; with so many instrumentalists at headquarters, you will soon have a boom." *

In 1888, tow-headed, ten-year-old Carl Sandburg of Galesburg, Illinois, slipped into Army meetings in the "low-ceilinged battered hall at South Broad Street on the public square." Later, he went there again when Pastor Nyblad formed the new Elim Church. But he didn't like the pastor much. "I couldn't think why he should give such attention in sermons to The Salvation Army, unless it was that he was afraid The Army might take away from him some of the Swedes who had stood by him. . . . I couldn't think of any other reason for his using a whole hour to slam-bang The Salvation Army. . . ." Carl "got pleasure" from The Salvation Army, sometimes

---

*The New York Staff Band has given unbroken service and established an excellent reputation both for instrumental and vocal renditions. It has performed for eight presidents, played throughout the United States and the British Isles and appeared on network TV and radio programs. It has also made several record albums. A Staff Band was organized in Chicago in 1907. This pace-setter has been called "a symphony in brass," but even more often, "the band with the sacred message." It has traveled widely, made records and not long ago played for the Midwest National Band Clinic held in Chicago. Dr. Edwin Franko Goldman, eminent bandmaster, stated of it: "The Chicago Staff Band is equal in performance to most professional bands I have heard."

played his guitar in meetings and stood on the street corner with Salvationists.*

———

During Brigadier Britton's visit to Marysville, Ohio, in 1888, the sheriff offered him the courthouse gratis for services. A report stated:

"The jury sat in the jury box as if the court was still in session; the sheriff kindly assisted in keeping the door, while his honor the mayor, with 11 lawyers and nine doctors, were among the audience. One soul sought salvation."

In Chicago, Nora Marks, a pseudonym for a reporter on the *Chicago Tribune,* jumped to her feet in dismay when asked by her editor, "How would you like to join The Salvation Army?" Her assignment was a series of articles published later in book form by Rand McNally and Company and titled, *Facts about The Salvation Army.* Before reading it, many thought the book was an attempt to discredit The Army, but it turned the tide of public opinion and The Army was respected in Chicago from that time on.

———

In 1889, the Booth family suffered a cruel blow. Catherine was told she had cancer and that there was no hope for recovery. After hearing the verdict, she drove home and told William. He sat down, speechless. She knelt beside him, saying, "Do you know what my first thought was? That I should not be here to nurse you at your last hour."

William sat facing a picture of Christ on the Cross which was hanging on the wall. He thought he could understand it then as never before. He could only kneel with her and try to pray.

———

* Young Carl became the world-renowned poet and historian.

For a few months Catherine struggled to continue public speaking and for an even longer time dictated letters and articles, but foreboding filled the home. Suffering intensely, she had to spend much of her time in bed. It was the most painful period of William's life. To go home was anguish. To be away was worse. Life became a burden almost too heavy to be borne. She was the family's seer, their molder, their rock. They were crushed.

Nevertheless, as month dragged after agonizing month, Catherine gave her soldier family the order they so often gave subordinate warriors: "At all costs, go forward!"

They advanced as best they could.

"I know what that woman used to be—
one of the worst drunkards in Hull."

Chapter Four
1890 / 1899

PERSECUTION
AND
PROGRESS

EVERYONE was reading William Booth's *In Darkest England and the Way Out*. Not even William could have guessed the reception. The first edition of 10,000 was sold out on publication day, October 20, 1890. A month later, 10,000 copies had rolled off the presses A third edition of 40,000 was under way. By the following October, 200,000 had been sold, and the book was being translated into Dutch, Japanese, German, French, and Swedish.

T. H. Huxley, prominent English biologist-surgeon, was the most ferocious critic. For a year he wrote denunciatory letters to the London *Times*. Professor W. J. Ashley, noted Anglo-American economist, in the *Political Science Quarterly*, was sure that "General Booth's 'panacea' " was no better than a quack medicine.

But thousands welcomed the book with no reservations. Archdeacon Farrar of Westminster Abbey answered Huxley in the *Daily Graphic*. Cardinal Manning, Roman Catholic archbishop of Westminster, wrote: ". . . every living soul cost the most precious Blood, and we ought to save it—even the worthless and the worst. . . ." Actor S. B. Bancroft offered to donate £1,000 to The Salvation Army if 99 others would do the same. The Duke of Fife sent £100, and the Prince of Wales (Edward VII) expressed extreme interest.

Drawing his title from Stanley's *Darkest Africa,* William had presented the plight of the "submerged tenth" of England and proposed a comprehensive plan for rehabilitation all done in the name of Christ. What appeared to be revolutionary had already been tested. The book was a record of proved experiments rather than the drawing of broad ideas. By the end of 1890, the following social services were listed:

Rescue Homes (fallen women)	33
Slum Posts	33
Prison Gate Brigades	10
Food Depots	4
Shelters for the Destitute	5
Inebriates' Home	1
Factory for the "out of work"	1
Labor Bureaus	2

Within three years, the following additional services were offered: homes for the homeless, inquiry offices, preventive homes for girls, temporary work in the city, temporary work in the country, children restored to parents, poor man's bank, poor man's lawyer, labor brigade, household salvage brigade, homes for children.

The underlying cause of the attacks on William appear to have been in his daring belief that religion should embrace social concern, and social amelioration be concerned with religion. William was not a social reformer; he was a preacher. He believed that God, and only God, could redeem and fulfill a man. He believed that Jesus Christ is "the Way, the Truth and the Life," and that no man comes unto the Father but by Him. He also believed that "thousands of these poor wretches are not so much born into this world as damned into it." He questioned: "Why all this apparatus of temples and meeting-houses to save men from perdition in a world which is to come, while never a helping hand is stretched out to save them from the inferno of their present life?"

Society felt the bite of his insistence that "while recognizing that the primary responsibility must always rest upon the individual, we may fairly insist that society which, by its habits, its customs, and its laws, has greased the slope down which these poor creatures slide to perdition, shall seriously take in hand their salvation." He proposed to deal with the undeserving poor exactly as he knelt with the deserving poor.

His "Cab-Horse Charter," about which he wrote in *In Darkest England and the Way Out* became the byword of the scheme:

"When in the streets of London a Cab-Horse, weary or careless or stupid, trips and falls and lies stretched out in the midst of traffic, there is no question of debating how he came to stumble before we try to get him on his legs again. The Cab-Horse is a very real illustration of poor broken-down humanity. . . . These are the two points to the Cab Horse's Charter. When he is down he is helped up, and while he lives he has food, shelter and work."

William asked the public for £100,000 to carry out his "scheme." By the beginning of February, 1891, he had received £108,000, and by September, 1892, the amount had reached £129,288.

Two weeks before the publication of *In Darkest England,* William was struck by the most intolerable sorrow of his life. On October 4, Catherine was promoted to Glory. She had discussed the book and read proofs for it until the end. She had worked on the book as she lay in her cluttered bed, backed by the tricolored Army flag.

Near the end, Catherine slipped her wedding ring on his finger and said, "By this token we were united for a time, and by it now we are united for eternity." At the last, the family stood around her bed while Herbert sang. Once, when the singing ceased, she said, "Go . . . on!" She called "Pa!" several times. As the morning broke the children kissed her, then she took hold of William's hand and love illumined her emaciated face.

"Pa," she said.

He laid his lips on hers, and she was gone.

One of womankind's Christian vanguards was gone. Her persuasive ability in public ministry is well indicated by a remark from a hardheaded Scotsman, father of Dr. Randall Davidson, then chaplain to the Archbishop of Canterbury: "If ever I am charged with a crime, don't bother to engage any of the great lawyers to defend me. Get that woman!" Another gentleman, who had intended to denounce Army doctrine in the press, heard her, apologized, and handed her a check for £1,000. The answer to her manifestly powerful life, she explained, was her faith in God. Near the end she said, "The waters are rising, but so am I. I am not going under, but over." Those who saw her suffer and die believed her.

Under a colored canopy in the Army's Clapton Congress hall, with her Bible, crested jacket, bonnet, and Army flag on the coffin, Catherine's body lay, while thousands filed by. At the cemetery, William, husky but controlled, spoke:

". . . Out of the dark tunnel she has emerged into the light of day. . . . First, she was good . . . second, she was love. . . . Lastly, she was a warrior. . . . My comrades, I am going to meet her again. . . . What, then, is there left for me to do? . . . My work, plainly, is to fill up the weeks, the days, the hours, and cheer my poor heart as I go along with the thought that when I have served my Christ and my generation according to the will of God . . . she will bid me welcome to the skies, as He bade her. God bless you all. Amen."

Kneeling, he kissed the coffin as 10,000 began to sing Herbert Booth's hymn:

Blessed Lord, in Thee is refuge,
Safety for my trembling soul,

Power to lift my head when drooping
'Midst the angry billows' roll.
I will trust Thee,
All my life Thou shalt control.

"All my life Thou shalt control" was soon to be sung in many tongues across the seas as new "invasions" took place all over the globe.

In America, Ballington and Maud Booth became naturalized citizens and Americans were pleased. Ballington, with his height, intense personality, and dark good looks, was irresistible to many. He possessed a brilliant mind and had compassion for his fellow man. He was also approachable. He could "play with an audience as a Paderewski can with his instrument," said biographer Alexander Nicol. In moments of high emotion as he pictured the power of evil, his unusually long hands reached out to audiences in a manner that seemed to touch each one who listened. Despite his innate dignity, he was not beyond twisting his heavy black hair into two horns to better describe the devil. He was also a shrewd businessman, acutely aware of detail. During the first hard days of the withering depression that hit in 1891 due to United States overexpansion, he instituted men's shelters. He raised $6,000 for the annual Self-Denial fund and preached across the continent, spurring his battalions on, while appraising the country's social needs.

Maud Booth concentrated on prison, slum, and auxiliary work. Personal counseling and meetings with prisoners were instituted. "Slum sisters" were appointed to live among the people they ministered to, telling of a Savior who can make the vilest clean and the poorest happy. This work had already proved highly successful in England, and the slum sister program was the beginning of modern Salvation Army family welfare, hospital, community center, and settlement work.

Auxiliary league membership required members to defend The Army, pray for it, and contribute $5.00 annually to support its work. In return they received a pin, a weekly *War Cry,* and an invitation to special meetings.

Of Maud's efforts in "drawing room" meetings, as her forays into high society were called and from which she drew many of her Auxiliary helpers, G. A. Davis wrote in Frank Leslie's *Illustrated Weekly:*

". . . Mrs. Booth needs no introduction to the world of New York, where her sweet, womanly presence and the force of her personal magnetism have done more, perhaps, to remove prejudice and misconception and to help the cause dear to her heart, than any other individual worker in the field. . . ."

Despite the popularity of the Booths, salvation soldiers were having a hard time.

"Are you bound for Heaven or hell?" shouted the soldiers. "It's none of your business," was often the reply. There were a few, in the pioneer days of America, who believed God was in this noisome, spectacular band—and enlisted or defended its program. But there were more, the vast majority, who saw The Army as a rowdy band of fanatics. Often the very people to whom they had come thought them intruders. They didn't *want* to be saved.

It has been said that The Army literally "took Christianity into the streets." This is probably one of the most significant compliments ever paid it, for William Booth's attitude had always been: "We take Christianity into the streets because men ought to have it, whether they want it or not."

In Newport, Kentucky, soldiers were "thankful to the authorities of the city for giving police protection"; at Pueblo, Colorado, the march was hit with a "heavy shower of eggs and rotten apples from the top of a saloon." Newton, Iowa, lassies, imprisoned in 1891, composed and sang this song:

The hoodlums they did roar,
Till their throats are getting sore,
But they can't do any more, Hallelujah!
With Jesus as our friend,
He'll guide us to the end,
And on Him we will depend, in the prison.

Joe the Turk was jailed in East Portland, Oregon, for tooting his cornet despite an ordinance against "blowing horns." Several other Salvationists were sentenced to ten days but Joe got 15 extra for shouting, "Praise the Lord!" when the sentence was pronounced. One night he got a new cell-mate, a drunken painter named Jake, who had brought his paraphernalia with him.

"I can't find a soft spot anywhere on this board," moaned Jake in the middle of the night.

"Tell it to Jesus," counseled Joe.

The next morning Jake wanted to know more about religion. Did it really help to tell Jesus about yourself? Joe said it did. The two had a long and earnest conversation and Jake got converted. Elated, Joe considered Jake and his paints and brushes, then shouted, "Let's paint the walls for God."

Freshly white-washed walls made a fine canvas and soon a rainbow of letters a foot high proclaimed: PREPARE TO MEET YOUR GOD, WHERE WILL YOU SPEND ETERNITY? JESUS IS THE DRUNKARD'S FRIEND, REMEMBER MOTHER'S PRAYERS, and other startling reminders. The stunned jailer wailed, "What does this mean?"

"That Decoration Day is coming," said Joe meekly.

The judge was notified.

"What does this mean?" stormed the judge.

"That salvation is come to this house," said Joe, pointing to the sign, JESUS IS THE DRUNKARD'S FRIEND. "Judge, you're always drunk. He's the Friend you need."

A report noted: "The judge lost his dignity, was gloriously saved and in church and everywhere he goes testifies to the saving power of Jesus." He often carried the Army flag in the open-air march and for years protected Joe's cell signs, which were viewed by people from all parts of the country. At one time the local railroad company allowed stop-over tickets for this purpose.

In the New York slums, Major Emma Bown reported that a young man, formerly a bartender, had been converted. "As he came out of the hall one night about 18 young men set on him and thrashed him."

Michael Lambert, a St. Louis No. 2 Corps soldier, was murdered without provocation. Assaulted by young toughs, "one pounded him over the head with a club and when he fell another stoned him, while a third jumped on his prostrated body." A witness said he cried out, "Lord, forgive them."

On her way home from a meeting, "a foul assassin's blow killed Sister Maddock" of Pontiac, Michigan.

But victories were impressive too, and these kept the rank and file on the firing line. The Youngstown, Ohio, *Vindicator* reported: "Officer Bob Williams marched Salvation Army to city lock-up for blocking traffic, but Mayor Montgomery immediately orders release. Army marches away with band playing, 'When the battle's over we shall wear a crown.'"

In South Manchester, Connecticut, a converted drunk testified: "The change is so great that my dog knows I am saved and instead of his running away from me, comes to be petted."

Captain Wilbur Hall opened fire in Tampa, Florida, and though he and his assistant, Lieutenant Welles, reported: "Prospects are good for a soul-saving work being done in this city," they had a "hard go" until Happy Jack Gross, one of the cussedest fishermen to sail the Gulf of Mexico, was saved. Roughs and religionists sat up and took notice when Happy Jack dropped a pail of fresh-picked oysters and shouted, "Hallelujah!" Today, some of Captain Hall's children and grand-children are officers, and both second and third generations have contributed service to the African field. His son, Clarence, is a senior religious editor of *Reader's Digest*.

In Omaha, Nebraska, lay Salvationist Ida Lewis, mother of a large family, was asked by the penitentiary warden to visit the men and became unofficial chaplain for 50 years.

The Atlantic, Iowa, Captain reported the story of a Jewish man called Uncle Jake. "He comes to the meetings regularly. When we have converts, he takes them by the hand and con-gratulates them; he is sure to give in the collection and even shouts, 'Glory to God!' when we sing, 'Building up the Temple.' Uncle Jake said he believed in The Army's God but not their Christ."

Joe the Turk paraded the streets of Youngstown, Ohio, in his gaudy uniform. He wrote his own *War Cry* report:

"First I knew the police grabbed me, and marched me off to jail. . . . During five hours in jail I got two drunkards on their knees and made them sing and the police sang, 'Oh, it was a happy day when Jesus washed my sins away.' I put on the walls with my indelible pencil, 'Jesus is mighty to save!'"

In Minneapolis, Minnesota, the march went through First Street, the red-light district. At an open door sat a girl with her giggling companions. When the Salvationists began to sing, the girl leaped up, shrieking, "Oh, I can't stand that. My mother used to sing it." She rushed down the steps, into their midst and was restored to right living.

Captain Bartlett and his bride were forbidden to use musical instruments in Lyons, New York. They ignored the prohibition and marched anyhow, the Captain with a snare drum, another soldier with a bass drum. They were convicted and Bartlett was held under heavy bail until the Grand Jury met some four months later. However, "two or three of the biggest sinners in town, one of them a brewer, posted bail and

Bartlett was released. The entire town turned out for the open-air meeting the following Saturday night. Captain Bartlett sang his own composition which was sold for five cents a copy to help "the work." Accompanying himself on a street organ, he soloed:

> The judge came in haste, there was no time to waste,
> The Army was getting too fast;
> He looked awful mad, and made my heart sad,
> To have him give me such a blast.
> The trial was soon over, the judge was in clover
> To think he succeeded so well;
> We failed to give bail, so now I'm in jail
> For trying to save men from hell.

In Manchester, Connecticut, matters had come to a head. Again, the drum was the culprit. Drums and all, the Salvationists were often dragged to jail but when they were released, it was always minus the drum. So many drums were confiscated that the soldiers made them out of every available material, even cardboard. A drumstick needed only to be raised and everybody went to jail. The case was finally settled in the Supreme Court. The provincial officer, Adjutant Walter Jenkins, who was later to be National Secretary of The Army in the United States, came for the victory march from the jail.

"May we have our drums now?" he said politely.

Fifty drums were returned, and fifty drums led a jubilant procession up Broadway, as the warriors sang lustily, "I'll stand for Christ, for Christ alone. . . ."

Depression hit hard during 1891-3. Thanksgiving and Christmas dinners were given to thousands and became an annual event. The idea came to Major Richard Holz's attention from one of his corps officers, Ensign James Allan. Thinking it especially good, he had put the project over with not much more than faith. A sit-down dinner was given to homeless tramps and a "basket" dinner to families.

The idea spread quickly in Army circles. Charity had, of course, been given since time began, but never on such a large, organized scale. For example, in 1894, "250 of New York's needy people were fed at 91 New Chambers Street by 'slum angels,'" and a Christmas dinner was served to 2,000 worthy poor at Princess Rink in Chicago.

Disturbed about the plight of many sailors on the San Francisco waterfront in 1896, Major Joseph McFee set up a cauldron suspended from a metal tripod to finance his program to help them. His German mother-in-law had used such a tripod to hold her cooking kettle. He topped the tripod with a sign which read: KEEP THE POT BOILING. This was the first Salvation Army Christmas kettle, the funds going primarily to help operate The Salvation Army sailors' home. The idea was introduced in New York in 1897. That first year, "by use of the street kettle, 15,000 Christmas dinners were given."*

The following notice appeared in the June 16, 1894, issue of the *War Cry*: "The Commander [Ballington] after consulta-

---

* Christmas kettles still are an important source of income for Salvation Army Christmas and year-round relief work. Some friends erroneously believe that Santa Claus is employed as a kettle worker. This has never been true, and confusion has sometimes embarrassed both the public and The Army, especially in such instances as the one which prompted a friend to phone Army headquarters, reporting: "You are such nice people, and I have such respect for you that I must tell you one of your Santas is lying dead drunk on the street near my home." Only uniformed workers are used. They ring bells or play horns near kettles clearly identified. Sometimes, bright red capes and black overseas caps with red shields are used for added warmth.

tion with the General, has decided on the opening up of the Hawaiian Islands, situated in the Pacific Ocean. They will be worked by the American field. . . . "

Brought in to work plantations when native Hawaiians proved unsuited to field labor, Chinese, Japanese, Javanese, and Puerto Ricans were moved about at the owners' will. In the late summer of 1893, C. V. Sturdevant, a leading Honolulu businessman, became concerned about the spiritual needs of this displaced labor force. He contacted Brigadier Keppel of the San Francisco headquarters, who relayed the request to Ballington. Mr. Sturdevant was told there were "no funds" to help. He and his wife started a collection among friends, especially those who like themselves were members of the Central Union Church, and enough money was raised to pay the transportation of an advance group of officers and rental of a meeting hall in Honolulu.

On September 8, 1894, five officers arrived in Hawaii: Staff Captain John Milsaps, Adjutant George Egner and Mrs. Egner, Captain Mary E. Zimmer, and Lieutenant Jennie Jeffers. A Honolulu paper noted that the first open-air service was held on the Opera House steps, attracting a large crowd and "two of the lassies had tambourines, one had a guitar, and Adjutant Egner had a cornet." Theirs was a new type of warfare the press said, for their crusade "was directed against all manner of inconsistency, from irregular habits among the upper class to the dark doings in the slums." Their initial work was primarily among plantation workers. On borrowed mules, they "rode to all the plantations where they found the managers helpful." Not long after, a second group arrived and in a short time corps had been organized on three other islands.

In San Francisco, others wanted special ministry also. "I do so long to see a Chinese work started and lead some of my countrymen to Christ," wrote Lieutenant Fong Foo Sec in the September 15, 1889, *War Cry*. But the 20-year-old writer who was to become a doctor of philosophy, an attorney, an author, educator, editor-in-chief, director and head of the Rotary International of the Far East, had to wait seven years. On March 18, 1896, Fong, now Captain, reported jubilantly: "The first Chinese Salvation Army corps in the world is now an accomplished fact. The hall is in a good location on Sacramento Street. Every seat was taken and a crowd stood on the sidewalk and looked through the glass doors, unable to get in." One of the accomplishments of the first year was a Chinese *War Cry* with a circulation of 300.

William Booth paid another visit to the United States in 1894, during the golden jubilee celebration of his conversion—50 years of preaching Christ's gospel of the changed life. Though often tormented by loneliness for his Catherine, and always suffering from dyspepsia, requiring the usual diet of eggs, potatoes, and a "bit of toast," William was always the General. His tall form was only a trifle bent, his throaty voice a shade more rasping. The American press, for the most part, was beginning to approve of him. The Waterbury, Connecticut, *American,* which only two years before had recorded violent attacks on The Army now noted that William had talked to Waterbury citizens for an hour and a half with no one leaving, and concluded:

"They found that interest, not in his English, which was very faulty; not in his logic, which was self-contradictory; not in his rhetoric, which was halting; but in the intense devotion of the man to his mission, the noblest and most self-sacrificing of careers, to reach and save the hopelessly degraded.

"As he stood there with the shaggy beard and blazing eyes of the typical prophet, pleading the cause of the criminal and the harlot, it was like a revelation—with entire reverence we say it—of what one might have heard from the lips of Jesus Christ, had He stood on the platform of the Auditorium last night."

Ballington and Maud had prepared meticulously for the American phase of the golden jubilee celebration, with goals for the year set at 50 new corps, stress on the Prisoners' Hope Brigade, an increase in the number of "sunbeams for the night of slumdom"—the popularly known slum sisters—and more rescue homes. Ballington urged: "In our ordinary work as well as in our saloon and dive visitations, we stand confronted with the awful need of rescue homes, into which can be received the poor, hopeless, sinsick, wandering woman. . . ."

Open-air and auxiliary league work were advanced, and the Band of Love, a religious-education, recreation organization, provided, in Ballington's words: "opportunity to declare war on his satanic majesty and rescue, by legitimate and lawful means, the children from his grasp."

Swedish-American corps work, in which services were conducted in Swedish, was also encouraged, for Viking descendants, according to Ballington, "when saved, sanctified, consecrated and trained, make excellent soldiers for the Cross."

There were to be 5,000 more junior soldiers and new methods and programs were specifically aimed at Negroes.

However, during William Booth's visit, the young Booths were defensive; they felt The General showed little interest in these plans and goals. Although his public triumphs were spectacular, he gave no public approval of his son's service.

The older Booth was fearful and fighting mortal fatigue. He couldn't understand why the American flag had to be carried in processions. The national flag of no other country played a part in Army work. Nor could he see why the eagle was so prominent in American Salvation Army circles. The visit ended on a note of dissatisfaction and wounded feelings for the Ballington Booths, and of apprehension and determination for William. Booth men were "cut of a piece." Brilliant, strong-willed, and imaginative, they often were oversensitive, particularly to those closest to them. Ballington and the talented youngest son, Herbert, had been "managed" under Catherine's perceptive and diplomatic administration. At her death William became more and more the roving preacher, leaving increasing administrative policy and detail to Bramwell, including the overseeing of his brothers and sisters. Ballington and Herbert, who had borne autocracy from William, did not intend to bear if from Bramwell. They felt they were his equal. They would work with him but not under him. Ballington wanted democracy for the American Salvation Army:

"During our experience in America we had gradually become convinced that the system of governing the work in this country from a foreign center by laws made by those unaware of the needs and conditions of the country is neither wise nor practical. . . . For years we had not been consulted on the important moves and innovations of The Army. . . ."

As he had expressed himself some years before, William was fearful that the Ballington Booths would become enamored of the United States, that they would want to remain there permanently, and would seek to set up an "American" Salvation Army. This national identity would argue for independence from London.

In similar fashion, Herbert, now stationed in Canada with his Dutch wife, Cornelie, would develop a "Canadian" Salvation Army; Catherine, a "French" Salvation Army; the Booth-Tuckers, an "Indian" Salvation Army, and world unity would disappear. William now wanted to put his arms around the world. In his mind anything that would detract from that goal was not only unwise but evil. Were rules stringent and regulations limiting? Of course they were, but officers joined the ranks on a purely voluntary basis with their eyes open. An international doctrine, uniform, song book, band journal, flag, book of rules, and regulations? To be sure, but also a united, international, and obedient force for Christ. There was the secret and the power and the success.

THE CHRISTIAN'S DESIRE.

LORD JESUS, make Thyself to me
A living, bright reality!
More present to FAITH'S vision keep
Than any outward object seen, —
More dear, more intimately nigh,
Than e'en the sweetest earthly tie.

Chapter Five

SCHISM

MEMBERS of the Booth family headed most of the important commands in the world. Late in 1895, Bramwell, as Chief of Staff and undoubtedly under orders from William, reshuffled all of them. Herbert and Cornelie were to go to Australia from Canada; Eva from London to Canada; the Booth-Clibborns, eldest daughter Catherine and husband Arthur Clibborn (who prefixed his surname with that of the Booths', as did the other sons-in-law) from France and Switzerland to Belgium and Holland; and the Booth-Hellbergs, youngest daughter Lucy married to Emanuel Hellberg, from India to France and Switzerland. The Booth-Tuckers, Emma married to Frederick de Lautour Tucker, were in London due to Emma's illness. Finally, the Ballington Booths were ordered to farewell from the United States command.

Ballington and Maud, however, had no desire to farewell. They were popular, competent, progressive, and democratic. A shift in command, they felt, would ruin the work. In January, 1896, therefore, they seceded to form the Volunteers of America, a group which was initially structured along similar lines to those of The Salvation Army. The "Great Schism" tore the ranks apart.

According to biographer St. John Ervine, Ballington called

a meeting of leading officers, determined to "withdraw the whole of the American forces from his father's command." Other sources disagree on the purpose of the meeting. Eva, who had been dispatched from Canada by William to dissuade Ballington and Maud, was not allowed in the meeting:

"For a few minutes she stood in the street, nonplussed and worried. . . . Then she dashed into Thirteenth Street . . . climbed up the fire escape . . . to the hall, crawled through a window, and coming unto the platform, vehemently demanded to be heard. Her emotional eloquence worked upon the feeling of the officers and they agreed to stay in The Army."

Some sources believed that had Ballington wanted to force the issue, Eva's words would have been ignored.

"Break In Salvationists' Ranks!" headlined the *Chicago Record,* and newspapers across the nation echoed: "Ballington Booths Have Withdrawn." "May Divide Salvation Army" declared the front page of the *New York Times.* The old General, it was inferred, was trying to "anglicize" the American branch of The Salvation Army. Anti-British feeling was already running high in the United States just at that time due to a straining of diplomatic relations over a boundary dispute in South America.

Although the previous Moore split had been shattering, it couldn't compare to the Ballington Booth split in demoralizing effect. Staunch friends were thoroughly sick of the public airing. Many of them, auxiliaries of the New York group, for a time at least, gave full financial support to Ballington and Maud. Old enemies circled like vultures around a death spot. Many soldiers, confused and hurt, or sincerely in sympathy with the new order, deserted. Loyal warriors met opposition coming and going and were, at times, distraught.

In Chicago, a young officer approached the provincial headquarters building and asked who was in charge. "I am," the janitor said. All leading officers had defected. In Cambridge, Massachusetts, the defecting forces "opened a hall right at the back of ours and annoyed us in so many ways and tried to get our open-air stopped by the chief of police." At one corps, the commanding officer made the following announcement: "From tonight on this corps will no longer be associated with The Salvation Army but will become part of the Volunteers of America." The corps sergeant-major, a noncommissioned officer, stood and addressed the officer. "If you are no longer connected with The Salvation Army please get down from that platform. I am in charge of this corps."

Eva, who had been characterized in the press as a "minion of British despotism," directed the forces until the new commanders, Frederick de Lautour Booth-Tucker and Emma Moss Booth-Tucker, arrived. "Many said we were an English Army and wanted nothing to do with us, but Eva Booth stood like a rock for The Army and helped us through the most critical period," recalled Captain Alice Parker. At one protest meeting in New York which Eva attended, she was hissed and booed on mounting the platform. Striding to the side of the stage, she seized the American flag and, whipping it about her, shouted, "Hiss that if you dare!" The audience was silenced and she won their co-operation.

William Booth, back in London from a whirlwind trip as far as New Zealand, exhausted and heartbroken, dictated a cable to "My Dear Comrades of America: A great calamity has fallen upon you, and a great sorrow upon The Army everywhere. . . . Your late beloved and honored commanders have refused to obey the General's orders, and have resigned. . . . In this day of stern trial I call upon you to stand fast to God, to the worldwide purpose of The Army, and to the flag. Be ready to suffer for the principles you have espoused."

Of this tragic occurrence he said a little later: "I say my children have helped me, but The Salvation Army does not belong to the Booth family. It belongs to The Salvation Army.

So long as the Booth family are good Salvationists, and worthy of commands, they shall have them, but only if they are. I am not the General of the family. I am the General of The Salvation Army. . . ."

Time proved both William and Ballington to be partially right. Within two years The Army in the United States was incorporated. More democratic measures began to be introduced. Although a central international control and uniformity remained, the rapport and co-operation between International Headquarters and all territorial commanders improved. These changes set the pattern of present-day Army structure.

———————————

Major Maud Clements (R), highly esteemed 91-year-old former slum sister, was a headquarters officer during the Ballington Booth administration. Major Clements had great affection and respect for Ballington and recalls meeting him on the street several times after the secession. He was always gracious and interested, and one time she couldn't avoid asking, "Commander, are you happy without The Army?" Ballington replied, "I should never have left The Salvation Army."

One of the steadying influences immediately after the break was Samuel Brengle, the American ex-minister William Booth tested with the challenge, "You belong to the dangerous classes." Through personal contacts and writing, this gentle, compassionate man attracted the devotion of multitudes. He was as shrewd as he was good. On March 10, 1896, a few weeks after the split, he wrote to Bramwell:

"When I wrote you last December that I felt there was need of The Army's striking deeper root in this country, and that there should be more prayer and heart-searching simplicity and burning holiness in our own ranks, little did I think of the terrific storm that was soon to smite us. . . .

"If we humble our hearts and seek His face and look only

to Him for deliverance we shall live and yet delight ourselves in fatness. It seems to me that now is the time to strike roots, to deal with our own people, to lead them back to the old paths, to make them mighty in God."

Brengle redirected the fight against sin rather than indulge in personal attacks. Indicative of his spirit was this excerpt from a letter he wrote shortly after being appointed to Chicago: "K— is coming here to take charge of the Volunteers. I am praying God to thwart his efforts to do us harm, but to bless him if he devotes himself to getting souls saved—and I believe God will do it. Glory to His name!"

Brengle wrote a series of articles entitled "Soul-winning" which were published in the *War Cry* and later as a book, *The Soul-winner's Secret,* which still is read by Salvationists and nonmembers. He detested flowery language and obscure thought. A leading staff officer said, "This book probably did more to turn the minds of our people from self to souls, from the 'Split' to Christ—thus saving them for The Army—than did any other person or agency."

Despite misunderstandings, secession, and persecution, conversions were still the order of the day. An outstanding convert was a young sea captain, John Carlson, whose ship was docked at Norfolk, Virginia. He heard two lassies singing and followed their voices up two flights of dingy stairs, where he listened to them speak of the joy of sacrificial living. Carlson accepted Christ. New converts were expected to show their "colors," and discipline was rigid. Carlson didn't mind. On his knees with a number of converted drunks, one or two teenagers, a few solid souls, and the lassies, he sang:

> While I speak to Thee,
> Lord, Thy goodness show;
> Am I what I ought to be?
> Oh, Jesus, let me know.

John Carlson came from a background of position and culture. He made an excellent salvation soldier, attending open-air and indoor meetings every night, and witnessing for Christ to his men. On the evenings he couldn't get ashore, soft notes from his guitar floated over the waves as he sang:

> Friendship with Jesus,
> Fellowship divine;
> Oh what blessed, sweet communion,
> Jesus is a friend of mine.

When World War I came, Carlson entered the United States Navy as an officer, and when hostilities were concluded, he was knighted by King Gustav V of Sweden and appointed as Swedish Consul to the United States. He served on the advisory board of the Norfolk corps and later, his daughter, Mrs. Hannah Carlson Lynch, served as corps treasurer. His grandson became bandmaster.

Ordered to America in the emergency, the new commanders, the Booth-Tuckers, arrived to face personal heartbreak. Their seven-week-old son, Tancred, was ill when they left, and they decided he should follow them later. The news of his death awaited them in New York. Emma, called "The Consul," was the gentlest of the Booths. Crowned with luxuriant, curly, chestnut hair, she was tall and handsome rather than pretty, her delicately molded features shaped for compassion. It was Emma who had cared for the younger children during Catherine's busy career, and Emma who had nursed her mother during the last days.

Fritz, as Emma called her husband, had met crises before. Having given up wealth and position as a Civil Service magistrate in India to establish an Indian territory for The Army, he knew hardship, sacrifice, and persecution. Once, when asked about the daring of such officers as the Booth-Tuckers, William Booth said:

"You see, we have no reputation to lose; we are not obliged to stop and consider what anybody will say; everybody has settled it that we are fools, if not a great deal worse; and therefore, we can go into a town and do exactly what we think best without taking the least notice of what anybody may say or wish. We have only to please God and get the people saved. . . ."

The first days in America were rugged for the Booth-Tuckers.

"Credit," stated F. A. Mackenzie, Booth-Tucker's biographer, "really must be shared by three people, the Commander and the Consul . . . and Colonel Edward Higgins." Higgins was sent from London as Chief Secretary during the crisis. He was skilled in management and possesed patience in dealing with men. His personal life and example left a powerful impression on all who knew him. He traveled 600,000 miles during his tenure in this country. His influence is recorded by the growth of Army work and the esteem of his officers, many of whom he supported through distressing periods.

Commander Booth-Tucker had a comprehending, fertile, and imaginative mind which overflowed with new projects, usually captioned in pithy slogans. His farm colony scheme was dubbed, "The Landless Man for the Manless Land." He had an indomitable spirit and a nose for news. He was not content to be a small-time fighter. His objectives were big. His first task was the press: confidence must be re-won. He knew the newspapers were often hostile, or at least suspicious. He was particularly fortunate, said Mackenzie, with his choice of national leaders, especially "in capturing men like Mark Hanna, the president-maker," who referred to Salvationists as "patriots of the Lord." Hanna introduced Booth-Tucker to Pierpont Morgan and other prominent men. Fred also knew how to take setbacks. In many ways he was like his father-in-law in spirit. "I am like a cork," William used to say. "You may submerge me, but I bob up again."

There was no necessity to look for the needy. The slums of the big cities overflowed with them. The Booth-Tuckers decided to attack sin and suffering in a massive way. Fred's approach was to get a firsthand account. He would dress like a bum, sleep in the cheapest lodging houses, eat where his gutter companions ate, and observe life during midnight forays. In one seven-cent hotel he was recognized and thrown out. His story of the encounter was featured in the New York *Sunday Herald,* with a photo of him in disguise. The story concluded with The Army's plan for inexpensive lodging houses and an appeal for funds.

Fred had even more bizarre encounters. In April, 1897, he was charged with "keeping an ill-governed and disorderly house." This occurred after an "All Night of Prayer," when complainants vowed that 2,000 people with five brass bands had "caroused" all night. Fred wrote of this to his friend, Dr. Cuthbert Hall, president of Union Theological Seminary:

"I don't know what you will think of my last adventure. The magistrate was extremely nice this morning and said that no offence whatever had been committed. My experience in the prison cell was of a decidedly interesting character and I left on the wall a little message for the next drunks who might be locked up there: 'Jesus will save you just now.' "

A few months after his arrival, he was received at the White House by President McKinley, who remained a warm friend of The Army until his death. There is a stained-glass window in the Canton, Ohio, corps building which was presented by the family of the martyred president and depicts him with the United States and Salvation Army flags crossed in the background.

The Booth-Tuckers got their campaign against poverty

under way in 1897. It started with a work-shelter program in which men were required to saw wood for lodging. When it was announced, there was opposition from the Charity Organization, which considered that sufficient accommodations already existed. But if organized charity in America was obstructive, Fred believed individual Americans would support the program. The scheme was begun but the need had to be dramatized. The Christmas kettle idea had proved successful so, throughout the country, pots on tripods signalled need and 150,000 needy people were given feasts that year. Ensign Allan's basket idea was promoted and baskets "containing fowl of fair size, tea, coffee, sugar and the like" were distributed. Madison Square Garden was used as the distribution center, and 24,000 families were helped in New York alone.

Also in 1897, Army work was begun in San Quentin State penitentiary by Sergeant-Major J. Brown of the Oakland, California, corps. A number of Alaskan Indians were the first converts. A few months later, when permission was obtained for inmate converts to be enrolled as soldiers and wear an Army badge, an outpost was officially established in the prison. Subsequently, a section of the prison was set apart so Salvationists could live together. Backsliders were quickly transferred "to the steel cells in the new prison wing." As the sergeant-major of the outpost was serving a 99-year sentence, it appeared likely no change in his position might be expected for his lifetime.

Both the Spanish-American War and William Booth hit the United States in 1898. When war was declared in April, Salvationists were immediately stationed at camps. Salvationist Major John Milsaps was appointed chaplain to the United States troops. The Salvation Army Naval and Military League, later to be known as "Red Shield Services," had been organized in 1894, primarily for spiritual aid to "visit sailors on board and hold meetings among them on shore, visit the camps of soldiers and follow them into battle as far as possible."

The General, more gaunt now, with white beard flowing, was delighted with his tour of the nation. Before he left for home, he saw his son, Ballington, and effected a moderate personal reconciliation. Record of this was kept by two respected gentlemen asked to audit the meeting, Dr. Charles Cuthbert Hall, president of Union Theological Seminary; and Dr. Josiah Strong, General Secretary of the Evangelical Alliance for the United States:

"1. General William Booth and Commander Ballington Booth met in the Windsor Hotel in the presence of Dr. Josiah Strong and Dr. Cuthbert Hall on Sunday, January 16.

"2. The interview was purely as between father and son.

"3. Nothing transpired calculated to lead to any union of the two movements.

"4. It was agreed that all public controversy, in the papers or otherwise, between the two movements, should as far as possible, come to an end."

When William left for home, one thousand people waved and sang him a farewell.

In 1896, the wild shout, "Gold in Alaska!" stirred the country and a trek to the Klondike began. With the swarm of gold-seekers went seven Salvation Army officers, Adjutant and Mrs. Tom McGill among them. At Skagway, a rip-roaring camp of tents and shacks, Adjutant McGill and Ensign Fred Bloss dug in while the remainder of the contingent battled in Dawson City. The miners were hard nuts to crack, and McGill wrote of his experience with them:

"Gambling halls, saloons and brothels were seemingly the main business of the place. We rented an empty store, put in seats and invited the people, but few would come. . . . We commenced meetings for the natives. Soon, things began to happen."

In April of 1898, Evangeline Booth, then commanding Canada, decided on a personal expedition to Alaska. This was to be the first of many such trips. Bramwell was against the idea but William said, "Let her go." Protected by Canadian mounties, she visited village Indians, more than 300 of them already Salvation Army converts, and was impressed by their "sincerity, intelligence" and willingness to accept religious discipline. Then she moved on to Skagway, the wide-open "devil's headquarters of the northwest," boasting neither police nor military protection, and crowds swarmed after her. She wrote:

"Sinners they were—the old and hardened—the young tenderfeet just from home and plunging into degradation—the once well-to-do but now debased, the once poor but now rich; the intelligent, the sharp and the brutal—there they were, in western clothes with big hats—men on horseback—boys standing on their cayuse—a most striking crowd."

They clapped wildly for her and knelt en masse to sing, "Home, Sweet Home" as a benediction. At one meeting, 25,000 miners sat on a mountainside and sang, as she directed, "Nearer My God to Thee."

Perhaps the most notorious sinner in all Alaska, at least by record, was Soapy Smith. A local celebrity, he'd made his name in Denver selling soap on street corners. In certain packages he wrapped one, five, and ten dollar bills, and thus did a thriving business. However, he always made sure that shills got the special bars. Eventually, the skalawags were booted out of Denver and ended up in Skagway. Here they rolled customers and terrorized the town. Now, dour-looking Soapy Smith listened to Evangeline's exhortation. Two members of his gang were converted and left him. One evening, while the Salvationists camped with others among the trees, a cry went up, "Soapy Smith is coming!" As he approached with a five-man bodyguard, his group was confronted by Evangeline's Northwest Mounties, guns drawn on both sides.

"Leave him to me," said Evangeline as she approached Soapy.

Smith took off his hat. "I'm Soapy Smith, and I've come to tell you how much I enjoyed your singing."

"Thank you, Mr. Smith," said Evangeline. "Supper is over, but we'd be happy to give you a cup of cocoa."

Smith sat down. So did his bodyguard. They drank the cocoa quietly. The bodyguard kept their eyes on their chief. Then Evangeline drew him aside and talked with him for three hours. At the end of that time they knelt together. Tearfully, Smith promised he would stop killing people and would give himself up. A witness said he overhead him promise to "live the life of a Christian."

Shortly afterward, a citizens' meeting decided it was time to rid Skagway of Smith. A gun battle resulted, and both Frank Reid, leader of the Citizens' Committee, and Smith were killed. Before he died, according to Adjutant McGill, Smith gasped, "The way of the transgressor is hard . . . Quit!"

Evangeline's visit had a mighty impact upon the Northwest, and many Indians and miners mended their ways.

Among the Indians converted during 1899 was Jim Hanson. The young brave trembled with emotion and "tears fell fast as he prayed in his native tongue for forgiveness of sin." After a few weeks he confessed to McGill that he and several other Indians had murdered an innocent young couple in what his tribe had considered retributive action. His tribe and his wife turned against him. On McGill's advice, Hanson told his story to the judge. After three months in jail, he was brought to trial.

"Do you understand that no one but the President of the United States can save you now?" said the lawyer.

"I don't care what you do with my body. God will save my spirit," Hanson said. Judge Brown asked him if he wanted to say anything before being sentenced.

"God has told me not to keep anything in silence," he said. "I gave all my sin up and told all. Now, brother, work as God directs you."

Sentencing Hanson to death, the judge choked, "May the God you worship be with you in the hour of peril and have mercy on your soul." As the bailiff led the condemned man away, his head high, the Salvation Army badge shining on his shirt, the judge buried his face in his hands.

A petition, signed by Judge Brown and General Friedrick, who conducted the prosecution, was sent to the Attorney General at Washington. The Attorney General referred to the incident as "the most remarkable case in the annals of American jurisprudence." President McKinley commuted the sentence to life imprisonment. At the federal prison on McNeil Island, Jim Hanson won many converts, held Sunday services, and taught himself to play the violin to accompany singing. Five years later he was pardoned. Just one day before the pardon arrived, he was promoted to Glory. Warden O. P. Halligan commented reverently, "He died confessing the Christian faith."

Another early convert was a young brave from Klukwan, William Benson (*Kelth-Sue-Eesh*), who pleaded with Evangeline to send messengers to his people. "You take the message to your people," she said. He traveled by canoe to southeastern Alaskan villages and, although unable to read, his earnest eloquence communicated the gospel of "Good news! God loves you!"

For America the cry was "Remember the *Maine!*" "Get that gold!" For The Salvation Army it was, "Never let the old flag fall."

Even the sturdiest Army pioneer couldn't have envisioned the challenges or successes of the days ahead.

Chapter Six
1900 / 1909

TRIUMPH
AND
TEARS

SENATOR Mark Hanna's elaborate dinner for General Booth was a flop. Power and prestige had dictated the choice of guests. The papers announced that the guest list for February 12, 1903, included "all the members of the Cabinet, the British Ambassador, and a number of Mr. Hanna's Senate friends." Except for the President of the United States, whom William was later to meet, almost every important figure in public life was present, including the Vice-President, the Speaker of the House of Representatives, members of the Supreme Court, the Senate, and the House. Most of them came to please Senator Hanna, with little but curiosity for William.

It was a restrained, cheerless meal. When Speaker Henderson jested across the table, Hanna said peremptorily, "Now, Dave, this is not that sort of a dinner." Mr. Hanna's introduction made matters worse. Suddenly he was embarrassed. His fumbling effort to present William was as lively as cold soup. William got to his feet, tired and disturbed. He was hoarse from earlier speaking engagements. His initial remarks brought no light to anyone's eyes. Hanna looked worried.

Then came the cry, "Louder." William was startled by the interruption, stared back at his audience momentarily, then threw up his eagle head to his full height.

"Oh, I can shout if necessary," he replied and proceeded to galvanize them "mind and soul" for an hour.

In Chicago's *The Continent,* the Hon. Henry B. F. Macfarland of Washington described the occasion as "the most interesting dinner ever given in Washington." He related how Senator Hanna had been introduced to The Salvation Army by Governor Herrick of Ohio and how his "heart had gone out to The Army." Hearing that the founder of the movement was coming to America, Hanna had planned the dinner. He had misguidedly created the stiff atmosphere to the discomfiture of both himself and his guests. Nonetheless, Macfarland was pleased and wrote the following reaction to the address:

". . . but the Salvationist chief took them captive without their knowing how. . . . It was evident that the speaker was genuine, and it was equally evident that he was speaking of real life. But it was most evident that he was speaking . . . 'like a dying man to save dying men.' . . . When General Booth sat down he had completely changed the atmosphere. . . .

"Senator Hanna, rising to speak, searched in all his pockets for a handkerchief and not finding one picked up his napkin from the table and wiped tears from his cheeks. He was not the only man who had not been able to repress the tears. . . ."

The General visited President Theodore Roosevelt by invitation, then opened the Senate in prayer, remaining for an hour of personal fellowship. In the Vice-President's chamber, before the prayer, he met many lawmakers and had a characteristic comment when a prominent senator was introduced by Hanna as "the worst man in the Senate."

"That's good," said William, "I want to meet all kinds— the bad I want to help, and the good I want to help me."

His whirlwind trip was 20 weeks long. He covered 16,000 miles, visited 52 cities, held 200 meetings, addressed 300,000 people, and watched 2,500 kneel in penitence at the "mercy seat." Two thousand Salvationists had welcomed him by sailing down the harbor in eleven tugs and two steamers, each ship carrying a brass band, and decorated with banners shouting, WELCOME, GENERAL.

The Chicago *Record Herald* commented on his visit with an editorial that humbled Salvationist readers:

". . . We do not know what Jesus would do about the drums and cymbals and the songs set to rag-time music . . . but it is a safe guess that if He were on earth He would preach to the populace in the highways and the byways and He would kneel in the streets to pray for sinners with the Salvation Army lads and lassies. He would go with them to the slums of the cities where the hungry and destitute are fed and sheltered by The Army. His heart would be in their rescue work, and He would lend a helping hand in the work of reclaiming the fallen. . . ."

The year before William's successful American tour, he had again tangled with members of his immediate family which resulted in four more resignations. Herbert Booth and his wife, Cornelie, assigned to Australia, chaffing under the General's tenets of unity and obedience, finally resigned, as had the Ballington Booths earlier. And in France, young Catherine and her husband, Arthur Booth-Clibborn, became absorbed in faith healing which took up more and more of their time. William ordered them to concentrate on their Salvation Army duties, saying, "Go and keep the regulations and save the people." But Booth-Clibborn's activities reached full-scale insubordination. Ordered to retract, he refused with the result that he and his wife also severed their connection with The Army.

Although the severance was a cruel blow to William, he remained a rock of resistance to anybody who would pull him or his Army from the rugged path of applied Christianity. "I am General first and father afterwards," he said.

In the United States the rank-and-file soldiers of salvation, inspired by the Booth-Tuckers' leadership and their General's visit, marched forward. Both evangelistic and "social wing" crusades recorded many victories.

Three farm colonies, one in California, one in Colorado, and one in Ohio, were in operation and were Booth-Tucker's special interest. Part of William's Darkest England scheme, they were planned to provide agricultural employment as a second step in the rehabilitation of people first aided in shelters. Unemployed city dwellers were first interested in the colonies in America, and for a time they prospered; however, many found adaptation to rural living too difficult. Eventually, the colonies were abandoned or converted to other uses.

Twenty-five thousand dinners were served in 1900. Industrial-salvage homes and women's rescue homes were stressed. There was also a Labor Bureau to aid the unemployed; an Auxiliary Department; Life Insurance Department for the poor; Missing Friends Department, which from the beginning proved highly successful in finding lost loved ones throughout the world; and a Scandinavian, German, and Italian Department to supervise corps in which most services were conducted in foreign languages. There was a national staff band, flourishing summer camps for poor mothers and children, and a considerable amount of emergency work was being done, especially the housing and temporary feeding of "down on their luck" transient visitors to big cities.

Another important ministry of these years was traveling "singing and revival" brigades. Comprised of from two to ten members, all of whom were talented vocally and often instrumentally, the brigades had a three-fold purpose: they conducted revivals, "opened fire" (established corps) in smaller cities and towns, and raised funds to support Army efforts in larger cities. Singing brigade work was used extensively after the Ballington Booth split so seriously depleted forces and caused financial havoc. Concerning brigade effort, the *War Cry* received this correction to a typographical error:

"Instead of the 300 converts it should have been 1,300."

The signature was Ensign George Bennard's. Bennard, composer of "The Old Rugged Cross," wrote it, according to reputable sources, as a Salvationist while traveling with Captain Robert Keeler in brigade work. Keeler, known as "The Musical Wizard," played 22 instruments, among them cornet, violin, mandolin, banjo, and guitar, plus "sticks of wood and tin cans." Another of his specialities was "converted whiskey bottles" which were picked up in alleys and filled with varying amounts of water. Strung between two poles, the bottles were played like chimes and afforded tinkling, extremely pleasant music. Playing mallets were constructed from corset stays which had been begged from Keeler's wife Maggie. Keeler used such instruments as part of music-drama evenings when, dressed as a tramp, he interrupted Army open-air meetings, succeeded in attracting large crowds to meetings and acted rather than preached sermons on such themes as "The Tramp," "The Drunkard's Home," and "Scenes from Life's other Side." Newspapers pictured "the wizard" as "a musician of unusual culture who plays with great beauty and delicacy . . . having a voice of rare power and sweetness and of wonderful compass. . . ."

Combined efforts of preachment, music, and drama were common during this period of The Army's warfare in America. A wave of interest in drama swept the country and not only special services but also Sunday services were reserved for such presentations. For example, a Carthage, Missouri, Women's Christian Temperance Union spokesman said that a currently enacted Salvation Army drama would "do more to create temperance sentiment than all the temperance lectures that can be given in one night."

Questioned about the propriety of Salvationists using "the world's devices," William Booth said: "I don't know what to think. It is against the rules of The Salvation Army to have anything that isn't followed by the penitent-form, and you know they do have the penitent-form after their plays. There are wonderful scenes from real life, giving the drunkard's home and all the misery that means. I tell you, sir, the people realize it when they have it brought home to them in that way."

The reporter raised the question of "good art."

"Good art?" barked Booth. "What has that got to do with it? It is life, real life, and the people who go to them know it. . . . Oh, there's a lot to be said for the theater—but, yet, I don't know whether it wholly meets with my approval or not. No, I don't know." He continued that many of the world's greatest preachers had relied to a great extent upon dramatic devices in their sermons to appeal to the masses.

The General's appreciation of drama was seconded by Bramwell, who added that the theater "rather caricatured" The Army, "emphasizing the odds and ends of Army life and experience," and not stressing its romance. "Yet caricature is good," he added. "One of our leading officers in America, formerly a worldly man, was attracted to The Army by a stage representation, caricature though it was." He also thought there were "the makings" of a great play in The Army. "Is there not room for a really wholesome play which would inspire as well as amuse? If the theatrical world says not, that is the measure of its lack of faith."

Whether in social or evangelistic fields, front-line fighting meant victory, defeat, and sacrifice, and successful battles were often marked by open conflict and subsistence on starvation rations. It was, as Bramwell said, "at all times a real warfare wherein triumphs can only be secured at the cost of struggles that are very often painful and unpleasant."

The manager of the Raleigh Coal Company in Hinton, West Virginia, was "so pleased he built a tabernacle for us, and gave us coal and light free." The miners shared their food, beans, fat pork and corn pone, and their beds, which were "filled with corn husks and often buggy."

In Youngstown, Ohio, The Army instituted a unique ice-water barrel system downtown to "quench the thirsty throat with cool drink." Several barrels were placed along downtown streets and furnished drinks for 20,000 persons weekly. No one seemed to mind the fact that everybody drank from the same tin cup.

At the busiest intersection in Akron, Ohio, a sawing bee was held to help the kettle fund. To music furnished by the Army band, "the Hon. Wm. Buschtel, 81 years of age; Ohio C. Barber, President of the Diamond Match Co.; Mayor Kempel; Judge C. R. Grant, and a number of other prominent citizens took part."

In Wooster, Ohio, Captain Bryce Phillipson asked an old Irishman not to spit on the floor, whereupon the gentleman turned his hat upside down and placed it between his feet, using it as a spittoon.

Bill Beacraft of Guelph, Ontario, Canada, arrived in Flint, Michigan, in 1904, to work for David Buick, an "internal combustion" engineer who had ideas. Under Buick's instructions, Beacraft built the first Buick engine to be produced in Flint. He and his wife linked up with the struggling Salvation Army corps in Flint, and he became its first sergeant-major.

"Beacraft," said Buick in 1904, "we must hire more mechanics!"

Beacraft smiled, anticipating a steady growth in the Buick Motor Company—and The Salvation Army—due to the increasing popularity of "horseless carriages." The first two mechanics Beacraft employed, Morse and Randall, were Salvationists and also instrumentalists, as were many more hired later. This was the beginning of the now famous Flint Citadel band. Eventually, Beacraft became president of the Motor Division, with 4,500 employees under his supervision. His noonday factory services, at which employees who were Salvation Army bandsmen played, became so popular that they were started in other Flint factories. Undoubtedly, they sparked interest in similar meetings throughout the state, although factory meetings have always been a favorite with Salvationists.

In Guthrie, Oklahoma, the George Bivans family, ten in number, never missed a meeting. As many as possible climbed in the buggy, toting a big lunch basket. The balance of the family drove in a spring wagon, followed by the pet dog. One Sunday, because of illness, the family stayed home but suddenly missed their dog. The following Sunday, someone commented, "We thought you must be in town because your dog came to meeting."

In Detroit, Michigan, Salvationists were repeatedly thrown in jail. Police ran horses through the open-air meetings, while firemen hosed "In the Sweet Bye and Bye" down singers' throats. The local toughs battled both authorities and Salvationists. Major Blanche Cox, pioneer of the Cellar, Gutter, and Garret Brigade (forerunner of slum work in The Army), and also provincial commander for Michigan and Indiana, decided to test the ordinance against outdoor drum playing and was arrested. "The ordinance against our drum is unfair and strikes at the very foundation of the principle of free speech," said the Major. The doors of the workhouse closed 11 times on Blanche Cox, each sentence stiffer and longer. Finally, her case was won in the Supreme Court. As she left the workhouse for the last time, one of her jailers apologized, "Major, we ain't your kind but we hate like tarnation to see you go. Please don't forget us."

"Six feet of devil and 180 pounds of hell" characterized a killer in the Kentucky mountains during the feuds of 1903. There had always been feuds, but none had been so widespread. When The Salvation Army invaded the mountains of Kentucky, the St. Louis *Globe Democrat* said: ". . . It is seldom that a fight does not result in a killing. The problem is can the tambourine and big drum oust the revolver and Winchester, and will The Salvation Army contingent of volunteers bring the notorious Breathitt County into line with the spirit of the hospitable and beautiful blue-grass region?"

Staff-Captain Richard Holz headed the khaki-clad brigade on horseback. They left Cincinnati headquarters for Jackson, Breathitt County, Kentucky, the center of the feud district. The town was under martial law when they arrived. They held their first meeting across from the Jackson courthouse and their first prayer meeting "on the very spot where Lawyer Mascum was shot." One of the feuders knelt for mercy, confessing that though he was a college graduate with four diplomas, "for three years I've never been sober." Tent, open-air, and indoor meetings followed in rapid-fire succession. These citizens lived under the shadow of great crime, and a "smiling face in Jackson is the exception."

Then on to Salyersville. A member of the brigade reported: "Six of us mounted and four rode in the supply wagon. . . . A crack of the whip was heard and we were off. . . . Staff-Captain Boyd was prepared to give first aid. . . . We climbed great mountains. Many have gathered to see The Salvation Army pass by; on one stoop were 30 men, women and children. . . ."

Crowds were huge. In a village of 300 permanent residents, a thousand people congregated. At first, many of them were frightened and fiercely apprehensive, having never heard of The Salvation Army: "We had to tell them we were 'preaching soldiers' before they could comprehend. . . . The people trooped to meeting as to a county fair. . . . It was a moving sight to see more than one hundred big mountaineers kneeling in the dusty road to pray with us."

Judge Redwine, speaking of Salyersville, stated: "The meetings have tended to draw the factions closer together, something quite significant when it is realized that these factions stand severely aloof from each other. They will not go in the same building at the same time; in fact, so bitter is the feeling that they will not stand on the same side of the street. The Salvation Army succeeded in attracting both factions around open-air meetings. . . ."

On the way to Whitesburg, the party got separated, and four of the men under Captain Escott were lost for days but were received by the hill people with great hospitality, and a large number of conversions were reported.

Generally, the summer of 1903 had been a good one. The Booth-Tuckers felt progress had been made, and they threw themselves into plans for the winter season. They were delighted with a new baby which made their family an even half-dozen. Their consummate tact and gentility, coupled with their dedication, had aided progress in America greatly. Hundreds of once indifferent, suspicious people had been won for their cause, and thousands of citizens who had never heard of The Army came to know and understand its work. "Their leadership has been distinctive in that it yielded nothing," stated the *St. Louis World,* "and in that it won its way to confidence by courage and simplicity. . . ."

In mid-October, Emma Booth-Tucker went to Amity, Colorado, to inspect the Army farm colony. Her speaking engagements along the way captivated the press. Fred Boalt of the St. Louis *Chronicle,* rhapsodized:

"A stronger and more magnetic personality I have never known. She has been called a beautiful woman. . . . It is more beauty of soul than of face and form. . . ."

On her way back to meet her husband at Chicago for

officers' councils, she was killed in a train wreck. Her body was taken to the Princess Rink corps in Chicago. Ten thousand mourners filed past the casket and there were ten conversions at the bier. At the funeral, attended by 3,000, Booth-Tucker insisted on speaking. "He tottered as he walked," noted the Chicago *Chronicle*. "His hands shook as one who suffered from palsy; his head drooped forward until it rested upon his breast. Only his determination made it possible for him to speak to the audience as he stood and looked upon the features of his dead wife." Fred talked from his heart. He bared his grief but also showed his determination not to become bitter, and he moved listeners to tears as he told the following strange story:

"How well do I remember the last meeting that I attended in this hall. I called upon a man and asked him to give his heart to God. He laughed at me. 'Give my heart to a Being whom I hate?' he asked. 'If your wife had been killed in a wreck—if her mangled form had been brought to your children—would you love God?' he asked me. Those were his words. 'Would you love a God that was cruel?' he went on. That was his story. He said that he hated God. But if that man is here I wish him to hear me say that I do love God—that Christ is sufficient—and my wife has suddenly been taken from me."

The man was there. He rose, walked down the aisle and knelt at Emma's casket. "If Christ will help us like that then I'll surrender to him," he said.

Booth-Tucker plunged into work—more campaigns, more "all nights of prayer," more counseling, additional men's industrial homes and rescue centers and new corps. He lived on his stubborn faith that if God was any God at all, He would see him through this trial of trials.

Early in 1904, Frederick Booth-Tucker was ordered to farewell and proceed to England where he became Foreign Secretary. Before leaving in June, he spoke on "The Landless

Man to the Manless Land," in Carnegie Hall. Farewell messages came from President Roosevelt, the Vice-President, two Cabinet members, and 24 governors. After a short time in London, International Headquarters assigned him to India, where he continued his dedicated work.

Evangeline Cory Booth was appointed to succeed her brother-in-law in America. Born on Christmas Day, 1865, The Army's founding year, she was always regarded as William's "Christmas box." After coming to America, Eva, as she was intimately known, changed her name from Eveline to Evangeline and also used her middle name, at the suggestion of Frances Elizabeth Willard, founder of the Women's Christian Temperance Union. Miss Willard believed a dignified name aided a woman with public responsibility. Eva had been called "The White Angel of the Slums" during her teen-age years in London. Stories of her battles with toughs and authorities were legion. She possessed more than her share of spunk in dealing with such emergencies as Ballington's secession. In Canada, she'd exhibited oratorical genius and shrewd leadership ability, coupled with a fearless and daring spirit. She had an innate sense of timing and of the dramatic. She loved costumes and pageantry. In Toronto, she rode her mount to territorial headquarters with a red cape flying like a banner over her uniform and a red hat topping her chestnut hair.

Evangeline had many opportunities for romance but as a commander of troops in the International Salvation Army, she felt there could be no other preoccupation or intrusion. She did adopt several children and gathered about her a retinue of helpers who gave her blind devotion. One of these was "Gipsy," a tender little woman whose life was lived through her Commander. Another was Lieut.-Commissioner Richard Griffith, her personal aide.

Evangeline's initial impact in 1904 was impressive. "The World for God!" was her motto. Although woman suffrage had yet to be realized in the United States, she headed a mixed army of men who were expected to jump at her command, and of women accustomed to male supervision. She was confronted on all sides with serious problems; but everywhere, she bid her soldiers, "March on!" One of her first innovations was the institution of school breakfasts, after she learned that in New York City alone, 70,000 children were going to school without food. This practice had its beginning in Christian Mission "breakfasts for the poor" and has been followed whenever need demands.

———————

In 1905, George Bernard Shaw's play, *Major Barbara,* set many Army friends back on their heels, both in America and abroad, though it caused little resentment among Salvationists. For one thing, they were used to both caricature and criticism. If Shaw did not have all his facts straight, he nonetheless had made a worthy attempt to understand The Army and its queer methods, and he warned Salvationists of dangers that otherwise might have become tragic certainties, and remain temptations even today. Shaw did not present his play as the truth about The Army and said: "Whosoever says that it all happened . . . that it is a record of actual occurrence, is, to speak according to the Scriptures, a fool and a liar. . . ."

The play was a consideration of whether a religious organization could accept tainted money. He held against The Army its belief that in the course of "undoing many of the injustices and wrongs which society itself has caused, it would take money from the devil himself and be only too glad to get it into the hands of God." He wondered whether in housing itself, keeping extensive records, and depending on others for support, its "staff of enthusiastic commanders should be succeeded by a bureaucracy of men of business." He did not like public testimony, termed it self-publication. At least at the

Corps building in Dawson City, British Columbia, 1900.

CONTINUAL COMRADES.

ENSIGN SECCOMBE.   CAPTAIN AGNEW.

TO BE UNITED IN MARRIAGE BY COLONEL EDWARD HIGGINS, AT FEDER-
ATION HALL, STATE AND FORTIETH ST., CHICAGO, ON TUESDAY, OCTOBER
SECOND, NINETEEN HUNDRED.

PLEASE PRESENT THIS AT THE DOOR.   FIFTEEN CENTS.

A

B

(A) *A Salvation Army wedding
invitation;* (B) *St. Louis* Globe-
Democrat *drawing of Salvation
Army work in Breathitt County,
Kentucky;* (C) *Chicago Rescue
Home, 1905;* (D) *Slum sisters,
early 1900's.*

C

D

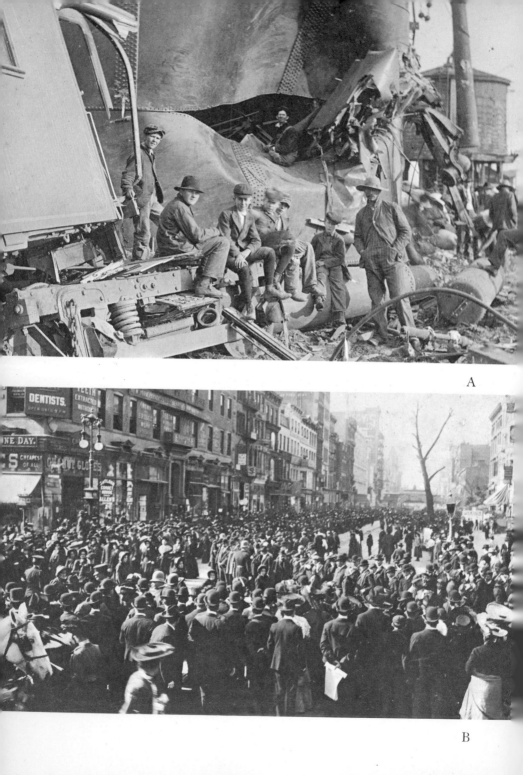

A

B

(A) *Scene at wreck which killed Emma Booth-Tucker and* (B) *funeral march for the Consul at 14th Street, New York City;* (C) *General Booth and his eldest granddaughter, Brigadier Catherine Booth (daughter of Bramwell), 1906;* (D) *Early League of Mercy workers.*

D

A

B

C

E

(A) *George Scott Railton;* (B) *Drawing of William Booth just prior to his death;* (C) *Funeral cortege for General Booth, London, 1912;* (D) *Christmas baskets ready for distribution;* (E) *Part of the American delegation dressed as cowboys at 1914 Congress of All Nations, London.*

D

Miss Sheldon and the Boys ready for the big doughnut drive. Cornay.

ON ACTIVE SERVICE

THE SALVATION ARMY
HOSTELS
REST ROOMS

WITH THE
U. S. A. FORCES

I'm always S.O.L.

Get in line there you big stiff

Don't push

Any seconds

Let's go

SALVATION ARMY

PETERSON
1918.

Cornay.

I just took a walk down to Cornay last nigt and oh, those doughnuts and Coco of Miss Sheldons certainly was great!

I was on guard and couldn't get away, that's always my luck.

Fleville.

Tchorgues,

France after the Argonet Sheldon Battle

Say, if we only had some of Miss Sheldon's Coco & Doughnuts I wouldn't mind this cold a bit, would you?

Buzancy.

You said it, Jack, they sure are great. Us Co. D boys certainly won't forget Miss Sheldon and Miss Swenson They sure deserve a lot of credit.

A

B

(A) *Cartoon as part of letter to doughnut girl, Margaret Sheldon;* (B) *Scene at front, World War I —doughboys line up for dough-nuts and coffee;* (C) *Salvation Army doughnut girls outside of dugout.*

C

A

(A) *Commander Evangeline Booth greets representative Life Saving Girl Guard;* (B) *Christmas dinner, 1917;* (C) *Pie Baking at Front, World War I;* (D) *Lassie ready to serve returning doughboys, New York City;* (E) Saturday Evening Post *cover honoring Salvation Army, 1919.*

B

C

THE SATURDAY
EVENING POST
An Illust___
Founded A? D___
MARCH 29, 1919   5¢

D   E

A

B

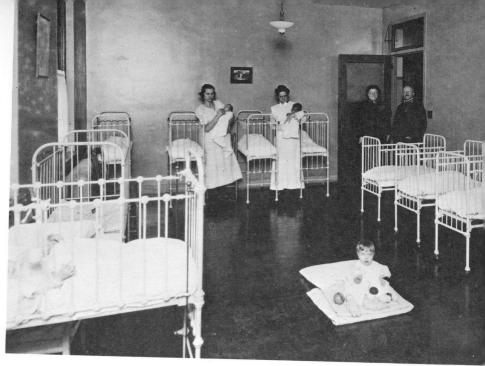

C

(A) *Open-air scene, Union Square, New York City, 1920;* (B) *Prominent citizen contributing to Christmas Kettle effort;* (C) *Nursery of Minneapolis Home and Hospital, 1920's;* (D) *open-air service, San Diego, California, 1920.*

D

A

B

C

(A) *Doughnut lassies entrain for Paris, 1926*; (B) *Salvation Army representation at Rose Bowl parade, 1922*; (C) *Rheba Crawford, "Angel of Broadway"*; (D) *Evangeline Booth "in rags"*; (E) *Salvation Army officer takes friends fishing*; (F) *Sunday school class.*

D

E

Keep the Demon Out Forever!

(A) *Cartoon appearing in newspaper, 1923;*
(B) War Cry *cover, 1921.*

time, he understood neither Divine forgiveness nor punishment.

Shaw had not always been so condemnatory. During the Purity Crusade in the eighties he declared he'd peddle W. T. Stead's articles, "Maiden Tribute to Modern Babylon," personally. "I'll take as many quires of the paper as I can carry," he told Stead, "and sell them in any thoroughfare in London." Also, not long after *Major Barbara* was produced he defended a Salvation Army band in print "as an act of justice." William Booth then invited him to a festival. Years later, Bramwell invited him to another, and Shaw exulted, "If only Strauss and Elgar had been here they would have been so delighted that they would then and there have composed an opening piece for the next festival."

Also in 1905, the General gave consent to the formation of a sub-territory in the United States, with headquarters in Chicago. Called the Department of the West, it was commanded by Commissioner George Kilbey, a man of sound reputation who enjoyed widespread respect and affection. He was, of course, responsible to Evangeline, the National Commander, and the Department of the East remained under her direct supervision.

Commissioner Kilbey and Brigadier Ashley Pebbles were on a train bound for San Francisco on April 18, 1906. At 5:30 P.M. the conductor handed Kilbey a telegram. It was from Chicago and read, in part: "SAN FRANCISCO SERIOUS EARTHQUAKE STOP CITY ON FIRE."

When Kilbey arrived, he found that Colonel George French, Divisional Commander, had set up shop in Fairmont Park. Equipment was taken from institutions still standing and a huge kitchen was established. Thousands of Salvation Army owned cots were the only beds many people possessed. The disaster was heightened by broken water mains. No water was available to fight the sweeping blaze which was fanned by a strong wind. Kilbey, after seeing the havoc caused by the earthquake, sent this plea to the *War Cry:*

". . . Also suffering are Santa Rosa, San Jose, Beulah, Lytton Springs etc. . . . Homeless, foodless, and clothesless . . . But we are face to face with the fact that our halls, headquarters, hotels and industrial homes and officers' quarters are wiped out. . . . Our rescue home and beautiful orphanage are most seriously damaged, and all of this ruin about us when our harbors are the most needed. . . ."

Ensign World, a girl corps commander in San Francisco, told of being awakened by screaming:

"I sat up in bed and watched the brick wall parting at the head of the bed. I stretched my hands over the babies [niece and nephew]. The house reeled and rocked, jerking and swaying. . . . Articles fell from the mantle; the bookcase fell over with a crash. . . . Then, with a terrible crash, our front walls fell to the street. . . .

"Rushed out—terrible confusion outside. A block away lay about six large dray horses—dead (electrocuted). A few feet ahead was a dead man and two others in the same street. Ambulances, patrol wagons, autos of all descriptions dashed here and there, picking up the dead and dying. . . .

"I could only give a word of cheer here and there. . . . The next day, the children, lieutenant and I moved to a dump heap. . . . The bedding, musical instruments and a few other things were placed in a hack. I was the only lassie in the crowd, I think, carrying a tea kettle. . . . Sights. Yes, I saw them—awful sights, and I had a share in them. . . . The dear old corps is not dead. Our hall and quarters are gone, but the corps to a man are here. . . ."

Eva visited the scene of desolation and was asked to describe the city:

"You ask me an impossibility. No picture can convey to

the mind any adequate idea of the change which has come over this western metropolis. Every spacious street is distorted, every busy mart and thoroughfare is a heap of ruins. . . . The bivouac of 50,000 tents marked off into streets and avenues with sentinels and watches, makes up a city in itself. . . . If calamity has reduced it to a wilderness, it is a wilderness that blossoms as the rose."

She was asked if military rules had forbidden public meetings.

"Not at all, for they relaxed them in our favor and lent our services every possible facility. . . . I never saw a more picturesque and appealing crowd than the one that sang, 'What a friend we have in Jesus. . .' "

A few months later the *San Francisco Examiner* reported: "Four thousand young refugees and 4,000 Christmas gifts— the sight has never been seen anywhere else in all the world . . . in seven refugee camps. In all the camps the Salvation Army representatives were assisted by the commander and committees appointed from the camp staff and/or camp refugees."

The Army's growing social service efforts came under attack repeatedly during this decade. On May 1, 1906, the men's work-shelters, at present termed Men's Social Service Centers, were professionally attacked during a conference that was widely publicized. A previous attack had alerted The Army. At the National Conference of Charities in Philadelphia, Edwin D. Solenberger, general manager of the Associated Charities of Minneapolis, read a paper titled, "Relief Work of The Salvation Army." He declared that the social work of The Army as carried on through its homes, lodging houses and other agencies, was poorly organized and poorly administered. He asserted that "so-called charitable work of The Army" was largely subservient to financial interests. During the discussion that followed, Brigadier Alexander Damon was allowed 10 minutes for a rebuttal. He won "the hearty approval of a large part of the audience." For the time being the matter was dropped.

The year 1907 was a dark one for all Americans. Financial panic hit and thousands upon thousands were thrown out of work. In the midst of this calamity, masculinity faced an even more devastating force: women were on the march for suffrage. The "bloomer girls" were having their say, and they were vociferous and persistent.

A popular Salvation Army department during the early 1900's was the National Trade, which had evolved from early Army days in London, when red hatbands, Bibles, and yellow-red and blue "recruits' ribbon" had represented almost the sole stock-in-trade. By 1881, the International Trade Department was a "going concern," at least with respect to uniforms, books, and tambourines. After publication of an article by William Booth titled, "Miriam, a Forerunner of the Prophetesses of The Salvation Army," which was illustrated with a drawing of Moses' sister playing her timbrel, Railton reported that 1,600 tambourines had been sold in six weeks and warned lassies that they "should not beat tambourines without at the same time singing."

By 1894 the National Trade Department* in the United States boasted a "Secretary for Trade Affairs," Adjutant R.

---

* The four present-day "Trades," now called Territorial Supplies and Purchasing Departments, though catering primarily to Salvationists, are open to the public. These should not be confused with Red Shield stores, in which clothes, furniture, and bric-a-brac contributed by the public and made saleable by Men's Social Service Center clients, are offered to the public. The latter stores serve all classes of people, many who cannot afford to buy new articles at commercial prices and many

Caygill, and sold all Salvation Army "equipment" necessary, including vocal and instrumental music books, uniforms (which it made) and "other details too numerous to mention."

The Army was busy fighting evil, which included anything that harmed "God's living temples." Liquor and smoking were attacked as "current ills." This was the period of the sampler and The Salvation Army had a wide assortment of card quotations on sale in its Trade Department. The cards usually were enhanced by floral decorations. This is a "motto" the Trade store sold:

> MOTTO FOR A CIGARETTE: "I am not much of a mathematician," said the cigarette, "but I can add to a man's nervous trouble. I can subtract from his energy; I can multiply his woes. I can divide attention from his work, and I can discount his chances for success."

There were also card indictments of whiskey. One could be purchased for a few cents:

> THE BOTTLE: Whiskey is a good thing in its place. There is nothing like it for preserving a man when he is dead. If you want to keep a dead man put him in whiskey, if you want to kill a live man put whiskey in him.

On February 11, 1907, the steamer *Larchmont* sank off Long Island Sound. Of the 200 passengers, 180 were drowned, among them 10 Salvationists, seven officers and three cadets bound for a Scandinavian congress. The *Larchmont,* an antiquated, iron-hulled type ship, was rammed at night by the

---

seeking the unique and unusual. Money from the Red Shield stores supports the Men's Social Services program. Also, both clothes and furniture are given without charge to needy people through welfare channels and in times of emergency.

schooner *Harry Knowlton*. Tons of water poured below deck while a 45-mile gale whipped up mountainous waves. In the darkness, passengers struggled on decks and companionways. Many didn't see the lifeboats and froze on deck. Mrs. Harris Feldman, one of the two women survivors, told reporters: "Amid all the confusion, the singing of the Salvationists, who were brave to the last, was the one redeeming feature."

Another survivor said that as the ill-fated steamer sank she heard a Salvation Army lassie's voice, "sweet and clear, singing that grand militant phrase, 'Onward, Christian soldiers!'" Salvationists had exhorted fellow passengers to prepare for death, assisted as they could, then knelt together, praying and singing to the end.

Speaking at the funeral, Eva called it a time of "tears and triumphs." Her address was reported as strikingly dramatic and simple:

"They wore the white robe (Rev. 7:13–7)," she said. "I don't know what price they paid for them. I know the price that some people have paid in order to get the white robe of Christ's righteousness. . . . I only know that they *got them*. And the white robes were their own. . . . Have *you* got the white robe? No borrowing of other people's names or reputation. No presuming upon the good deeds of the organization they belonged to. . . . *The work must go on!* Is there not somebody here tonight who will say, 'Let me go'?"

Ten Salvationists had been drowned. Eleven volunteers marched forward to "take up the sword laid down by their promoted comrades."

It is not certain why William Booth, in 1908, produced a personal statement regarding women to be read to all Salvationists "straight through without comment." Probably he simply felt the time had come for a restatement of what had long been his belief: "My best men are women." In his statement, he declared women to be equal to men, except, perhaps, in physical force:

"Taken as a whole I say that woman is equal to man in the value of her gifts, and the extent of her influence, and I maintain that if she is given a fair chance she will prove it to be so. . . . Whether married or single, let every man treat the woman with whom he is acquainted with respect, with patience and with care, and let us determine to pay woman more regard in the position assigned to her as a wife, as a mother and as a daughter.

"It is true that some of the more remunerative forms of earthly labor are frequently closed to women. But thanks to The Salvation Army, positions of respect, fields of boundless opportunity for usefulness and the highest interest of the race are now open."

For the American front-line salvation soldier, the first decade of the twentieth century was a time of lessening physical persecution. Unfortunately, this was replaced by a widespread, somewhat condescending attitude. The children of Army officers were humiliated by classmates, often called "scum" and "gutter babies." "Put a penny on the drum!" "Salvation Army, save my soul, trying to go to heaven on a telephone pole," and other such taunts were flung at them. A favorite chant was:

> Hallelujah, I'm a bum;
> Hallelujah, bum again.
> Hallelujah, give us a handout
> To revive us again.

Parents and children fought side-by-side against such indignities, often victoriously. Sometimes, however, parents could not withstand the abuse and could not remain faithful to The Army. Then "Deserted!" was penned blackly in the record book. Occasionally, scandal would break. Sometimes, corps officers handled money incompetently. In Gary, Indiana, for instance, the new officer with a wife and three children, sold the furniture from his living quarters to pay off bills left by his predecessor. But, for the most part, the spirit was always high. "Miss Eva" was a powerful and colorful commander, and it could rightfully be said of her, as it was of Napoleon, that her troops brightened when she merely walked on the field. The stock admonition to Army children was, "What would the Commander think?"

From the beginning of his ministry, William Booth had been concerned about children and youth. Nothing had been done to attract boys and girls to Christian living through recreational programs.

During 1903, Major Alexander Damon interested some affluent friends in providing vacations for slum mothers and children. Mrs. Francis Fowler, wife of one of the managers of Swift and Company, improvised accommodations at the family farm near Hinsdale, 30 miles west of Chicago. The Fowlers were particularly interested in children's camping—their ten-year-old son had died the year before. During 1904 Mr. Fowler formed a committee of business people, mostly stockyards men, to secure a suitable property for a fresh-air camp. A site was found at Glen Ellyn, Illinois, and for 15 years the camp filled a great need. In 1920, the village had surrounded the camp and a new site was purchased at Camp Lake, Wisconsin, where the camp flourishes today. The original camp board became the first advisory board in The Salvation Army and included as charter members besides Mr. Fowler, Francis S. Peabody, Frederick W. Moore, Henry H. Kennedy, Judge Henry Varnum Freeman, William R. Perrin, Edward F. Smith, and Samuel A. McClean.

In Yankton, South Dakota, Captain Wesley Jerome, a sports enthusiast, was asked to help with the city baseball team.

He agreed to help on two conditions: that no profane language would be used, and that nothing impudent would be said to the umpire when he made a decision. In Jerome's next appointment, he started what probably was the first Salvation Army sports team, a baseball team among young band members. This team played others in the city with great enthusiasm.

The Captain had a richly resonant bass voice. When the bass singer of the Episcopal church choir became sick just before a concert, a member of that church inquired, "How about the Army Captain? I heard him on the street. He's mighty good!" Captain Jerome happily substituted.

In 1907 a cavalcade of borrowed autos, recorded as "big Thomas cars, white Steamers, Rambler cars, Franklins, Knoxes, Red Dragons, Black Racers," enabled 225 of Chicago's slum children to have a day's outing at Glen Ellyn. The Staff Band played as Brigadier Mary Stillwell, secretary of rescue and slum work, and her slum angels arrived with various detachments of children, each wearing a neighborhood badge. Streetcars were stopped when the band led the way down State Street for the grand send-off. Leading the motorcade was Colonel George French and a carload of boys, all waving flags. The frolic "was increased by two tires blowing, one car going off the road into a bog, and two cars sticking in the mud." Staff Captain Fletcher Agnew was "head boy, arranging games, races and prizes."

The Department of the West had enjoyed three good years of progress by 1908 under Commissioner Kilbey. He had arrived with both vision and faith. Until 1900 few Army facilities were owned. Commissioner Kilbey was anxious to house his forces. Part of the answer, he felt, lay in a substantial and commodious central building and, consequently, he built the Chicago Temple property. He advocated the smallest cash payment that would handle the arrangements and the largest loan possible. Unfortunately, he failed to give sufficient information regarding his actions to International Headquarters, an infringement of regulations.

The building was erected at a total cost of $118,000 on Madison Street across from the Princess Rink corps and was dedicated on April 5, 1908. It had a large youth hall in the basement and a senior auditorium on the first floor which held about 800. Rent from the stores and living apartments on Madison Street was to provide the greater part of the annual income to meet payments on the loan.

Always cautious and fearful of debt, International Headquarters pronounced the financial scheme unsound and called Kilbey to London. Immediately after the trip, he resigned. His staff was reassigned.*

The succeeding Financial Secretary, Brigadier Arthur Smeeton, proceeded to borrow the necessary money and float a successful bond issue. Commissioner Kilbey's claim that money could be borrowed was vindicated.

Many midwest Army personnel and supporters were distressed over the Kilbey incident, but despite personal feelings, they felt the war must go on. Commissioner and Mrs. Kilbey must have shared their belief, for they retired from the ranks with dignity and grace. In a *War Cry* farewell, he spoke of matchless opportunities in the West for the triumphant march of The Salvation Army into a position of strength, blessing, and usefulness second to none in the world, and urged his comrades to be true to God, strengthen the hands of their leaders and "push the war in the west for God and souls."

In 1909 a Boston Back Bay woman, Mrs. Mabel Hunt Slater, paid a visit to Captain Sulzer with a surprising offer. She was worried about Boston's under-privileged during that

---

* "Kilbey's building," still the largest corps building in Chicago, has just been remodeled. It is the principal meeting place for large united meetings in that city.

cold winter. Had the Captain heard that children were going
to school without food? Could something be done—without
red tape and immediately? Captain Sulzer suggested hot dinners served at the Army hall. As a result of meetings, all winter
long and for many winters to come, a "big hot supper" was
served to 100 children three times a week, supervised by Mrs.
Slater. The menu included "chowders, beef and lamb stews,
cocoa, cake, bread, butter, jam, and fruit. Also a box of crackers." Aid in free meal programs was not usually so generously
offered. Though common throughout the country, such large-
scale meals more often challenged Salvationists to much
prayer, work—and begging.

That same year brought a major conflict in Boston with
the Board of Overseers of the Poor, a powerful local organization. The "Battle of Boston" began just before Thanksgiving.
The Board of Overseers barred The Army from Boston streets,
prohibiting collection, including kettles, on public property. A
member of the Board stated in the press:

"I object most strenuously, as do most members of the
Board of Overseers of the Poor, to begging in the public streets,
by an association, organization or person. It is degrading and
demoralizing to the public. The method is spectacular and
showy, directly opposed to the quiet, unobtrusive way in which
the other charitable organizations by personal solicitation and
letters collect for the poor. The spirit of giving charity before
it is asked is *wrong.*"

Army people replied that they must have money, lots of
money. They urged that the need had to be dramatized. People
should have something beyond themselves to look toward and
support, even if it *was* only a drop in the bucket. That drop
might mean hope for some despondent Nellie or Joe.

"Come, stand in front of my house," said private citizens.
"You can stand inside my door," said the merchants. But that
wasn't enough. By the time citizens awakened, Thanksgiving

was almost at hand. From somewhere, money had to be found for thousands of dinners and toys. Without warning the Boston press (*Journal* and *Post*) took over in a big way:

To The Public of Boston, The Greater City and New England

Send your checks to the *Journal* to aid The Salvation Army of this city in its great heartfelt helpful annual charity for the benefit of the city's poor. One dollar today will be worth five-fold the day before Thanksgiving.

A leading citizen, John F. Fitzgerald, made an extremely substantial contribution. Immediately, Amos T. Luther, candidate for mayor, stated in print: "John F. Fitzgerald has led the way as a contributor. I follow." The feast was in the bag.*

The Overseers of the Poor backed down but too late to be of help. The press reported: "Salvation Army feeds 5,000 poor today," (3,500 dinners to homes and 1,500 at People's Palace). Three thousand toys were given away, and Adjutant Annie Eastwood asked for more automotive power to bring in more needy.

The "Battle of Boston" was over, but it was only one incident of many more to come.

---

* A large Thanksgiving turkey, presented by the turkey industry, was given to The Salvation Army by John F. Kennedy, President of the United States and grandson of John F. Fitzgerald, on November 19, 1963, just 3 days before the President's assassination.

Chapter Seven

1910 / 1919

PROMOTED
TO GLORY

AS THE second decade of the twentieth century arrived, William Booth was almost blind but as determined in his purpose as ever. On May 9, 1912, the 83-year-old warrior addressed 10,000 people in Royal Albert Hall, assisted by Eva, who'd come to visit him. He was expecting to undergo a second eye operation. His message, a recapitulation of his life, concluded on the same dynamic note with which his career had begun:

"And now, comrades and friends, I must say good-bye. I am going into dry-dock for repairs, but The Army will not be allowed to suffer, either financially or spiritually, or in any other way by my absence, and in the long future I think it will be seen—I shall not be here to see it, but you will—that The Army will answer every doubt and banish every fear and strangle every slander, and by its marvelous success show to the world that it is the work of God and that the General has been His servant. . . .

"While women weep, as they do now, I'll fight; while little children go hungry, as they do now, I'll fight; while men go to prison, in and out, in and out, as they do now, I'll fight; while there is a poor lost girl upon the streets, while there remains one dark soul without the light of God, I'll fight—I'll fight to the very end!"

On the twenty-third of May the operation was performed, unsuccessfully, and William was left completely blind. He took the news calmly, saying, "God must know best," and in the days that followed his concern remained for his soldiers.

On August 20, the hoarse voice that had demanded, "Go straight for souls and go for the worst," was silenced. The next day, a banner was stretched across the full length of International Headquarters at Queen Victoria Street:

THE GENERAL HAS LAID DOWN HIS SWORD. GOD IS WITH US!

The world now wept for the man who had loved it more than his own life.

The President of the United States, William Howard Taft, wired Bramwell: "In the death of your good father the world loses one of the most effective practical philanthropists. His long life and great talents were dedicated to the noble work of helping the poor and weak, and to giving them another chance to attain success and happiness. Accept my deep sympathy."

The press beat his drum: "Amid the world-wide sympathy extended to the family of the creator of The Salvation Army on his death, no one will be more real than that of the members of the Jewish community," said the *Jewish World*. "The Army and its General have always shown Christian tolerance in the best sense of the word Christian. . . ."

The London *Daily Chronicle* reported: "The world has lost its greatest missionary evangelist, one of the supermen of the age."

The Washington D.C. *Times* noted: "It is not exaggerating to say that no other man of his time has contributed more than William Booth to the world's work of practical moral uplift for the unfortunates of society. . . ."

The *Chicago Tribune* commented: "General Booth gave

the unfortunate bread and soup, but he also gave them what they needed far worse—a coherent reason for going on, for suffering, for striving and, best of all, for hoping. . . ."

W. J. Lampton wrote in the *New York Times:*

> "Taps!
> Lights out!
> The soldier who has fought his fight,
> Who never feared to lead
> His army where the battle raged
> For any human need;
> The soldier fighting sin always,
> Wherever it might be,
> Yet always ready to put out
> His hand in charity,
> Has quit his earthly work at last,
> Has laid his burdens down,
> And for the cross he bore so long
> Has taken on the crown.
> Taps!
> Lights out!
>   The soldier sleeps until the Dawn;
>   His spirit leads his Army on."

The General's body lay on a catafalque in Congress Hall for three days. On the coffin lay his cap, his Bible, his song book, his fountain pen, and his flag. A portrait of Catherine hung above his head and could be seen through a window in the coffin. T. E. Calvert, a Cadet helper, described the crowds:

"For the next four days rain poured down on the people who walked past the coffin. All sorts and conditions of men and women were in that company. I saw barefooted newspaper boys come, look and salute as they passed by, the Bethnal Green costermongers, all pearly buttons and ostrich feathers, brought their floral tribute. The Cadets sang and played soft music during the long hours, but nothing mournful.

" 'Sweeping through the Gates' and 'Promoted to Glory' were paeans of praise indeed. A typically Prussian figure from the German Embassy handed over a wreath from Kaiser Wilhelm II which I placed at the foot of the coffin. Then from their Majesties, King George and Queen Mary, came a magnificent wreath which I placed at the head of the casket—together with one from Dowager Queen Alexandra with a card written in her own hand. . . ."

The Wednesday night before the interment, William's body was removed to the Olympia, the largest obtainable building in London, for a memorial service. The coffin was then taken to International Headquarters, from which the funeral procession marched on Thursday morning. As the catafalque was wheeled down the aisle, the throng sang, "When the roll is called up yonder I'll be there." It was a mammoth meeting of praise and prayer, no doleful dirges, no wild weeping—only triumph. Five thousand Salvationists marched to Abney Park Cemetery. The fifty-eight countries in which The Army fought were represented, soldiers marching behind national flags and the "yellow, red and blue." Rain poured down but stopped as the procession marched, six abreast, through densely packed streets. The coffin was placed on an open hearse drawn by two chestnut horses. On each corner of the hearse was the Salvation Army flag, while two draped the plain pine coffin on which lay the General's Army cap and Bible. The cortege was more than a mile long. Forty bands participated. As the procession passed the Mansion House, the acting Lord Mayor, Sir John Knill, saluted. It took three hours for the last of the procession to reach the cemetery gates. Thousands had to be turned away.

The London *Times* reported: "The only comparable occasion in this country in modern times was the burial in 1874 of David Livingstone, who, like Booth, was a man of no worldly position, and who won the universal respect of mankind by devoting his life to the service of his fellows."

And the London *Daily Chronicle:* "The last journey of General Booth through the East End streets was the most wonderful march the old warrior-missioner ever led. The poorest of the poor were there to say good-bye . . . among the marching Salvationists there was no outward spirit of conventional mourning, but among the East Londoners there were few dry eyes. They were seeing the last of an old friend, but it was the loss that was nearest to them, the sorrow and not the triumph."

The following evening, before returning to the States, Eva led a thanksgiving meeting, rousing soldiers with her restatement of their old General's message and the command to go forward under the new General, Bramwell Booth. Eva possessed a striking resemblance to her father. She related the incident of an army of tired and weary soldiers, footslogging at close of day. Suddenly along the line came a message that made every soldier lift his head and march snappily forward: "The head of the column has gone into camp!"

The head of The Salvation Army column had gone into the Camp Eternal. William Booth had received the highest honor of spiritual warfare, he had been "promoted to Glory." He left his battalions behind to fight in small or large corps. Not only in the streets, tenements, saloons, and brothels, but also in children's, inebriates', and maternity homes, women's and men's social service centers; labor, missing persons, and immigration bureaus, homes for ex-prisoners, lepers, and the aged; farm colonies, general hospitals; camps, home leagues, and leagues of mercy; antismoking and antisuicide leagues; instrumental and string bands and songster brigades. Circling the world, William's battalions fought on.

———————

In the United States of America, the field was far from conquered. Physical need in America was still overwhelming.

In 1911, The Salvation Army distributed 1,593,834 pounds of "penny" ice, 4,579,788 pounds of coal, and 18,335 Thanksgiving dinners were served. Army slum work was often the single force for good in deprived areas. A report stated:

". . . Our officers are made welcome in the vilest dens of iniquity. Where police must go in pairs, our unprotected slum girls can march unharmed. In brothels, opium dens, saloons, gambling halls and common lodging houses, hands begrimed with dirt and possibly stained with human blood, are stretched out to bid them welcome."

Slum sisters were appointed in two's and lived in the area they served. They wore very plain, dark navy or brown cotton or wool dresses, covered by voluminous white aprons, often pin-striped in blue or brown. Colored tape running across the bottom denoted their rank: yellow for "lieutenant," red for "captain," and white for "adjutant." The headgear was usually not the bonnet, but a sailor type, wide-brimmed felt or straw, or a higher crowned affair which a former slum sister referred to as "terrible looking things but good for our pride." The girls often did not identify themselves as Salvationists, in order not to be separated from the needy. "We didn't even carry a hand-kerchief," explained one. "This would have immediately alienated us."

They spent their days in house-to-house visitation, doing whatever needed to be done, ready to scrub, drive out rats, tend a jaundiced woman, bathe a dead baby and arrange for the funeral, deal with a drunken father, chat with distressed boys and girls. The Bible was in their pocket and prayer on their tongue. Often, neither was initially permitted and not infre-quently the girls were driven off with broom or mop. They spent their nights bombarding saloons and dives, using the *War Cry* as an introduction, talking, singing, and praying.

They grew accustomed to the worst aspects of life and quickly discovered that God's love, as shown by a helpful dust-cloth or a scrub brush or a bar of soap or, more simply, a cup of hot tea, was usually more welcome than when expounded from a pulpit. But the work required a stout heart and utter devotion to the war against distress.

At the New York No. 3 slum post, the lieutenant finished her meeting discouraged because young men had ruined it by "noisily singing at the top of their lungs" parodies to Army melodies. One boy, however, remained and discussion led to the subject of his soul. The lieutenant recorded: "So we got to our knees." That boy later became an officer and served The Army faithfully until his death.

In Chicago, Captain Margaret Sheldon visited the dives at midnight. In basement rooms, girls who were so debauched that men no longer desired them, slept on slabs fastened to the wall. One night, she found "a little girl of about 13, who had run away with a peddler and had been sold into white slavery." She took the girl with her, washed and fed her, and put her to bed. The girl, half delirious, screamed and tore her hair in an agony of guilt. The Captain tried to console her, but nothing availed until she made her peace with God. Then, clasping her Bible tightly, she slept. The girl became an outstanding worker for God after her conversion.

Slum sisters also were required to have a sense of humor. Slum worker Dunn, a nurse, found an 18-month-old baby eating canned lobster. "That's not good food for the baby," she told the mother. "Are you married, lady?" said the mother. "No." "Then I think I know much more about feeding and bringing up children than you do. I've buried five already."

Slum sister work was so successful that rescue homes were opened to accommodate abandoned and needy girls and women. Prostitutes were brought to them from "midnight raids" of both streets and brothels. In addition, they provided shelter and care for women drunkards, drug addicts, and women referred from the courts.

Day nurseries, children's homes, summer camps and outings, already successful, became an established part of the program. Bigger halls were acquired to meet multifarious needs.
Sewing and cooking classes were conducted for neighborhood
women, and some even brought their laundry to the slum post
buildings on Monday morning, having no washing facilities of
their own. Children played in the halls after school. Out of
these early efforts the Army's present settlement houses, community centers, homes and hospitals for unmarried mothers,
general hospitals, clinics, and day nurseries evolved.

A young poet named Vachel Lindsay tramped from
Springfield, Illinois, to Los Angeles, California in May of 1912.
His plan was to take no money but to earn it by reading his
verse and by doing chores. Apparently, the poems didn't always provide income, for Lindsay later explained:

"Everywhere I went I saw The Salvation Army at work,
its men and women singing on the street corners of villages,
small towns and especially the larger cities. Whenever I got
stuck for a place to stay and for a meal, I always knew that I
could go to The Salvation Army and get food and lodging.
Frequently, the Army folk listened to my chanting, singing
and reading. And they never turned me away. . . . I made up
my mind to write a poem in gratitude to the organization and
to pay tribute to the spirit of service in The Army and to the
memory of General William Booth."

The poem, which opens with the line, "Booth led boldly
with his big bass drum," was published in the January, 1913,
issue of *Poetry,* and immediately spread around the world.

"They say—those who ought to know, Edgar Lee Masters,
for example," said Lindsay, "that this poem made me famous
and that it is much better known than anything else I have
ever written. . . . I wrote it because I have always looked upon
The Army as Christianity with its sleeves rolled up. . . . 'General
William Booth Enters into Heaven' opened the door to oppor-

tunity to me. The poem is *my* monument as well as General Booth's, and I hope that my entrance into Heaven will be as certain as his."

In 1913, The Army was involved in the Los Angeles charities battle, and the serious legal fight that ensued. Millionaire Dr. Milbank Johnson captained the opposition and Commissioner Thomas Estill, territorial commander for the Department of the West, led the defense, backed by "the best legal advice available in Chicago and Los Angeles." The Municipal Charities Commission had been created through a city ordinance and given broad power to regulate all public solicitation. Without the Commission's endorsement, no agency could solicit funds publicly. Dr. Johnson, president of the Commission, disapproved of The Salvation Army, charging it with inefficiency, not meeting actual needs, and unwise handling of funds.

In an effort to meet approval, The Army was incorporated in the state of California but Dr. Johnson was not satisfied. Furthermore, he bluntly stated that even if The Army conformed to all the conditions of the Commissioner, the Endorsement Committee would add to the requirements other and new conditions that The Army had not met.

Advised by Los Angeles attorneys, Commissioner Estill ordered the industrial home and ten salvage stores closed and the relief and rescue solicitors "to cease operations until the legality of the ordinance could be tested." On January 26, 1915, Major William Dart opened a store, sold some clothes and was arrested. A report stated "that he remained in the city jail for some time and was made jail chaplain and conducted meetings with the prisoners."

Petition was made by The Army's attorneys to the Supreme Court of California for a writ of habeas corpus. A temporary writ was granted, releasing Major Dart from jail, and the hearing before the Supreme Court was set for April

12, 1915. The decision had significance because several other cities had prepared similar ordinances and were watching the Los Angeles case for results.

"Salvation Army Cleared" was big news when it hit the stands. Two significant lines written into the decision of the Supreme Court by one of the justices, are these:

> "The organized charity, scrimped and iced
> In the name of a cautious, statistical Christ."

The two objectionable provisions of the ordinance were voided, and very soon the city council cancelled it completely. The victory had cost The Army $25,000. At a mass meeting the next year, Commissioner Estill received unqualified support from prominent Los Angeles citizens. A spokesman at the meeting said, "Whatever position we took a year ago, Commissioner, today we are all-out for The Salvation Army."

In the early days of 1913, another pioneer fought his last battle, the beloved first Commissioner of The Salvation Army, George Scott Railton. He had been William Booth's commando, spending his later years exploring new territory and laying ground work for expansion. He could learn a language comfortably in a few weeks. In each country visited, he wanted THE SALVATION ARMY emblazoned on the front of his scarlet guernsey in the national language. Mrs. Railton's needle could hardly keep pace with his frantic travels and he decided to use a large yellow cross emblem instead.

On his final campaign, he collapsed at the train station in Cologne, Germany. Officials telephoned to the local Army officer: "A Salvationist is lying dead at the station." George Scott Railton, one of the most widely known and loved soldier-saints of The Army, was only known as "a Salvationist." He would have shouted, "Hallelujah!" about that.

"Congress of the Nations" year for The Salvation Army came in 1914. The American contingent, 450 strong, included mounted western officers dressed like cowboys, a Negro singing brigade in costumes of stars and stripes, several corps bands, and both the New York and Chicago Staff Bands.

Late in May delegates left for London, many of them traveling on the *S.S. Olympic,* which also carried former President Theodore Roosevelt. He had his photo taken with the American delegation and attended daily band rehearsals. "His broad smile of approbation gave the bandmaster and bandsmen inspiration to reach and maintain peak performance," commented Sam Monk, a bandsman of the Flint, Michigan, band.

Canadian comrades left simultaneously, sailing on the *Empress of Ireland.* Included in their delegation were territorial leaders Commissioner and Mrs. Rees, Colonel and Mrs. Maidment, and the Canadian Staff Band, 176 in all.

"Empress Of Ireland Sinks With Over 1,000 Aboard!" yelled the newsboys in Toronto streets on Friday morning, May 29. With her went 150 Salvationists. Thirty miles east of Father Point, Quebec, in the dark foggy hours of early morning, the *Empress* was rammed by a Norwegian collier, and sank in 14 minutes. Four hundred forty-six passengers were reported saved, 26 of them Salvationists.

In London, Bramwell Booth ordered everyone at International Headquarters to pray. Colonels George French and Samuel Brengle from the American Salvation Army were dispatched by Eva to do what they could in Toronto. In funeral preparations, public meetings, consolation of the bereaved, the spirit was captured by Bramwell's telegram: ". . . I rely upon you. Living or dying, we must go forward."

The loss in personnel caused many vacancies, but a year

later the American *War Cry* reported: "The *Empress* disaster has caused Salvationists to look to the foundations of their faith, to ask themselves whether they had remained true to the first principles of Army soldiership, and whether they were personally ready for a similar sudden call. . . . The Army is in stronger numerical position than before the disaster. All gaps have been filled by experienced officers. . . ."

The international Congress was strongly colored by the disaster. However, despite sorrow and apprehension over Europe's political problems, the Congress was a great success. Delegates gathered from 58 countries, wearing Army uniform or picturesque native costumes.

Many of the two weeks' meetings, which began June 11, were open to the public. Large halls were engaged including the Strand built especially for the Congress, the Royal Albert Hall, and the famed Crystal Palace, where 50,000 gathered.

One impressive event was the Congress parade, called "The March Past." The press commented: "London has never seen a more remarkable religious procession than that of The Salvation Army on Saturday afternoon from the Victoria Embankment in Hyde Park. Walking eight abreast, in very close order, the processionists took 50 minutes to pass through Oxford Circus. Nearly 60 bands, including four from the United States and one from Canada, took part. . . ."

A reporter wrote of the American delegation: "From the standpoint of military smartness and physical efficiency the American contingent, many hundreds strong, was far ahead of any of its rivals. Commander Eva Booth, head of The Salvation Army in the United States, rode on horseback, as also did Commissioner Booth-Tucker, head of The Salvation Army in India. . . ."

A deafening ovation was given the Staff Band from Chicago, which was "outfitted in gaudy gray uniforms splashed with crimson and white braid to complement crimson cowboy hats." It marched along the Strand playing from manuscript Captain William Broughton's new march, "America."

The official reception for the delegates in Royal Albert Hall was spectacular and awe-inspiring according to the London press:

"It was a colossal fancy dress parade—a religious variety entertainment—a revivalist assembly—a concert of 10,000 performers, a prayer meeting in which all the world, white, yellow and black, prayed for the world's salvation. There was no sort of human assembly that it failed to be, with the possible exception of a political meeting. . . ."

The previous night the Anglo-American peace ball had been held in the hall and all decorations remained in place, slightly camouflaged. Hiding the organ was "a vast representation of the *Mayflower* but they had hung it with 'Blood and Fire' flags, so it became the ship of salvation. . . ." The boxes were draped in white, and flags of many nations hung from the balconies. More than 1,200 bandsmen "played triumphantly the music of the world to come. . . ."

To the staccato introduction of drums and trumpets, the Bramwell Booths marched briskly on stage for the "military marshalling of the world's delegates." After a hymn and a prayer, the audience of thousands burst forth in acclamation: "Come, let us all unite and sing, 'God is love!' "

Delegates then filed on stage, where Bramwell and Florence stood "beaming radiantly with handclasps for as many as could be reached." The Koreans were first, with hats like beehives or diminuitive "toppers." Applause was vigorous as simulated barks of dingo dogs heralded the approach of Australian delegates, waving flags and singing as they came. Danish representatives "created a big sensation" by unexpectedly hurling hundreds of tiny paper "Blood and Fire" flags among the people, while thousands more came fluttering down from the gallery. Indian delegates were handsome and resplendent in saffron yellow and crimson native robes. "Amazing" was a war dance by befeathered Zulus, first on the platform and then through the hall. The United States delegation was not surpassed though, according to a press report:

"The United States contingent, hundreds strong, swung in to Sousa music and in a tornado of applause: Negroes, wearing whole suits composed of stars and stripes, cowboys in tremendous hairy breeches, miners with spades, and a band with what must surely be the largest curly brass wind instrument in the world.

"General Booth fell on the neck of his sister, Commander Evangeline Booth from New York, in true Biblical fashion, much to the delight of the whole gathering. . . . A little later he was to be seen wearing over his gray locks one of the red felt American wideawakes, which he would occasionally remove in order to beat time with it to the music, in a sort of rhythmic greeting. . . ."

The silent entry of the Canadians was in striking contrast to all that had preceded as they marched toward Bramwell, wide white ribbons draped diagonally across their chests. The Army substituted white arm bands and sashes for the traditional bands of black.

When the last delegate had taken his place, "All Hail the Power of Jesus' Name" was enthusiastically sung, with right hands raised during the final verse. Bramwell spoke "in very touching terms" of his father, then of the central problem of the Congress, "how to make this world of grief and suffering a little less a place of sin and strife, a little more like the Kingdom of God."

One of the most popular singing brigades was "The Commander's Own," the Negro singing group from the United States. Their singing of "When Trouble Come in Noah's Time, My Didn't It Rain?" and "Good-bye, Pharaoh, Good-bye" evoked tumultuous applause. "Good-bye, Pharaoh" was composed by Tom Ferguson, who was a member of the brigade.

During the music festival at Royal Albert Hall, the versatile New York Staff Band set their instruments aside to become a male chorus. Under the direction of Bandmaster George Darby, they sang his oratorio, "Wonderful."

On June 23 an exhausting program of events was held in the famed Crystal Palace and on its grounds, where a giant bandstand had been erected. At 8:45 A.M. the "sounding of the bombs" signaled seven bands to march from various parts of the grounds to the bandstand, where flags of the 58 nations represented were hoisted. The day closed at the bandstand with a mass meeting, in which the New York, Chicago, and International Headquarters Staff Bands played and Bramwell made his farewell charge, reiterating William's commission to his soldiers to bind up the world's wounds and seek the lost. He bid them God's speed and urged them to press God's holy war by loving all men.

On June 28, while some delegates were still in London, and many were on the high seas going home, their world commission was violently challenged when Archduke Francis Ferdinand, heir to the Austro-Hungarian throne, was assassinated at Sarajevo. This started the chain of aggressions that led to Germany attacking France by marching through Belgium, and in so doing brought a declaration of war from England for violating Belgium's neutrality. World War I had begun.

Salvationists in belligerent nations were heartbroken. On all sides they hated war, yet national loyalties were strong. Some officers enlisted as chaplains and Salvation Army Red Shield workers, some laity as medical assistants. But many young men hurried to enlist as infantrymen.

Salvationists in the United States did the job at hand. Activities of The Army's Naval and Military League were stepped up as the country enlarged its defense program. The Life Saving Guards, a virile nonmembership girls' work was begun in

1915, serving girls as succesfully as the Life Saving Scouts, initiated in 1913, served the boys. Camps for poor mothers and children were popular and many camp matrons seconded the statement in the *New England* magazine:

". . . A seldom heard fact is that almost everyone of the children treated have to be clothed from head to foot in order to be ready for camping. Each child is given a thorough bath and, when necessary, a shampoo and haircut."

Work with drunkards was now a major effort: they were contacted by visitation in the worst big-city districts, aided spiritually and physically in men's social institutions and regarded as special challenges by many Army officers. One of these was the Central Provincial Commander, Colonel William A. McIntyre, rock-jawed, rasping-voiced pioneer who loved the men of the street enough to experiment with many approaches in order to win them to God. One of these, his "Boozers' Convention," started on Thanksgiving day, 1910, was an all-out attack on "Bums' Row," in New York City.

Posters which read FREE EATS ALL DAY were posted on "almost every telephone pole and billboard in the underworld." From 4:30 A.M. Salvationist-manned buses cruised the Bowery, public parks, Hell's Kitchen, and municipal lodging houses, taking their "captures" to a central Salvation Army location, Memorial Hall.

In the afternoon, a "Boozers' Parade" was held, in which the entire force of The New York Salvation Army participated, supported by several brass bands, a waterwagon, floats, depicting scenes in the life of a drunkard and, most striking of all, the "Walking Whiskey Bottle," ten feet high, to which was chained a reeling, bloated "drunk," followed by a shawled, poverty-stricken woman and her ragged children.

A much publicized feature of one convention was "The Trial of John Barleycorn," presided over by a judge from the First Police Court of Jersey City, New Jersey. Marching in the parade with the judge were the jury, the witnesses, and the defendant.

Becoming increasingly popular and influential, the conventions were continued until the Eighteenth Amendment was passed. In 1915 the program was spectacularly successful. It was featured as "Thanksgiving with Mr. Boozer" in the New York press, which said of one officer's efforts: "Early in the morning out finding the neediest of men and women is Ensign John Allan of the Bowery. He spread a net through the dark waters of that neighborhood. Of 100 topers who breakfasted with him, about 80 came to the hall and were taken by bus to National Headquarters where in the afternoon Colonel McIntyre was on the bridge with his message. . . ."

Many conversions were reported.

Always on hand for these meetings was Henry F. Milans, a former editor of the New York *Morning Telegraph*. Milans, converted as a result of the first Boozers' Convention, had lost everything through drink. His bed became the Bowery gutters. Eventually he landed in Bellevue Hospital as Exhibit "A" of the most hopeless chronic drunk:

"Gentlemen," poor muddled Milans heard a Cornell University professor say to a group of medical students, "look at this man. . . . Note the dancing eyes, a sure sign of approaching insanity. . . . This man can never be cured, and you are looking at an example of alcoholism at its worst. He must die a drunkard, nothing can save him. You are looking, gentlemen, at a hopeless incurable."

When Milans was released, he ended up at McIntyre's Boozers' Convention, brought in by a lassie. He turned to God who released him from his driving thirst. Not long after, he accepted a position in a prominent New York printing firm, the Brieger Press, and for the rest of his life spent his free time counseling other needy men through The Army. Dr. J. Wilbur Chapman, noted American evangelist, said of Milans: "I know all the famous converts of America, but Milans is the greatest of them all." *

Between 1910 and 1920 there was also steady progress in prison work. A report stated:

"One of our provincial officers has been made a justice of the peace and county jail chaplain, while in several towns our officers are recognized as probationary officers of the courts. The deputy sheriff in one county is a staff officer's wife."

Corps officers throughout the country paid regular visits to city and county jails and state penitentiaries for counseling and worship services.

On April 6, 1917, the war "to make the world safe for democracy" bugled the American doughboy to attention and "Over There!" became the song hit of the year.

During the spring, Eva campaigned harder than ever for prohibition, considering it a moral issue. The *War Cry* published antidrink articles, including strong statements such as the following: ". . . If a man sells poison to another and the other is killed because of the poison, the man who makes the profit on the poison selling should pay. . . . More effective would be stopping the sale of alcoholic poisons entirely. . . . A first and big step in the direction of temperance would be to treat whiskey as we treat opium. . . ."

Salvation Army forces in America officially went on record

---

* Of course, many converts both in pioneer days and now do not remain faithful or become genuinely rehabilitated. Many cause heartbreak to themselves and to those working with them. Often, it is long-term loving patience that brings success with alcoholics. Recently in Chicago a man testified to a lengthy period of sobriety due to faith in God, but added, "Faith didn't 'take' till the seventeenth time I tried!"

opposing the use of strong drink in May of 1917. The *Philadelphia Inquirer* reported that during congress meetings in Philadelphia, a resolution introduced by Evangeline Booth was adopted in protest against "the waste of grain for the manufacture of liquors. . . . The delegates rose to their feet and adopted it unanimously."

"We should all help to cleanse the country of this foul pollution," said Eva. "This is the time to push the fight." A telegram urging the administration to insist upon the enactment of a law prohibiting the manufacture and sale of intoxicating liquors was sent to President Wilson.*

During the same congress, the *Inquirer* reported: "The delegates are looking forward with great interest to some action by the congress on what part The Salvation Army will take in the war. A hospital unit has already been organized and will probably be sent to France. . . ."

Shortly after, Eva announced the Army's attitude toward all war: "The Salvation Army is ready for the emergency but The Salvation Army is an international organization. Our flag is interlaced with the flags of all peoples. As our great Founder was, and bade us be, we know no man after the flesh, and yet recognize our brothers in all the families of the earth.

"There is only one war in which we can glory—that supreme struggle in which we are ceaselessly and desperately engaged—the triumph over sin and strife and death—all other war we deplore. But the Salvationist stands ready, trained in all necessary qualifications in every phase of humanitarian work, and to the last man will stand by the President for the execution of his orders. . . ."

---

* Soon after, sale of liquors to servicemen was prohibited, and in December, 1917, the proposal for a prohibition amendment was passed by Congress and submitted to the states for ratification or rejection. By January 16, 1919, it was ratified by three-fourths of the states and took effect on January 16, 1920.

Chapter Eight
1917/1919

DOUGHBOYS AND DOUGHNUTS

THE ARRIVAL of The Salvation Army in France in August, 1917, at least broke the monotony for many doughboys. One commented, "The Salvation Army! I believe they'll be waiting when we get to hell to try and save us." But it had taken a great amount of both planning and perseverance to get the first small group of Salvationists overseas. Two unusual incidents were partly responsible.

With the entry of America into the war, The Salvation Army was also put on a war basis. A National War Board was created and Colonel Edward J. Parker was appointed War Secretary. Religious, social, and entertainment services were provided at most large United States Army camps. Eva wired Washington, placing at the President's disposal the personnel of The Salvation Army in the United States, for any overseas service needed. The offer was refused because, she was told, the need was already met by the Young Men's Christian Association, the Knights of Columbus, and the Red Cross. That was enough.

Undaunted, Eva appointed Lt. Colonel William Barker to lead the overseas contingent of The Army. He was a man of brilliance and courage. Speaking of Barker, Eva once said: "If you want to see him at his best you must put him face to

152

face with a stone wall and tell him he must get on the other side. . . ."

Despite the official attitude, Barker planned to look over the European field of action to determine the best way to serve. Needing official permission to do so, he asked for an interview with Joseph Tumulty, Secretary to President Wilson. Tumulty was talking to a man at the far end of his office when Barker entered. After Barker made his request, they were interrupted by the other man.

"Joe, give the Colonel what he wants and make it good. The boys over there will need help, and when I think what Major Winchell has done for me. . . ."

Barker then recognized a prominent Jersey City lawyer, now a volunteer on the Attorney General's staff. His conversion had caused a sensation in New York society circles. He told his story to Tumulty, concluding, "You know what The Salvation Army has done for me. Now, do what you can for The Salvation Army."

A letter to the American Ambassador in France, William Graves Sharp, was speedily written, and Barker hurried out, "praising God and wondering at His way of doing things." The Ambassador in turn gave him a letter to John J. Pershing, General of the Armies. General Pershing was extremely friendly, giving The Army immediate clearance and ordering that whatever it needed was to be supplied. He suggested that Barker go to the camps, assess the need and report back to him. A car was even put at his disposal. The General's attitude was not a miracle but a simple case of casting one's bread upon the waters and having it come back buttered toast, as Salvationists sometimes put it.

In September, 1915, General Pershing, then stationed at the Presidio, San Francisco, California, was at Fort Bliss, Texas, on business. While the Presidio was shrouded in fog one night, a disastrous fire occurred. The next morning when the fog

lifted the shocking discovery was made that the General's wife
and children had been burned to death and his home completely destroyed. Lt. Colonel Henry Lee, West Coast provincial officer, wrote the General on behalf of The Salvation
Army, expressing deepest sympathy and "the assurance of the
prayers of all Salvationists." The General told Barker that he
had never forgotten "The Army's expression of sympathy." *

Barker found a mixed attitude toward Salvation Army
participation in the war. Many high-ranking officers and chaplains welcomed the idea, but "among the regular officers there
was rather a pessimistic attitude. It was nowise hostile, but
rather doubtful." Several specific problems which The Salvation Army might help solve were indicated. Homesickness was
a scourge. At St. Nazaire, the reception base for American
troops, camp followers were preying on soldiers. Perhaps the
sight of Salvationists would help. The report to General Per
shing resulted in official authorization and was accompanied
by the suggestion that Salvationists rush to the American training area to see what could be done about "the terrible epidemic
of homesickness."

When Eva received Barker's report, she promptly borrowed $25,000, cabled Barker to that effect and added, "Eleven
officers are being dispatched at once." Barker immediately
bought a tent and a touring car and sped over the French
countryside reconnoitering.

In the States, Eva's bold action furrowed many brows.
The Salvation Army's overseas program was now a fact, but
there was no money to support it. She asked subordinates to
see what they could do about repaying the loan. Her troops

---

* On the back of a printed acknowledgment, General Pershing
penned this note: "Dear Col. Lee: Your message of sympathy touched
me very deeply. I cannot tell you how much it has meant to me. Will
you please extend my thanks to the other members of The Salvation
Army? Very sincerely, John J. Pershing."

dug in for a kind of campaign wholly familiar but known to be sometimes disastrous—the finance fight. After six months of vainly trying to raise war funds, Major Fletcher Agnew, Special Efforts Secretary in Chicago, a former Northwestern student, marched into Commissioner Estill's office with a unique plan.

"Would you approve getting the letter carriers of Chicago to go over their delivery routes one evening in uniform to solicit for war work?"

It was a "ridiculous proposal" but it worked. In one night $49,267.25 was raised for war work. On the strength of this success, evangelist Paul Rader* volunteered to tour the principal cities of the West, holding mass meetings, following each with a local postal carriers' drive. By March 2, 1918, a total of $200,670.89 in cash had been collected for war work in the Department of the West. Of this, $124,503.27 was collected by postal carriers.

The fever of giving was infectious. Business and professional men began to push the campaign. Furthermore, once people were persuaded to give, they often became more receptive to religion, and The Army wielded its two-edged sword. During the fund-raising activity in Portland, for instance, Mayor H. R. Albee gave his free time to both spiritual and financial aspects of the campaign. By December, 1918, the West had raised two and a half million dollars for war work.

On August 12, 1917, eleven Salvationists set sail for France. Hand-picked by Eva, the seven men were younger or older than enlistment age, and the four women were over 25.

At Bordeaux, by General Pershing's order, they were fitted

---

*Paul Rader's brother Lyell was a prominent chemist and lay Salvationist leader. His children and grandchildren are Salvationists.

in regulation khaki uniforms with red S.A. shields on hats and red epaulets. The touring car Colonel Barker had bought was, for a while, the sole transportation system for all Salvationists. "Heartlessly overdriven and overworked," it also served as Barker's home. Someone reported seeing it tearing through the countryside at 40 miles an hour, "loaded inside and on top with supplies, several passengers clinging to its fenders and a load of lumber or trunks trailing behind."

The advance guard of the American Expeditionary Forces was quartered in small French villages. To one of these, Demange, the advance guard of The Salvation Army headed. The first Salvation Army overseas hut, a portable tent 25 by 100 feet, was put up. When it was completed Colonel Barker sped back to Paris where the women had been left temporarily. There was a stir among the enlisted men. Real American girls! Women! The French were aghast.

In order to do the most good, The Salvation Army placed its huts where other volunteer groups were not operating. However, a "Y" unit had followed on the heels of The Army, and on the opening night of the first Salvation Army hut, "Y" workers requested help at their meeting. A male cornetist and two lassies volunteered. They found about 1,000 soldiers still sitting around a ring where a boxing match, then a band concert, had been held. Soon, "Nearer My God to Thee" floated into the night. Women's voices. Doughboys crowded nearer. "When the trumpet of the Lord shall sound and time shall be no more. . . ." Then one of the girls told an old story about a Man who died for other men, promising, "If the Son therefore shall make you free, ye shall be free indeed."

At the Salvation Army hut it was the same. Meetings were always song services with brief talks. The boys went away calmed, they said. The huts were also used as canteens, serving a variety of packaged foods, gum, figs, nuts, cookies, and necessities such as razors, watches, gun oil, knives, shaving sticks,

writing paper, etc. Salvationists offered "jawbone," the soldiers'
term for credit, but no accounts were kept. A soldier paid at
his convenience or he didn't pay, and no soldier without money
was ever turned away.*

Most nonfood supplies were bought in France. At first,
$300 was the limit of purchases in Paris but as confidence in-
creased the ceiling was raised, until The Salvation Army was
purchasing $10,000 worth of supplies at a time. In early war
days, Bramwell loaned $100,000 from the international treasury,
urged by Eva, who said: "It is only a question of getting to
work in France, and the American public will see that we have
all the money we want."

In a dripping tent on the edge of the wood of Montiers
in September, 1917, Helen Purviance and Margaret Sheldon,
of the first and second overseas parties respectively, were distressed. Their regular supplies were gone, and the mucky roads
held little hope that more would arrive.

"We ought to have something more than just chocolate
to sell the soldiers, anyway," said Margaret, a former slum
sister and an expert cook. She looked across at the drooping
shoulders and discouraged faces of the boys around the Vic-
trola. "We ought to be able to give them some real homemade
cooking."

Private Braxton Zuber of Auburn, Alabama, was drinking
coffee. "Oh, would I like to have a doughnut."

Soon, the entire group was chanting, "We want doughnuts."

But flour could only be obtained in small quantities. Lard
was scarce and there was no stove available.

"You fellows get the stuff and I'll make the doughnuts,"
Margaret promised. The hut emptied. Within a very short

* Proceeds from the canteens were contributed to memorialize
United States divisions on the Western Front. This included all division
monuments and their bronze inscriptions.

time, an adobe stove of mud and stones was constructed by some of the men who had served on the Mexican border. The stovepipe was made of empty gallon fruit cans with the ends removed, stacked one on top of another. Soon, soldiers returned with everything but lard. And then, suddenly, one panted in with a huge kettle of bacon fat. To take out the salt, Margaret fried potatoes for the boys. Then she began to mix. The tent blew down, so the girls worked in the rain. A wine bottle was the rolling pin, and as there was no cutter, the first doughnuts became crullers, fried seven at a time in a small frying pan. Helen had to kneel before the tiny stove to cook in it.

The first batch of "doughnuts" was made from eighteen pounds of flour, nine pounds of sugar, six cans of milk, six cans of water, a pound of baking powder, and a tablespoon each of lemon, vanilla, and mace. One hundred and fifty doughnuts were made the first day, and the second day's production was doubled. However, the girls wanted to make doughnuts, not crullers, and in the next few days experimented with a variety of "cutters." A blacksmith welded together an evaporated milk can and a shaving tube; baking powder can tops with both camphor ice caps and coffee percolator tubes were tried. The most ingenious but also heaviest cutter was a seven-pound shell fitted with a one-pound shell. When fully equipped, the girls made from 2,500 to 9,000 sinkers daily. Soon, other Salvation Army huts specialized in doughnuts too, and their fame spread far and wide.

American aviators flew many miles to pick up doughnuts for their buddies. One dropped a note which read: "Will return for doughnuts tomorrow." Another time, a balloonist landed just for his share. A scout, sent on a reconnaissance mission, cleared No-Man's-Land and two nights later watched enemy forces retreat. He cautiously advanced and noticed smoke rising from behind a stone pile. Sure it was enemy soldiers, he drew two pistols and lunged, yelling a command in German as he did. "Behold, my enemy was two Salvation Army lassies, sleeves rolled up, hands covered with flour and dough." They were Swedish girls making doughnuts.

Pie had been the original baking idea but was abandoned for lack of ingredients and ovens. They were baked later however and soldiers stood in line for hours waiting for one piece. Often, there was a company of men hovering near the line but not part of it, looking on hungrily. After a while, a lassie would announce: "All of the men who have already had pie, please step out of line and all who want coffee and pie but have no money, please line up." *Stars and Stripes* had this to say of the pie-making:

> Tin hat for a halo;
> Ah, she wears it well,
> Making pies for homesick lads,
> Sure is "beating hell."
> In a region blasted
> By fire and flame and sword,
> This Salvation Army lass
> Battles for the Lord.
>
> Call me sacrilegious,
> And irreverent too;
> Pies? They link us up with home,
> As nothing else can do.
> "Home is where the heart is,"
> True, the poet sang,
> But "Home is where the pie is,"
> To the Yankee gang.

Supply lines often failed and the girls had to resort to imagination and improvisation. But transportation improved and space allotment was more generous. In a single month,

120 tons of flour were shipped to the Salvation Army overseas, in addition to local purchases. Within nine months, 600 tons of chocolate bars were purchased, plus those bought through French sources.

At Tartigny, soldiers rushed from the Salvation Army hut to their dugouts when a bombardment surprised them. One, helping a lassie, shouted, "Come on! Follow me to your dugout." A tray of freshly baked lemon cream pies stood on the table, and the girl's sturdy new boots under it. She rushed after her escort, tray in one hand and boots in the other. Having crossed a little gulley on a plank, the soldier turned and saw the lassie swaying as she crossed. "Drop the shoes," he shouted. "I can clean the shoes, but for heaven's sake don't drop the pies."

Another Salvation Army service was banking. The American soldier was well paid compared to other allied soldiers. He often had more money than he could spend but there was no way to send it home, even if his family was in need of financial help. The Salvation Army transmitted the money, sending it by money-order to New York and from there to officers commanding in local areas, who delivered it in person to the appropriate family. This meant a personal contact, often comforting, and if there was need in the home, Salvationists helped.

The Salvation Army forces overseas were never large. At no time were there more than 500 representatives on active duty. Despite the claim that there was no place for them and that women could not stand the rigors of combat duty, the girls managed incredibly well. The overseas program seemed perfectly natural to Eva. In an exclusive to *The Ladies' Home Journal* in 1918, she stated:

"What more natural thing? It must not be forgotten that The Salvation Army, wherever it is established in 61 countries on this earth, has been trained to endure hardship and privation, to deal with the miseries and wants of unfortunates. . . . Our workers . . . skilled and experienced in practical relief work, and long since consecrated to God and His service, are the 'little mothers' of the battlefield. . . ."

In an effort to obtain recruits, Eva advertised in the *War Cry* for Salvationist helpers, but they must be "neither tourists nor butterflies." She was right. The girls lived in huts, tents, ruins, dugouts, and haystacks. Some went weeks without a change of clothes. Margaret Sheldon reported in her diary:

"The rats made such a noise over our heads, we didn't get to sleep. Made 76 pies this morning. Didn't have enough to go around." They made doughnuts, but they also baked pies, rolls, tarts, fried ham-n-eggs, made coffee, cocoa, lemonade. "Made rolls and coffee for the 91st Division as they passed our hut. . . . They had been traveling 48 hours and were so tired. . . . Miss Billings and I made 3,120 butter rolls."

They also sewed buttons, mended uniforms, talked and listened, sang, preached and prayed, and cried, too, as the wounded boys were brought back. There wasn't, however, much time for tears. One worker was notified that her brother had been killed in action and she was urged to take the day off. Her reply was, "I didn't come to cry. I came to make doughnuts."

Salvation Army lassies somehow had the knack "to fit in." American doughboys sometimes speculated about it. "Why have they become so popular? It wasn't like this when we came over." "No," was the reply, "but you got to remember, they've always been popular with the homeless. Now, we're the homeless."

A military colonel once said the Army lassies were the only women in France who were safe unchaperoned. They were the only women ever permitted to sleep in the underground passages at Verdun.

Salvationists stationed overseas, both men and women,

followed American troops into the trenches. For example, when the Allies opened their drive on the Germans, so great was the demand for nurses that Salvation Army lassies by the score were thrown into action along "with their food trucks, which were transformed into ambulances."

Nothing stood in their way. Told that they couldn't get permits for the Montdidier sector as the French were opposed to any relief organization going there, the girls went without permits, riding in the United States Army trucks. Two dugouts were made just behind the trenches, and there they looked after the needs of their fighters.

One dark rainy night in the trenches, Roy Ahrend and his buddies were stunned to see a Salvation Army girl "come wading through the mud and give us each a cootie bag. These were tied around the neck and were filled with a substance so foul-smelling that even a cootie couldn't stomach it."

At the field hospital in Cheppy the wounded arrived in droves, a thousand when only two hundred had been expected. Salvation Army girls were asked to take charge of wards. They were under fire for five days when the General ordered them to leave. The Salvation Army major in charge came to report. "General, my girls say they won't go." The General's face softened. "Well, if The Salvation Army wants to stay, let them stay." Frequently, nurses asked if "Ma" Sheppard, a middle-aged officer from the Midwest, could find time to come and sit with a dying boy who was calling for her. She never let a boy who was going "over the top" leave her hut without a word of personal prayer.

On Decoration Day, Eva sent word that she was sending American flags for all soldiers' graves. Near Treveray, a censor called in a lassie who'd written home about the service. "I understand by one of your letters that you are thinking of decorating the American graves. We would like to help in that, if you don't mind. I'd like the company to be present."

Early on Decoration Day, the girls gathered armfuls of crimson poppies, snowballs, and blue bachelor buttons. Each grave received an apple-tin vase of flowers and a flag. The girls offered a prayer, a squad of riflemen fired a volley for each man buried there, a bugler played taps "and the little service was over." Similar services were conducted at all locations.

Songs were written and poems composed about the Salvation Army lassies, but the Salvation Army men who worked with them, and others who served as chaplains also distinguished themselves. Major J. E. Atkins, a widely loved chaplain who served with the First Battalion, 26th Infantry, became affectionately known as "Old 53," his badge number. Soldier Herman Heydt referred to him in a poem written about a dying doughboy calling for his mother:

Old Fifty-three then drew the lad unto his flattened breast,
And held him firm against his heart as if by her caressed.
The happy boy no longer feared the battle's new alarms,
For he was most content to die within his mother's arms.
And so I sing the praise of him whose noble, simple heart
Was big and strong and tender, too, to play a mother's part.

Other doughboys recall their own individual experiences.

Henry L. Moody who was in the Rainbow Division said that "in the worst part of the Chateau Thierry battle two Salvation Army men arrived at the front lines and passed out cigarettes and chocolate bars." He wanted chewing tobacco and was lucky to get the last two plugs of "Brown's Mule."

Floyd I. Silk met The Salvation Army just below division headquarters in Cacarat, France, where a sign read: "Come and Eat and Then We Shall Pray to the Good Lord." "Salvationists," he recalled, "seemed always to be with us in the front lines and trenches with hot drinks or lemonade and candies." John O. Findlay, Co. B., 316 Supply Train, was close behind combat lines during the Argonne battle where shells whined overhead, machine guns spit, and planes strafed. He noticed a group of soldiers. "A Salvation Army man and two lassies were frying doughnuts over a blazing fire within an improvised stone firebox." Soldiers slipped away briefly from the front and "there was gratitude and near disbelief that anybody cared to make existence a bit easier."

Asa G. Ellis, stationed with the Chemical Warfare Service, reported that their village had been shelled continuously: "A mammoth shell was on the way. A S.A. lady had started across the street. She stopped, knelt, and after the shell passed went calmly about her business. . . . They always seemed to know when we were due back from the front lines and met us. . . . I wish to stress the fact that your women were out there. It was not just your men."

Anna May Kamp, widow of Charles Kamp, Fifth Marines, Second Division, quoted her husband: "We were in the front lines. It was as black as pitch and raining like the hammers of hell. We heard the sentry halt someone and when we looked it was two S.A. lassies carrying a milk can of coffee and some doughnuts. The girls were soaking wet and up to their knees in mud."

James G. Barber, attached to a motorcycle unit, had lost his helmet and wrapped a legging about his head. A Salvation Army girl serving him coffee told him he shouldn't return to combat without a helmet. He explained he didn't have one nor did he have money to pay for another. "We'll find you one," she said, "if we have to give you one of our own. We're here to serve not to sell." Barber, like many other servicemen, later became a warm friend of The Salvation Army. As Judge Barber of Evanston, Illinois, he helped build a strong advisory board and served as board chairman for many years.

Some ex-servicemen joined The Salvation Army and became full-time officers. Representative of these were David Brown, who was with the army of occupation in Coblenz, and

Fred Wilkes, who fought with General Pershing in the Mexican War and served with the "Fighting First" in France. During World War I, he told a friend: "Charlie, when I saw the Sallies with their ever willingness to help a fellow in need and expose themselves to all kinds of danger . . . I knew there was something in life I'd missed. I can't get The Salvation Army out of my mind." He joined and was a faithful officer until his death.

Howard Fritz, who had attended Salvation Army meetings in Europe was waiting for discharge at Staten Island. While there he visited the local corps. When the Captain was absent one night, he volunteered his services: "I decided to have an open-air service, and I had to go alone so rode on a trolley car an hour to get up courage. At sight of a lone soldier playing a clarinet, a large crowd gathered. I preached to the best of my ability for a half hour and asked if anybody wanted to decide for God. Thirty-two people knelt and there were so many standing around that traffic was stalled, including the trolleys."

Ed Beckwith, a member of the U.S. Army Medical Corps and a Salvationist, took part in five major battles. It was part of his duty to give a tetanus shot to all wounded brought to the first-aid station. He records: "We still were using old-style needles, and this shot was given in the stomach." Beckwith had thought about the possibility of death and wanted to make a last witness for God. He pinned a Salvation Army cap band to his undershirt so whoever opened his shirt would consider his condition before the Almighty.

A very young German boy was brought to the first-aid station in bad shape. He'd been told the Americans shot prisoners with poison needles and begged hysterically, "Please! Please! I want to see my mother again." Suddenly Beckwith thought of an idea that might help. He opened his shirt and bent over the boy so that he could see the cap band. "Oh, The Salvation Army." The boy smiled and relaxed.

When the armistice was finally announced, "Cease fire!" was passed along trench lines. There was an uneasy feeling in the silence. Two hours after the first report was received, runners arrived to confirm the news. "Slowly, almost unbelieving, men lifted themselves from the ghastly trenches," recounted one of the McAllister doughnut girls, "stretched weary, cramped limbs. . . . There was no hilarious demonstration, no shouting, no loud hurrahs, no blowing of trumpets." Slowly they began to talk in normal voices. Having whispered for so long, this was a luxury in itself. Having crawled in the trenches for so long, just to walk upright was a rare treat. Then came the bonfires. All light had been prohibited during battle. Both sides began to build fires, and the leaping flames themselves heralded peace.

Twenty hours after the armistice, Salvationists Harold and Mildred Smith accompanied one of the American generals with his staff across No-Man's-Land into German trenches. Mildred Smith spoke fluent German and acted as interpreter. At another sector, two girls took huge trays of doughnuts across the lines to the German forces.

At home, the country went wild. Everything stopped, everybody took to the streets. Salvation Army Commissioner Estill in Chicago grabbed the Army flag, took all his territorial headquarters staff and paraded with thousands of other Chicagoans through the Loop.

The Salvation Army overseas group stayed with the army of occupation while the stateside forces expanded services to receive homecoming heroes. Dockside, their first concern was for the wounded. While the rest of the boys waited to entrain, the girls who had been too young to go overseas and who served in clerical capacities at New York and other port headquarters, gave out chocolate, answered questions, hunted up relatives, passed out stamped post cards, wrote and sent free telegrams—services that were most appreciated by the enlisted man. The girls were on 24-hour duty and reported any time a troopship arrived. After duty at the docks, they often hurried back to the office to spend the night sending telegrams. In one day, April 20, 1919, they sent out 2,900 telegrams for servicemen. Other women Salvationists visited hospitalized servicemen regularly.*

Harry E. Negley, with his poem, "The Little Dougnut Girl," capsuled the thinking of American doughboys during postwar days:

> I went thru the bloomin' fracas,
> From Thierry to the Rhine,
> And the trimmin' that we gave 'em
> Was a hummer, you will find;
> But of all the folks that mixed up
> In that beastly bloody swirl,
> I cannot forget the graces
> Of the little Doughnut Girl.
>
> I've done my bit for Uncle Sam,
> Three thousand miles away.
> I have had my fill of fighting,
> And I'm home this time to stay.
> I think they'd have to drag me in,
> For another such a whirl,
> But I'd wade through hell barefooted,
> For the little Doughnut Girl!†

---

* This work is still a function of The Army and is performed by the League of Mercy, augmented by local bands and songster brigades. Special emphasis is placed on Easter and Christmas visitation when small gifts, candy, and copies of the *War Cry* are distributed.

† One doughnut girl, Irene McIntyre Walbridge, became national president of the American Legion Auxiliary. The daughter of Salvation Army pioneers, Commissioner and Mrs. W. A. McIntyre, she was under enemy fire for 256 days and was twice cited by the U.S. Army for courage and devotion "under high explosive fire and gas."

In March, 1919, The Salvation Army received a letter from Franklin D. Roosevelt, Acting Secretary of the Navy. It read, in part: "The Department desires to express the gratitude of the officers and men of the United States Navy for all the many good things you have done for them during the World War. . . . The Department is desirous that your excellent work be continued . . . whether the country be in peace or at war. . . . There is a very constant need for your services."

In October of that year Evangeline Booth was awarded the Distinguished Service medal by President Wilson for her personal contribution to the American armed forces, and that of her "peace soldiers."

Years after the armistice, W. L. Stidger told a story that best exemplifies the meaning of the service Salvationists shared with American doughboys. Stidger had been stationed near Toul, France, when the burial of the first American soldier took place. It was a strange burial, for not only was an American buried but also a Frenchman and a German. A participating sergeant asked the U.S. Captain in charge, "Shall we fire a salute and play taps for the Boche, sir?"

"Yes, after all, he's just some German mother's son."

A French woman attending the service, whose husband had recently been killed in battle, protested, "Bah, Boche." That night the chaplain spent two hours telling her how the Americans had no hatred for the Germans, only for evil. She told her neighbors about the "crazy Americans" and took them to see the three graves. Just before Christmas, she came to the chaplain.

"If you Americans do things differently at burials, you must have your own way of celebrating Christmas. I have nothing for my boy. Could he have an American Christmas?"

The chaplain discussed the incident with two Salvation Army girls. Toys simply were not available. In fact, all they could offer was doughnut dough.

"Then we'll have a doughnut Christmas."

"And we'll invite the whole company," said the chaplain.

The girls made dolls, trees, tables and chairs out of dough, a bed with a soldier in it, a house with windows, a big star, and imitation candles and bells. Then they made a crèche— the stable, the manger, the Child, with white bone buttons for a halo. Christmas Eve arrived and into a French cottage crowded excited children, their mothers, American soldiers, and Salvation Army lassies. The big party ended with carols and the final one was, of course, "Silent Night."

It was a magnificent moment. Finally, a soldier broke the silence.

"A German wrote that song we just sang. Ain't that something?"

The French woman again came to the chaplain.

"You don't hate men, only the evil they do. You love the good, the beautiful. I understand. Yes, I undertsand."

So it was that doughboys and doughnuts brought the Christ meaning to a French village.

THE POPULAR
TWENTIES
AND JEOPARDY

THE METROPOLITAN Opera House in New York City was packed from floor to ceiling and "the golden horseshoe looked like a Caruso night." Thousands waited expectantly. On the stage, Salvation Army leaders had finished spirited preliminaries. Now the dropped curtain hid them, lights were cut and singers, clad in hooded robes of red and white, softly took their places on stage, forming a gigantic red-rimmed cross. Terraced at the rear of the stage was the New York Staff Band, playing "as if symphony critics were in the boxes. . ." Lights dimmed to blue. A single shaft of brilliance picked up a figure coming down the center aisle.

Evangeline Cory Booth, as a cockney tune hawker in rags and a fringed shawl and playing a concertina, walked on stage. Fifty slum sisters in gingham dresses and voluminous muslin aprons fanned out on either side of her. Addressing the audience, Eva began one of her widely acclaimed "lectures," this one entitled, "The Commander in Rags." In it she told of her teen years when, termed "The White Angel of the Slums," she ministered incognito in London's East End. Her presentations more closely resembled dramatic monologues. Massed bands, songsters, and soloists were important to her pageant-sermons, as were lighting effects and "props" of all kinds, including her harp, a huge lighted cross, live sheep and, at least on one occasion, a live horse.

Eva's lectures, always concluding with an invitation to accept Jesus Christ as Savior, were widely sought. STANDING ROOM ONLY signs were posted hours before her appearance, and the press invariably reported: "Doors opened one hour ahead of time to prevent a riot in crowds outside." "Every seat taken within five minutes after public admitted." "Thousands turned away." Audiences included bankers and laundresses, titled visitors from overseas and cab drivers, fashionable socialites, judges, lawyers, educators, clergymen, business leaders, women from the red-light districts, and the most odious and odorous drunks.

Conversions were numerous, sometimes spectacular. For example, before Eva left the stage after one lecture, a tough-looking man dashed up the proscenium steps, pulled out a pistol and handed it to her. "You take it," he said. "I won't be needing it any more." Eva prayed with him on the stage.

Indicative of her impact on intellectuals was her 1922 visit to Princeton University where she delivered her lecture, "The World's Greatest Romance," before students and faculty. Introducing her, President John Grier Hibben said:

". . . By our presence here tonight, we wish to express to Commander Booth and also to her associates, our very deep appreciation of the manifold work of The Salvation Army, and also to express, in some measure at least, our feelings in regard to the deep debt of gratitude we owe to this institution for the self-sacrificing work it has for so long carried on, not only in this country but right around the world. . . ."

In the lecture Eva not only described The Army's rise and progress in the social service field but also gave an outspoken and, to some, surprising testimony to the "fact and efficacy of the sacrifice of Calvary, and the power of God unto salvation." Reporters said no word of hers could have been received with more rapt attention or more sympathy. Upon her return to New York, she was inundated with telephone calls from Princetonians, expressing their appreciation for the strengthening of faith and renewal of spiritual perception which her visit had brought.*

The press, growing bored with ornamental religion, had glowing words of commendation for this actress-preacher-militarist, and for her tactics. They said she had strong personal magnetism, a genius for administration, a quick brain and "the unconquerable endurance of the Booths"—and she was the "spitting image" of her father. They said she could have been one of the world's leading actresses, that she had her mother's emotional oratory and her father's sense of politics.

It was no secret that she gathered around her leading lights of society's important professional and business people. Even the starchiest members of the clergy who had once decried the methods The Army used and doubted its sincerity were also part of her following. Prominent Jews, as well, enthusiastically supported her Christian crusade. Her purpose was three-fold: Such friends aided in maintaining sympathetic relations with the public, assisted in the interpretation of The Army's aims and purpose, and advised Salvationist leaders on matters of community service. Among her staunchest supporters were these nationally known citizens: John and Rodman Wanamaker, William Jennings Bryan, John Markle, Thomas R. Marshall, Henry B. F. MacFarland, Helen Gould, Myron T. Herrick, Herbert Hoover, Rabbi Joseph Silverman, Allison V. Armour, Joseph W. Harriman, Otto H. Kahn, George Gordon Battle, Henry W. Taft, John H. Finley, Bishop W. T.

---

* In 1964 Princeton sophomore John Bowers made a significant statement to a Salvationist undergraduate, who regretted that The Army often is misjudged as wholly a social service organization. "You should be glad," said Bowers. "No other church is misunderstood because its social service ministry is so intertwined with its worship of God."

Manning, Finley J. Shepard, William G. McAdoo, Felix M. Warburg, Edwin Gould, Adolph Ochs, Frank L. Polk, Minnie Maddern Fiske, and Samuel Untermeyer.

She made these friends Advisory Board members and campaign managers; she took them on guided tours of Salvation Army installations and had them chair her huge public meetings. In her dramatic persuasive manner she exposed dire needs to them and asked their personal advice and co-operation. They gave both.

Illustrative of their practical interest is an excerpt from a speech made in 1922 by "the merchant prince of Philadelphia," John Wanamaker, at the unveiling of a memorial bust of William Booth in New York City: ". . . This is not my speech at all. I am simply talking to you. There is not anything I could do that I would not do to help the Commander in the work. . . . She does not ask me often enough." Later in the speech he revealed the reason for his continued interest in The Army: ". . . At the best Salvation Army meeting I was ever in, there were only 70 or 80 workers present, and they were praying together on their knees. They called on me to pray. . . . It was the most gracious season I ever experienced. We every one got nearer to God. . . ."

Many of Eva's influential friends said they had a selfish motive in joining The Army's battle against distress. In John Wanamaker's words, they too "got nearer to God."

Evangeline Booth never pulled her punches. She never watered down the Atonement, her hatred for strong drink, her abhorrence of Christian love that does not act to alleviate want, soften sorrow, and challenge sin. She was knowledgeable. When certain officers expressed a desire to study psychology in order to better equip themselves to serve their fellow men, she said:

". . . Modern methods? Yes, if they mean greater efficiency in the discharge of our God-given duties—I welcome them.

Yes, if they mean grander results in the numbers of souls saved—I rejoice in them. Yes—if they add strength and solidarity to our forces—if they give more wisdom to our leaders—if they assist more poor—if they set at liberty more captives—if they unstop more deaf ears—if they give more sight to blind eyes—if they bind up more broken hearts—I love them.

"But we must remember they are nothing in themselves. They must be devoted to the service and subject to the influence and inspiration of God if they are to be servants of the Kingdom. They must be His not ours. They must be means, not ends."

Eva's critics said she was autocratic and even, at times, abusive. They said she was emotional, melodramatic, and difficult to persuade. All of this was at least partially true. But it was also true that she captained Salvation Army forces in the United States with dynamism, imagination, and daring—that no one deprecated. A few rebelled at her authoritarianism, but most accepted and even rejoiced in it. In elite circles she *was* The Salvation Army.

Under Evangeline Booth, The Army in America prospered in the twenties more than at any other period before.

By 1919, postwar needs had lessened so Salvation Army local needs were reviewed. Properties were sadly run down and work had been sharply curtailed until the war was won. A Home Service "drive" was launched, the first of its kind, to raise $10,000,000 throughout the 48 states. Salvationists had always deplored having to beg support for their work with a tambourine. Now, for the most part, panhandling was replaced by organized fund-raising. The idea appealed to the public and some influential friends rallied in unconventional ways. For example, the receipts of the annual New York Horse Show were donated early in the twenties. A feature of this show was the presence of the Prince of Wales, who appeared with Eva.

When Eva took command much of the work was carried

on in rented buildings. Doughboys and their families now contributed generously to house The Army. By the end of the twenties in almost every city and town where The Army operated, there was an Army owned building, though inexperience in choosing professional campaigners and in building meant near financial disaster in some cases. Also, as inflation set in, building and maintenance costs skyrocketed.

Helping in the financial drives in the Midwest and West were advisory boards of local professional and business people. When Commissioner Estill was transferred to the command of the Eastern Territory in 1921, he formed boards throughout the East.

The first advisory board, an outgrowth of the original camp board and the model for all of them, was formed in Chicago in 1904. Today, there are 7,496 Salvation Army advisory boards in the United States, with 106,697 members, including such men as Frederick Kappel, Chairman of the Board of American Telephone and Telegraph Company (New York); Edgar Forio, Senior Vice-President of the Coca-Cola Corporation (Atlanta); John T. Pirie of Carson Pirie Scott and Company and C. E. McKittrick, Assistant to the Publisher, the *Chicago Tribune* (Chicago); and Benjamin Swig, owner of the Fairmont Hotel (San Francisco). Advising, aiding, promoting, advisory board men and women are The Salvation Army's trusted "citizen soldiers."

During the 1920's, The Army revolutionized its practice of family social welfare at holiday time, "turning from the more spectacular charity of the sit-down dinner to the goodwill basket." It also served an increasing number of children and youth. By 1924, the year the Boozers' Conventions were discontinued because they were no longer considered necessary, Eva said: "It means in the future that we shall have less to do with the grave and more to do with the cradle; less binding of life's broken plants and more training of life's untrammeled vines;

that more of our energy, our ingenious methods, will be thrown into the work of prevention."

Although Eva's dream of a nonalcoholic society was not realized and The Army soon felt impelled to redouble its efforts on behalf of the drunkard and his family, increasing emphasis was given to youth work, nevertheless. When Eva arrived in America, The Army's chief youth work was in its relatively small Sunday schools, called "company meetings." Now it offered a wide variety of activities and services, including singing companies and youth bands; Young People's Legion and Corps Cadets, which offered leadership training and education-recreation programs; Boy Scouts and Girl Guards (similar to Girl Scouts), Chums (now Cub Scouts) and Sunbeams; and the mushrooming Red Shield youth clubs, "The Army's contribution to the solution of the underprivileged problem. Their aim is the bringing of the sports and games of outside youth off the street and into a clean and wholesome atmosphere."

In Rome, New York, the first Salvation Army boys' club, or post, as it was called, was organized by Captain Jack Seddon. Today, there are 291 clubs and community centers. Seddon, a former English slum boy, sympathized with the rebellious children of Rome's mill hands. Cutbacks after the armistice heightened the problem, and the captain walked the streets talking to boys, discussing and gaining support for his dream of a clubhouse. In an old warehouse he set up a gym, game room, craft room, and a snack bar specializing in penny candies. Soon he hired a young Salvationist, J. J. Simonson, a psychology major from Indiana University, to direct it. Simonson later became an officer. It was probably in Rome that the well-known term, "Red Shield" services, originated, for "using the red shield of The Army as our guide," said Simonson, "we developed as our insignia a shield, outlined in red, with the initials RSP (Red Shield Post), in red diagonally across it."

With the opening of the club, juvenile delinquency in Rome showed a surprising decline. Judge Parker Scripture of Children's Court estimated it at some 60 per cent to 70 per cent in the first three years, and he appointed the club superintendent as a probation officer. The club welcomes about 200 boys regularly now, "from welfare boys to sons of teachers and city officials."

There was also a great amount of home missionary work being personally done by Salvationists who were concerned about wayward boys and girls. Sister Justice, a soldier of the Bowery Corps in New York City, was one who cared about other people's distressed children. She simply "went down to the Bowery and made friends." In 1923 the Houston Streeters, a gang of "Dead End" kids, came under her influence, and she formed a Bible class. It might be one of the toughest Bible classes in the world, she admitted, but it was a good one. Asked to give testimonies, the boys responded characteristically. One said: "During the week I shot craps. I threw a brick at a policeman and got arrested. I stole money from my mother. I played hookey from school. I got into four fights and got a busted nose." Seeing that Sister Justice was obviously disappointed, the boy hesitated. Then he said in a rush, "Next week I'm not going to do any of them things." He produced a much used pair of dice and asked her to throw them away. In a few moments all the boys had made "contributions."

During the previous decade there had been discussion between Bramwell and Eva concerning the division of Army work in the United States. Bramwell leaned toward the appointment of three territorial leaders (later, four) directly responsible to International Headquarters. Evangeline thought this would be disastrous because it would destroy a unified command in the States. In 1922 she confirmed a press announcement that she was being farewelled, stating, "I shall obey the order when the date is set for me to go," and cabled Bramwell for further instructions. Longtime friend Myron T. Herrick, United States Ambassador to France and formerly Governor of Ohio, wrote that "it would be as disastrous to the people of the country as to The Salvation Army in America if Evangeline Booth were moved." Former Vice-President Thomas Marshall also quickly protested. An impressive list of people cabled Bramwell that if Eva were succeeded by three leaders with limited powers "there would result a diminuation in the popular interest for The Salvation Army and its work." Bramwell replied that there was no thought of an immediate farewell, and the war front in America settled down.

Work was now divided into three territories. The new Western Territory, established in 1920, was headed by Lt. Commissioner Adam Gifford; Commissioner William Peart commanded the Central Territory (formerly part of the Department of the West); Commissioner Thomas Estill, the Eastern Territory; and Eva became National Commander. In 1927 another new territory was born—the Southern—with headquarters in Atlanta and commanded by Lt. Commissioner William A. McIntyre, a pioneer of many battles, about whom Eva said in her inaugural address, "Cast him into a den of lions and he will pray them lockjawed and come out unscathed."

Each territory was divided into a number of provinces or divisions, which supervised local corps. Specialized work such as hospitals, men's work-shelters, and prison ministrations, came directly under the supervision of territorial headquarters.

The open-air ministry, always a major method of attack, was greatly extended in the United States during the 1920's, and officers often employed large brass bands and proficient songster brigades. Services were geared to local conditions. In small farming towns hour-long Saturday night meetings were common. Near factories, lunch-hour programs and "praise" meetings were provided. And in the big cities, crowds swarmed around downtown meetings.

Between 1921 and 1923, Times Square in New York was besieged by The Salvation Army. Captain Rheba Crawford was appointed to the reactivated New York #2 Corps, which specialized in street meetings. She obtained permission to conduct meetings from the side steps of the Gaiety Theater on 46th Street. There was some resentment at first—a few buckets of water, some coarse remarks. Then a Catholic priest addressed the crowd.

"Stop harassing the Captain," he demanded. "After listening to her, I'm inclined to believe that wayward members of my own flock who also listen may return to our church better members than before."

The underworld passed the word to let her alone and give to her fund for the destitute of the street. Gamblers, girls from the red-light district, discharged soldiers, and a police captain from the "tenderloin"* district attended her meetings and sought help. Returning from circuit tours, theatrical people checked in at the National Vaudeville Association down the street and then came to the meeting. They always sang with gusto. One of the reporters assigned to the Bright Light Beat who came to listen was dapper young Walter Winchell. He said Rheba Crawford was the only "doll," except for the girl he later married, who could look beautiful without lipstick, powder, or gook. Winchell named her "The Angel of Broadway."

No bass drum was needed to attract attention. Crowds

---

*An area in which lies the greatest opportunity for graft and corruption. In New York City the old 29th police precinct, from 23rd to 42nd Street, west of Broadway. A police officer assigned there was reported to have commented that he had always eaten chuck steak, but henceforth would have tenderloin.

grew and so did the number of converts, as Captain Crawford "orated about being saved." Between five and six thousand listeners awaited her on "good" evenings. One night she was arrested for obstructing traffic, and hundreds of furious listeners crashed down a door at the police station trying to free her. Walter Winchell heard of her arrest and rushed from the Palace Theater with former police captain Reardon to obtain her release. The next morning the charge was changed to "disturbing the peace," on evidence that the captain waved her arms when she led hymn-singing. The case was dismissed.

Winchell "got religion" under Rheba Crawford's ministry. When columnist Donald Freeman heard this, he told Damon Runyon, star reporter for Hearst newspapers, who knew "more than somewhat" about the Great White Way. Intrigued, Runyon wrote a story about Rheba Crawford, called it, "The Idyll of Miss Sarah Brown," and published it in a series, *Guys and Dolls*. Freeman said Runyon changed very little of the original story. He described "The Sky," his main male character, as "by no means as innocent as he looks. The Sky is smarter than three Philadelphia lawyers, which makes him very smart." Sky, while walking along Broadway, "comes upon a little bunch of mission workers who are holding a religious meeting, such as mission workers love to do of a Sunday evening, the idea being that they may round up a few sinners here and there." Sky sees a young "doll" in the group:

"She is tall and thin, and has a first-class shape; and her hair is a light brown, going on blond, and her eyes are like I do not know what, except that they are one hundred per cent eyes in every respect. . . . He hears her make a speech in which she puts the blast on sin very good, and boosts religion quite some, and says if there are any souls around that need saving, the owners of same may step forward at once."

Later, this story and another, "Pick the Winner," the chronicle of gambler Nathan Detroit and his "ever lovin'" fiancée, Miss Cutie Singleton, became the basis for *Guys and Dolls,** the very popular musical comedy, which later became an equally popular movie.

The Salvation Army National Commander, then Commissioner Ernest Pugmire, and an aide, Brigadier William Parkins, were invited to a preview of the play. Parkins was somewhat apprehensive, but Pugmire said, "Any presentation that relates The Army to city life doesn't do any harm." Although parts of the story were obviously unrealistic, increased interest in The Army's federation of services has been the result.

———

The enrollment of officer candidates shot up during the twenties, "crowding to capacity its three large training schools where twenty years ago one small school sufficed."

Vocational training was interesting Salvationists. So many unfortunate people had no job skills and no self-discipline regarding work. Like their old General, William Booth, Salvationists believed in "work for all," not degrading charity. "I do not want my customers to be pauperized by being treated to anything they do not earn," the General once said. Some Salvationists encountered special problems in job placement for those they tried to help, and used methods not outlined in their *Orders and Regulations.*

Major Carrie Sabine and Commandant Rachel Payne, in charge of the Waioli, Hawaii, home for girls, were greatly concerned about the need for vocational training. George Norton Wilcox, a generous friend of The Army who had earlier provided 50 acres of land in Kaimuki for a boys' home, heard of their plight and donated $50,000 for a tea room. The idea for the tea room reportedly came from the presentation of a

———

*Words and Music by Frank Loesser. Book (for play) by Jo Swerling and Abe Burrows.

coconut-frosted birthday cake which the two officers baked for
Mr. Wilcox. Delighted, he suggested, "Why not have a little
tea room and serve cake and juices? Your girls will be trained
and your home will benefit." In the fall of 1922, "Waioli"
opened its doors, staffed entirely by girls in the home. It served
coconut cake and Hawaiian fruit juices. Waioli has become
world famous as a tourist attraction, and the tea room and gift
shop are now included on tours in Manoa Valley. Due to its
phenomenal success, girls are now drawn from the community
to staff it, although the program of classes in homemaking
still continues. Proceeds support the home and contribute to the
support of The Salvation Army's expanding youth program in
the Hawaiian Islands.

Particularly in New York City assistance to immigrants
included a variety of services, such as caring for small children,
providing clothing and other necessities, finding loved ones,
providing temporary shelter and, as in the case of the widower
in Wheeling, West Virginia, helping in family problems. He
had written his mother in the Old Country to choose and send
him a new wife. When the woman arrived in New York she
was met by an Army Immigration Department representative
and headed for Wheeling. There, Captain and Mrs. Bryce
Phillipson, corps officers, took her home, arranged for a Catholic priest to marry the couple, helped choose the ring, and even
tied cans on their car to make the celebration 100 per cent.

The method of The Army's ministry was changing to
meet the needs of people in a more sophisticated era. Its halls
were not quite so bare, its processions were more orderly, its
preaching a trifle less ebullient. However, in many places pio-
neering was still going on. In Twin Falls, Idaho, Captain and

Mrs. Purdy campaigned by motorcycle. A mining camp in Tarbridge Range was one of their stops. "We expected to find real mining people," they said, "and we did, but to our surprise learned they had an unwritten law that no minister would be permitted in town." The Purdys sang, knelt, and prayed in the street. When they stood up, the street and windows were crowded with listeners, although some were frightened as it was "the first religious service in more than 10 years."

The Men's Industrial Department, aiding homeless men, was amazingly successful during this period. Founded on William Booth's "Darkest England and the Way Out" plan, the program was an effort to effect men's rehabilitation by giving them temporary housing, clothing, food, and work, while simultaneously striving to point them to God. In his book, the General had dealt with this subject under two headings: "The Factory" and "The Household Salvage Brigade," stating: "Any person who comes to a shelter destitute and starving will be supplied with sufficient work to enable him to earn the fourpence needed for his bed and board." His desire to make the work self-supporting included the salvaging of waste materials: ". . . I propose to establish in every large town a civil force of organized collectors who will patrol the whole town as regularly as policemen, who will have their appointed beats, and each of whom will be entrusted with the task of collecting the waste of the houses in their circuit."

As part of the plan, paper and rags would be baled and sold to paper mills, and wearable clothes, shoes, and furniture (refinished by men being rehabilitated) were to be sold at modest prices. This still is the practice, although antiques and other precious articles now bring higher prices. In times of emergency and special need, clothing and furniture are given without charge.

The first men's lodging house in the United States was opened in 1891 in Greenwich Village, New York, and by 1895 others had been added in Buffalo, New York; Waterbury, Connecticut; Boston, Massachusetts; Seattle, Washington; and San Francisco, California. During the Booth-Tuckers' administration, social work of all kinds was given extreme emphasis. However, a man usually sawed wood in exchange for temporary care. In October, 1897, a young industrial officer sent 12 homeless men out with pushcarts to test the General's idea. They returned—loaded with empty bottles. By the end of the month, "20 men with four carts were doing the rounds." By 1905 all centers had horses and wagons and by the twenties the Industrials were doing a thriving business, supporting themselves financially and, what was so much more important to Salvationists, doing miraculous work in reclaiming men, chiefly through leading them to God.

In 1929, Commissioner Edward Parker said of the work he had supervised for 27 years:

"The purpose of these centers is the rehabilitation of men, spiritually, physically and mentally. . . . These are not residential hotels or jobs, but treatment centers for men.

"Physical relief is just one of the minor considerations, although a very important one. We look upon our real job as the salvaging of wrecked humanity. Just as we pick up old wrecked stoves and furniture and shoes, and rebuild them into articles once more usable, so we pick up wrecked, discarded men and recondition them so that they may once more become useful, happy members of society. Above all, we try to save their souls."

Emergency and disaster service was greatly expanded during the twenties although it had always been part of every Salvationist's life. "Dedicated to the Unexpected" is a motto that could well be added to the already popular "Others!" and Eva's favorite, "A Man May Be down but He's Never Out."

Such service was purely a personal effort during pioneer days, but as experience and knowledge increased, procedures were standardized, and quick communication between corps and headquarters facilitated the pooling of personnel, equipment, and commodities. Refreshment, clothing, and furniture were provided.

Salvationists hunted lost relatives and friends. They helped the bereaved identify dead loved ones. They were on hand to comfort, to pray, and to assist, and often the helping hand became the holding hand as the shocked, the suffering, and the heartbroken clung to someone in a midnight blue uniform they called "friend." This was no easy ministry.

During the late twenties one of the most devastating hurricanes ever to strike Florida brought Salvationists from throughout the state bumping over unpaved roads in touring cars and trucks. They reported scenes of indescribable desolation as they rushed into stricken areas, and said of locations in the Everglades: "They are charnel houses of death and human woe. Sixteen thousand persons are without a change of clothing; 95 per cent of property is damaged. The situation in Lake Okeechobee area beggars description. Bodies piled in decomposing masses are being buried as quickly as possible to prevent plague. In one huge trench on the outskirts of this city, 600 victims were laid away near midnight. . . . Salvation Army women visited the melancholy field and ministered . . . to the staggering diggers. . . ."

A tornado that struck southern Illinois and parts of nearby states in 1925 was fiercely destructive, and Salvationists were happy that "relief work started six minutes after the tornado swept the countryside." Within a half hour of the disaster William Peart, now territorial commander in Chicago, also had sent a party of nurses from the Chicago Home and Hospital and the officers' training school. Other parties were immediately detached from St. Louis and Indianapolis. Dr. H. H.

Pillinger, a Chicago physician who was one of the first on the scene of disaster, commented: "It was like a scene in France after a great battle when we arrived. . . . The Salvation Army workers were doling out doughnuts and sandwiches and coffee."

A report some days later said: "There was also an order for cooking utensils to be distributed to the tornado sufferers living in tents. Many of them have been cooking on old bent pieces of tin roofing over open fires. . . . A number of funerals were conducted by Salvation Army officers today. All bodies not claimed for burial by some church are being interred by the Army officers. In addition to this, all the work of digging graves, and there is an immense amount of this, is done under Army supervision."

When a series of tornadoes and floods in the South flattened many homes and took a heavy toll of life in 1927, The Salvation Army did what it could to help 150,000 homeless and destitute people. It distributed food and clothing, made homes fit for habitation and helped combat general unsanitary conditions. It also publicized the need in the *War Cry:*

"Salvationists were among the first to begin work in the inundated areas of the Mississippi Valley, and they are remaining at their posts and broadening their activities. . . . WE MUST PROVIDE MONEY AND CLOTHING."

Aid to the masses was always important, but the resolution of grave if singular problems often brought the greatest satisfaction to Army workers. For example, Captain Clarence Hall of Valdosta, Georgia, was helping in a flooded area in 1927 and recounted this story: "The loss of stock has been keenly felt. One old Negro was found fearfully standing in water to his waist feeding his cow with water-soaked corn. At first he refused to leave when told the cow could not be taken aboard. It was finally agreed that the cow be pulled behind the barge. . . ."

Brass bands and songster brigades came into their own now though music had always been one of The Army's chief weapons. William Booth had often stated his conviction: "Soul-saving music is the music for me!" He said, "Why should the devil have all the good tunes?" and had religious words set to secular tunes. He also employed any instrument that could be used to "make a pleasant sound for the Lord."

The first Salvation Army brass band was started in 1878, and brass instruments were used in the earliest meetings of The Army in the United States. However, often stringed instruments proved more acceptable for indoor use. The concertina and guitar starred. The latter, particularly, was inexpensive to buy and relatively easy to play. An acceptable accompaniment could be provided by one person. Before World War I, numerous local bands and the staff bands of New York and Chicago had served well, but cost of instruments and lack of technique hampered the quality and quantity envisioned by good Army musicians. In the twenties, however, music became the signature of The Army.

In 1920, Staff Captain John Allan, upon his return from wartime chaplaincy, conceived and directed the first music camp to be instituted in The Army. Eager to train young Salvationists, Allan conducted the first summer encampment at North Long Branch, New Jersey, for junior vocalists and instrumentalists.

A second camping period was conducted for several corps in 1921, and in 1922 the camp was moved to Star Lake, Butler, New Jersey, the territorial camp site. Incorporating intensive study and practice with recreational camp life proved an excellent idea. Young people went home inspired and challenged and with enough new knowledge to spur them to high-standard accomplishment. Ensemble and band rehearsals were an incentive to practice for those who belonged to very small and sometimes ineffectual corps bands.

The camps immediately became popular and rewarding, and in 1935 a territorial music camp was begun in the Central Territory by Commissioner McIntyre, under the direction of Staff Bandsman Bernard Smith, former "boy wonder" director of the Flint, Michigan, band. In the Southern and Western territories music camps were first conducted in 1937.

"May none of our musicians ever ape the skill of the world in the production of merely pretty sounds, not only disconnected with the quickening truth of God but often almost inaudible to those whose hearts they ought to stir. . . ." This strong pronouncement by William Booth was often reiterated by Army leaders. The purpose of The Salvation Army was not to be a colossal music-participation or music-appreciation class but to be a militant arm of the Christian church. Throughout the twenties, Bramwell Booth urged Army musicians to concentrate on the tunes of salvation, always looking to the Creator of all harmonies, who provided and sanctions the unadorned melody of the ages: "Jesus Christ, the same yesterday, today, and forever!"

In the summer of 1928, although unplanned, a most successful Salvation Army program of services, first called Rural Service, then Service Extension units, was initiated. Envoy William A. Nichol, a noncommissioned officer, was seeking funds for general work in Bennington, Vermont, the center of a mountainous rural area and a noncorps town. Bennington's bank president reported happily that $500 had been raised as an annual contribution to The Army. The funds would help needy urbanites and also help support institutions which rural citizens might use in times of special distress. As Nichol left, the banker mentioned an elderly woman he knew of who needed fuel for the winter. "We can't have that," said Nichol. "Give her $100 of the money you raised."

When he returned to Boston and reported the incident, it was decided to repeat this kind of action in other noncorps areas. In this manner, "service units" were pioneered. Twenty per cent of the amount raised annually by Salvation Army designated community leaders was retained for local need.

The principle of the service unit was, and still is, mutual aid for The Salvation Army and for the rural community. Local men and women community leaders volunteered to represent The Army. They raised funds annually and controlled the use of the allocation kept locally for emergency needs. Primarily, the units existed for unusual and emergency relief which no local agency could meet. Although already benefiting from statewide and interstate services of The Army, the noncorps areas would now have a part in the regular support of such services as homes and hospitals for pregnant, unmarried girls, camps, emergency-disaster services, missing persons bureaus, service for armed forces, aid to prisoners and their families, children's homes, emergency shelters, and centers of rehabilitation for alcoholic and other distressed men. Examples of service given included these:

A wig was bought for Dolly, a little girl born without hair; a "deaf and dumb" Christmas party was arranged for 150 parents and their afflicted children, and Santa conversed with them by hand signs; financial assistance was given a family who lost everything in a fire; glasses were supplied to a little boy who was doing poorly in school because of defective eyesight; an unwed mother was cared for in an Army hospital; a telephone was installed in the home of an aged couple; an artificial limb was bought for an eight-year-old girl; hot lunches were provided for school children; a blind couple were sent to camp for a week; and a cow was bought for a farmer whose barn had burned down.

It was an ingenious plan to reach rural America, where millions of people were still beyond the reach of The Army's program of spiritual-social service.

Illustrative of the public's changing attitude toward The Army in the twenties was its inclusion in the Palace of Education and Social Economy during the Sesquicentennial Exposition in Philadelphia. Joseph R. Wilson, director of the section, considered especially notable the inscription, "The World for God!" on a revolving globe in the exhibit. The Salvation Army was becoming more and more difficult to categorize. Nevertheless, it won the grand prize for its socio-religious exhibit.

By 1927, stirrings of unrest regarding Army government were evident among Army leaders throughout the world. They wanted to have the privilege of electing Bramwell Booth's successor at his death. Bramwell did not agree. When, at his father's death, he was declared General, he said, "I take my stand upon the living God, my father's God." It was not a new stand. Long before, he had assumed responsibility second only to that of William and Catherine for training an army composed of soldiers who had been prisoners of war. He had given his life to The Army and felt he knew what was best for it.

Bramwell was The Army's master organizer and in many respects was resilient, understanding, and foreseeing. On one matter he was not—the manner of choosing a General to succeed himself. William Booth's way, established legally by a foundation deed in 1878, was for a General, upon taking office, to write on a slip of paper one of two things: the name of his successor or "the means which are to be taken for the appointment of a successor." The slip was to be placed in a sealed envelope and given to the Army lawyer to be opened on the death of the General "or upon his ceasing to perform the duties of the office." In 1904, a supplementary deed was added. Two clauses dealt with a number of contingencies—unsoundness of mind, mental or physical infirmity, bankruptcy or insolvency, dereliction of duty, notorious misconduct, or "other circumstances." A third provision stated that the Chief-of-Staff with four other Commissioners or seven Commissioners without the Chief-of-Staff might call together the High Council, which consisted of all Commissioners and territorial commanders. By a majority of three-fourths this council was empowered to adjudicate a General "unfit" and remove him from office. A General so removed could not resume office or appoint his successor. The High Council would then elect a new General and dissolve itself.

Throughout the twenties, dissatisfaction grew. Some Salvationists supposed the sealed envelope contained the name of a member of Bramwell's immediate family, that of his wife, a son, or a daughter. There was concern that there was undue influence in his household, that The Army would become a Booth dynasty. Correspondence criticizing Bramwell and his family was circulated and a series of pamphlets on the subject of successorship and the dangers of too much Booth power, published in Texas and ascribed to a W. L. Atwood whose identity never was disclosed, had a wide readership. Colonel George L. Carpenter, a highly respected officer and close fellow worker of Bramwell, went to his chief personally, describing the seriousness of the criticisms and pleading with Bramwell to democratize the manner in which Army Generals were chosen. Bramwell, bound to his duty as he saw it, ignored the entreaty. Later, Carpenter, greatly disturbed over the situation and fearful of worldwide criticism, wrote Bramwell a letter telling of the disturbed feelings. He was ordered by Bramwell either to name the sources of criticism or retract the letter. When he would do neither, for what Bramwell termed "rank insubordination," Carpenter was sent to an Australian appointment he had held 20 years before. Carpenter later became the fifth General of The Salvation Army.

Bramwell could not believe that democratic measures were necessary in the military Salvation Army, and he could not believe that subordinates would seriously question his judgment. He also could not perceive the extent to which his beloved Army was marching with the times, which demanded that every man not only have equal opportunity but also the privilege of representation on important matters.

At this time Eva felt obliged to act, partly because she had been appealed to by Salvationists throughout the world and partly because of her knowledge of William Booth's attitude: ". . . My father had talked to me as he had talked to no other concerning dangers involved in the position of my brother and his family, although of these I could never speak except to my brother himself, which I did. . . ."

She believed that "more and more as the years went by" Bramwell was encouraged . . . to look upon The Army as a dynasty which was to descend to his children. And more and more The Army all around the world sensed this, with all its tragic dangers."

In the fall of 1927, the tenth anniversary of the United States' entry into World War I, Eva was the special guest of the American Legion at their convention in Paris. She was orator and emblem for the veterans, and sometimes she made her own opportunities. Visiting the tomb of the Unknown Soldier with Legionnaires, she had been told that no religious rites were permitted, but when they arrived "there was an awkward silence when it seemed as if somebody ought to say something." Evangeline stepped forward and prayed eloquently.

On October 11, a special thanksgiving service was held in the Cathedral of Notre Dame, and Eva was invited to attend. When she arrived, a military officer escorted her to a side room

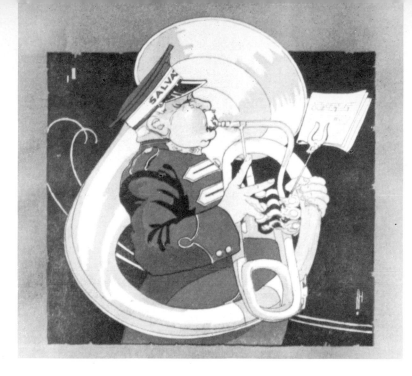

Representative War Cry covers, 1920's.

A

B

C

(A) *Men's shelter, 1930's;* (B) *Library at Gold Dust Lodge, New York City, 1933;* (C) *Scenes like this of people being dispossessed were common in the early 1930's.*

A

B

C

*Cecil Brown, Shepherdess of the Hills, used (A) schoolhouse cabin
as meeting house for Salvation Army and (B) trailer as her chapel.*

A

B

C   D

(A) *Congress parade down Michigan Avenue in Chicago. Commander Evangeline Booth standing in car;* (B) *Commissioner Samuel Logan Brengle in annual Memorial Day service, 1934;* (C) *Eleanor Roosevelt, wife of the Governor of New York State, staunch friend of The Army;* (D) *Will Rogers, famed American humorist who devoted time and supported The Army financially.*

A

B

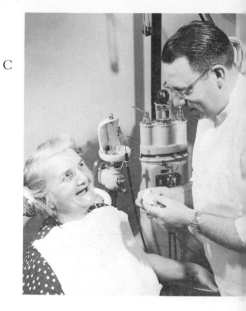

C

(A) *Pet show at recreation center, Philadelphia;* (B) *Counseling women prisoner;* (C) *Service performed at dental clinic of Salvation Army Chicago settlement house;* (D) *Open-air service, Atlanta, Georgia, 1940's.*

D

A

B

(A) *Canton, Ohio Corps woodyard. Note stained glass window in building, containing picture of President William McKinley, which is reproduced above* (B). *This window was donated to the Salvation Army by the family of the President;* (C) *International Headquarters, London, England, after air raid in 1941;* (D) *New International Headquarters building dedicated in 1964.*

C

D

A

B

C

"A Home Away From Home"

D

(A) *Sailor outside a Salvation Army operated U.S.O. Center, World War II;* (B) *Midnight round in mobile unit, Hawaii;* (C) *Lassies standing by to receive telegrams to be sent to servicemen's relatives;* (D) War Cry *drawing of servicemen's Christmas party.*

(A) War Cry *cover reproduced and now hanging in the office of U.S. Army Chief of Chaplains;* (B) *Evening at U.S.O.;* (C) *Wartime mobile canteen in action;* (D) *American G.I.'s served by World War II doughnut girl;* (E) *General Albert Orsborn with blind veterans at Valley Forge Hospital, Philadelphia.*

A

B

C

D

E

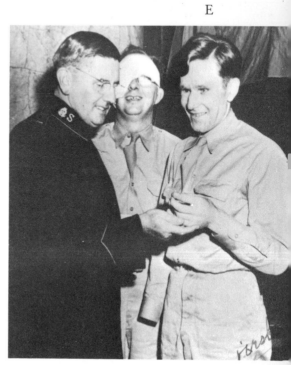

A

B

(A) *Supreme Allied Commander, Dwight D. Eisenhower enjoys Salvation Army doughnuts;* (B) *General Omar Bradley with Commissioners Ernest I. Pugmire and John J. Allan.*

where, after greeting her warmly, General Pershing and Marshal Foch asked her to march between them up the middle aisle to the high altar as they represented their countries in thanksgiving to God for peace. It was a memorable day. But it was also, for Eva and for Bramwell, a day of heartbreak. After the church service she crossed the Channel to International Headquarters and presented formal suggestions for democratizing The Army to Bramwell. The chief consideration was:

"To have the High Council or some such body within The Army select the succeeding Generals would provide a safeguard for the future which would be of great strength to the organization, and do more to elicit and maintain the confidence of our own people than anything else, and this would not in any way interfere with the purpose of the Founder."

Bramwell would not accept it.

The sense of urgency grew stronger within the ranks. On Tuesday, March 6, 1928, Bramwell, now 70 years old, found on his desk a letter signed by seven active and two retired commissioners, all residents of Great Britain, in support of the more democratic position. One was Frederick Booth-Tucker, a veteran of both America and India, and now retired.

Bramwell was stunned. He showed his wife, Florence, the letter. "Unless I had seen it with my own eyes," he exclaimed, pointing to one name, "I could not have believed it." Throughout the day he repeated again and again, "Why didn't they speak to me?" He didn't understand that Colonel Carpenter's experience had dissuaded them from trying that course.

That Bramwell believed he was right, no one questioned. "You will, I am sure, realize that a great responsibility rests upon me," he wrote Eva, "I received it from the dear General— nay, I received it from God. . . ." That both God and William Booth now willed otherwise, the great majority of Army leaders were positive.

It was a tragic impasse.

Bramwell was worn out from a lifelong encounter with evil. Now, the strain of a shattering burden bowed his spirit and his shoulders. In May, 1928, he was ordered by his doctors to have complete rest. His wife and the Chief-of-Staff, Edward Higgins, managed administration for six months. Then the assumption became widespread that his health was now precarious and that any moment death was imminent. Successorship became a matter of crisis to Army leaders. Yet there was no thought of secession, for their frenzied concern to have modifications made before Bramwell's death could only be interpreted to mean that they were eager to remain within the ranks.

The fateful action was taken. On November 14, 1928, the required number of seven commissioners invoked the deed poll of 1904, which provided for removing a General from office. A legal requisition to the Chief-of-Staff requested him to summon a High Council. Bramwell was too ill to be told the news till near the end of December. Then his daughter, Commissioner Catherine, a member of the High Council, went to him. Looking steadily at her, he said, "They have called the High Council."

She nodded, too distressed to speak.

"If I die, Catherine," he murmured, "remember, there must be no bitterness. I forgive, you and the others must forgive too. They want to change the General's plan. They know I will never agree."

From throughout the world territorial commanders and all other commissioners were summoned to London. It was apparent to all who saw or conversed with them that they were in great distress of spirit. They loved Bramwell and honored him for his skill and superbly practical Christianity, but the winds of destiny were blowing, and they must do what they thought right.

A motion stated that at Bramwell's advanced age he could not hope to "recover sufficiently to take up the burden under which he collapsed." He was requested to "co-operate with the High Council in securing the future welfare of The Army" and allow himself to be retired. The motion was laid on the desk of the presiding commissioner and signatures were invited. Old comrades wept as they signed. Some could hardly hold the pen.

The documents were taken to Bramwell by a deputation of officers whom he personally admired, among them the venerable Commissioner Gunpei Yamamuro of Japan and Commissioner Samuel Logan Brengle of the United States. They were shocked at his wasted appearance.

"I must have a little time," he told them. "I must have light to see what I must do and how I must do it. . . ."

He wrote the Council that his medical advisers said in a few months he would be fully recovered. He felt the request to retire was "little less than threat of expulsion should I fail to comply with it." For this there was no foundation, but an ill and beleaguered old warrior could not be expected to recognize that. He was making a last-ditch stand for what he felt to be right.

General Bramwell Booth was deposed. The Chief-of-Staff, Commissioner Edward J. Higgins, was elected as the third General of the international Salvation Army.*

It is sometimes a tragic necessity that progress drags per-

---

* After The Salvation Army's first election in 1929, General Higgins changed Eva's rank from Commander to Commander-in-Chief; he appointed a London advisory committee to study current problems and suggestions for solution, then present findings to a full conference of commissioners to be called during November of 1930. Eva attended this conference, a proponent of further democratization. Agreement on important issues was reached rapidly; in the future, Generals were to be chosen by the High Council, which was "thus transformed into a permanent organ of Salvationist opinion." Generals were to retire at age 73.

sonal disaster in its wake. In retrospect, one leading officer said, "It was the right thing at the wrong time." However, final division might have resulted had the democratizing been delayed. The Army's legal adviser, George W. Wickersham, senior partner of the Cadwalader, Wickersham and Taft law firm, said to Brigadier George Darby of Eastern Territorial Headquarters:

"What are you doing to Bramwell? Isn't this a dirty trick to oust him?"

When Darby explained the matter fully, Wickersham said, "Not another organization in the world could have effected that change without a schism."

On June 16, 1929, Bramwell Booth was promoted to Glory.

The impact of the entire experience was a jolt to American Salvationists as it was to all others throughout the world. It would take time to get their feet on the ground. But there was no time. On October 11, they were suddenly thrust into a whirlwind of dismay when "EXTRA!" was shrieked across the nation. "EXTRA! STOCK MARKET CRASHES!"

Citizens swooped on banks. Banks closed. Businessmen jumped from windows. The apple man appeared on the corner. And at Salvation Army halls the needy began to make a line—a long, long line.

Chapter Ten
1930 / 1939

DO
SOMETHING

THE DEPRESSION of the thirties was no respecter of persons. When the crash came, it made no difference whether a man had two million, two thousand, or two dollars in the bank; the money was gone—at least temporarily.

For a while, all banks closed their doors. Loans were a luxury of the past. "Mortgage" was a dirty word. And The Salvation Army had a full-grown dilemma on its hands. Not only was there the specter of William Booth shouting, "Do something!" (as he had done to Bramwell at the sight of men sleeping under bridges), but also the struggle to keep itself in operation. It depended on wealthy friends, but most of these had sustained severe losses. It depended on the public, but the public's pockets were empty. Cutbacks of every description were made: benefits to officers were sliced, headquarters staffs were reduced, some posts were closed. Yet, somehow, material aid had to be increased and facilities expanded to meet the growing need.

Consider a representative town, Canton, Ohio, where Adjutant and Mrs. Earl Lord were in command. It was a city of industry and hard-working people. It was also a city of poverty and corruption. Market Street was kept respectable by ordinance, but on Walnut Street in the red light district where the Army building stood, hopeless and desperate men and women swilled cheap liquor, strained Sterno through filthy socks, or stole bottles of flavor extracts. Maudlin and bleary-eyed they staggered through the alleys or lay sprawled in their own vomit. Here also were the bookies, the dope dives, and houses of prostitution—bad houses—as many Salvationists called them. One such house operated next to The Salvation Army hall, where voluptuous girls rapped energetically on sateen-draped windows from two in the afternoon until mid-night. On hot summer nights, Army worshipers and several radios in the house next door spread their gospel simultane-ously: "This is my story, this is my song. . . ." "You're drivin' me crazee. . . ." "Praising my Savior. . . ." "Be glad when you're dead, you rascal, you. . . ." "Praising my Savior, all the day. . . ." "Goodnight, sweetheart, till we meet tomorrow. . . ."

On that fateful morning in October, Earl Lord walked into the Dime Savings Bank, or tried to. The trust officer, Frank Damato, stood in the doorway.

"Adjutant, this bank has failed."

"Failed?" said Lord incredulously. "What do you mean *failed?*"

Exactly that. Army money, like all other money, was frozen, perhaps irrecoverable. Dazed, the Adjutant started back to his corps building. *Failed. Failed? Maybe the banks had but God hadn't, and neither had The Salvation Army.* Lord began to lay plans for the massive relief operation that must come. Hitherto, it was the tramp, the drunk, the parolee, the abandoned, the ill, the erring, who had come for a hand-out. Now the line would be lengthened block upon block by Everyman—desperate in his need. Despair at financial loss was widespread, and many once wealthy champions of The Army, still proud though shattered, waited behind closed doors for the Captain to assure them that God was still on his throne. In Canton, and across the nation, the corps officers rallied their

soldiers, explained problems and needs. If they couldn't pro-
duce minimum supplies, they'd pray and they'd beg, anywhere,
all the time. And they'd learn how to make do.

Now the Canton hall was packed day and night. The
needy crowded around the pulpit, waiting for relief. They even
sat on the penitent-form. Families sought groceries, rent pay-
ments, clothing, and medical aid. What about the where-
withal? Beg for it. Bakeries donated stale bread and pastries,
coal companies donated coal, the Timkin Roller Bearing Company donated coke. Employment was slackening sharply.
Another suicide. Another baby frozen to death. Another old
man dying from malnutrition. Find them! Pray with them!
But tuck a blanket around their skinny shoulders and get some
oatmeal in their stomachs while you do.

Edgar Guest, "The Common Man's Poet of America,"
wrote "The Christmas Spirit," extolling The Army's efforts at
this time:

> He who gave us Christmas Day
>   Would be very pleased, I'm sure,
> Meeting her along the way
>   Bearing baskets to the poor.
>
> This He wanted, this He taught,
>   This He gave as service holy;
> Dedicating time and thought
>   To the troubled and the lowly.
>
> Lassie, bonneted of head,
>   May your heart a little faster
> Throb today because you tread
>   In the footsteps of the Master!

In the summer of 1930 economic conditions were alarming.
Unemployed men were sleeping in every kind of improvised
shelter, municipal lodging houses were exhausted, and the ex-

isting soup kitchens were distressingly inadequate. The plight of thousands upon thousands was indescribable. The Army mobilized for relief as it had mobilized for war a few years before. Men's industrial institutions, men's and women's transient relief shelters, and children's homes were all used to capacity but without solving the problem. In order to help as much as possible, corps across the nation altered programs drastically. For example, in Canton, the soldiery vacated the Army facilities on Walnut Street, a commodious building, and moved its worship-service and character-building program to a store front on Market Street. In the Walnut Street building, beds were put in both upper and lower chapels, and a well-equipped kitchen and dining room installed. A woodpile was provided in the backyard, the double benefit being sought-after work for some and fuel for others.

Sometimes, unusual work-shelter programs were offered. Such was the case when on Thursday, December 18, 1930, the S.S. *Broadway,* a paddle boat of 3,600 tons, 320 feet long, was dedicated at a Brooklyn pier. Rented to The Army "for an indefinite period for one dollar" by C. G. Dimon of the Dimon Line for the relief of destitute seamen, it had a capacity of 1,500. Ensign Fritz Nelson, a qualified sea captain as well as a Salvation Army officer, was appointed to command the vessel.

In the big cities the need was crucial, yet The Army had to turn away men for lack of room. These were not the usual knights of the road but the depression poor. Leaving homes to seek jobs, they became embittered and despondent, hid their shame behind pseudonyms and liquor—professional and business men, skilled artisans, artists, musicians, and day laborers, plus the usual itinerants. What could be done? Often at such times another hand appeared to direct.

When Chicago's chewing-gum king, William J. Wrigley, Jr., was going home late one summer evening in 1930, for some reason his chauffeur drove him via the lower level of

Wacker Drive. There Wrigley saw hundreds of men trying to sleep beneath the superstructure of the Drive. Aroused, he phoned his real estate manager and asked if he owned a vacant building that could be used as a shelter and 509 N. Union Street was chosen. The Salvation Army was called on to assist in the operation. On October 5, six days after taking possession, Brigadier Sam Wood opened the Wrigley Lodge to homeless men. On its busiest day, October 12, 1931, 8,142 men were fed in that building.*

Wrigley Lodge became the working model and training school for the equipping and manning of Illinois shelters by the Emmerson Commission and its successor, the Illinois Emergency Relief Commission.

The Wrigley Lodge was a great blessing to Chicago, but in the cold winter of 1932, New York City, with a still greater problem, had no such facility.

Major and Mrs. Andrew Laurie were assisting the indefatigable Lt. Colonel Wallace Winchell with New York area shelter administration. There were 24 soup kitchens in Brooklyn and New York City alone. One wild winter night, Andy Laurie came home distraught. "They're dying right on the ground in the parks."

"But you can't help it, Andy," his wife Annie said.

"I could talk to Colonel Welty."

"He has more than he can manage now."

Laurie couldn't sleep. He tossed restlessly all night and got up in the morning, muttering, "There must be a key. Something must be done."

---

* Today the Wrigley structure is one of the largest Men's Social Service centers in the world in terms of men aided; in 1964 there were 3,655 men in its "Service to Man" program, with 241,535 meals served. The center operates three emergency mobile canteens which, in 1964, made 192 calls and served 896,554 cups of coffee, and 297,828 doughnuts. Added to this is a comparatively new service, the contribution of 1,700 pairs of gloves to firemen who lost theirs in the line of duty.

On the way to work, an enormous empty building, the Heckers Flour Building, caught his attention. He noted the name of the building's owner and went to his offices, but a secretary tried to prevent him from seeing the president.

After a long wait, threats of breaking down the door finally gained him entry. His first words were: "I want that building at 40 Corlears Street to house 2,000 men."

The president started, then, leaning back in his chair, surveyed Laurie coolly.

"My wife sent you here, didn't she?"

Laurie said he didn't know the man's wife.

"Well," said the president, "yesterday she and I went for a ride through the park and saw what you saw. She said, 'Why doesn't The Salvation Army do something about it?' She couldn't sleep and woke, saying, 'Something must be done. The Salvation Army can do something about it.'"

Laurie got the green light. He called Envoy Red Sheppard, in charge of Army prison and parolee work, and asked for 20 parolees to clean up the building. He figured on a month to get it ready, no more. The first meal was served on Thanksgiving day, 1932, and the Gold Dust Lodge (named for a product of that generous president's corporation) accommodated 2,200 men daily throughout the depression.

Still a line of gaunt men waited for a bed. So about 300 more were sheltered on a nightly basis and allowed to sleep on the backless benches and tables in the dining room.

One of the major problems was lice until someone thought of using a commercial presser on the men's clothing. Everything alive was exterminated and the clothes were brushed and cleaned. "It worked fine," explained Mrs. Laurie.

In the cavernous building, 34,000 meals were served in a week—2,100 pounds of prunes, 10,000 pounds of potatoes, 7,000 loaves of bread, 2,000 pounds of beef, sacks of peas and beans, nearly a ton of coffee, rice, onions, carrots, and oatmeal. On

Easter, 10,000 breakfasts were served, using 20,000 eggs.

"Gold Dust" proved to be more than a shelter. It became a rehabilitation center. The newspapers were generous with space. Dorothy Kilgallen lauded it in her column. Eleanor Roosevelt paid a personal visit. Professors and social workers descended to study Exhibit "A." According to records, the men came from 45 states and 43 different countries. Ninety-six different trades were represented and every conceivable kind of shop was maintained by the men. Qualified doctors, aides, and technicians among the homeless staffed the infirmary which occupied the entire top floor.

Perhaps the most important service besides the spiritual aid given through meetings and counseling, was the school. If a man had any talent, the Lauries encouraged him to develop it. Instructors for several subjects, including bookkeeping, mathematics, art, economics, and English were recruited from the lodgers. Music was taught by the Major. Even other Salvationists smiled when the Lauries mentioned diplomas. But it was no joke. The courses were tough; so were the examinations provided by the state. Even poetry flourished, and one New York paper published a column of "Gold Dust Gleanings." For example:

THE GOLD DUST WELCOME

We welcome you as one of us,
To share our freedom, cot and crust;
We don't believe in don'ts and musts,
In you we do believe and trust.

The beds are clean, no cooties here;
The beans are—well, are, extra fair.
Those bow-wows, too, but faugh, who cares?
Soon they'll be served ex-millionaires.

> Oh, yes, we'd ask you, if you can,
> Respect our rights as man to man;
> Or, after one—just one—good "pan,"
> You'll get, for sure, the Gold Dust "can."

Sometimes there were miracles. The success story of Joseph E. Vance, 25, a confessed failure, was one of them. Five weeks before coming to the lodge, he'd sent his young wife and children back to her family. The last job he held was as a tire salesman, but he really yearned to draw. The Lauries encouraged him, and the Major hung above his desk a pencil sketch Joe had made of Franklin Delano Roosevelt, the New York State governor. Ten businessmen toured Gold Dust one day. One stopped in front of the drawing.

"That's very good," he said. "Who did it?"

Joe Vance was called, and C. M. Washburn, an investment counselor and an artist himself, gave Joe his start on the spot by becoming his sponsor. Joe's drawing was later presented to the wife of the governor.

There were exceptions to the success stories, of course. For example, there was the time 40 of the men were scheduled to give a concert in Carnegie Hall. One of the stage hands had some liquor, and when the men marched on stage to sing, "He sends the rainbow, the lovely rainbow; He sends the rainbow with the rain . . ." several advanced jovially, waving bottles. But shelter, cheer, education, spiritual foundation, and refoundation—this was the real story of the Gold Dust Lodge.

The Army benefited in many tangible ways as a result of its concern for people. In several instances, borrowed and rented buildings were repaired and improved by appreciative welfare recipients who disliked accepting charity. Later, even counties and states helped.

The Army mobilized for relief in a big way. A variety of new relief programs were effected and, soon, Army officers were asked to handle state and local emergency relief programs.

The county welfare board of Clarkesburg, West Virginia, appointed Mrs. Major Campbell chief investigator with seven investigators under her direction. In North Dakota, Adjutant Flora Edwards chugged over the dusty trails in her redoubtable Chevvy investigating family needs for the county. In Lynchburg, Virginia, Captain Lewis Phelps arranged with barbers to cut school children's hair free, with the largest department store in town to repair ten pairs of shoes a day, and with drycleaners to clean clothes donated in a citywide clothing drive.

In Bristow, Oklahoma, The Salvation Army announced that due to canning efforts, reliefers would have "food fit for a governor," for all Oklahomans knew that Governor Murray's favorite dish was poke greens and hog jowl. Captain Garrison, Bristow commanding officer, also supervised the planting of 33 acres and required the head of every household being fed by The Salvation Army to give at least two days a week to the gardens. It was reported: "The plan interested social workers all over the United States."

The mayor of Camden, New Jersey, called in Captain David Brown and asked, "What would you recommend in the way of relief distribution?" The Captain suggested that firehouses should be adequate. "We're already using them in Philly." Firehouses were designated. Also in Camden, one of Commissioner McIntyre's sons, a bakery manager, daily channeled all leftovers through The Army to breadlines that stretched for blocks.

In Atlanta, Georgia, city representatives met and decided that The Salvation Army should expand its efforts to include a 24-hour-a-day food-shelter-clothing program for all types of transients. They were also designated to operate a community kitchen and take charge of the collecting and disbursement of free clothing for the city of Atlanta.

In Bismarck, North Dakota, Major Herbert Smith, with

206 / BORN TO BATTLE

a growing family, an active corps, and severe local needs, was instructed to meet a train from Chicago. He was surprised to find not only his divisional commander, Brigadier Albert Chesham, but also the territorial leader, gruff, visionary Commissioner William McIntyre.

"Smith," said McIntyre, "we're here on real business. Judge Christiensen believes in what you're doing. He wants you to take over the North Dakota relief program. What do you think? Can we make an impression on the depression?"

Still nominally in charge of the local corps, Herb Smith was released to the state. He effected a program that became the basis of budding nationwide welfare efforts.

Army officers were now carrying a heavy burden of state, county, and city relief, but it is improbable if this could have been done without the tremendous help of lay and nonmember volunteers. Home Leagues perhaps made the greatest contribution. These women's groups, whose motto was "WORSHIP, SERVICE, EDUCATION AND FELLOWSHIP," primarily organized for non-Salvationist friends, began a "bee" that lasted for years. Previously they had included service projects with activities of self-interest. Now, as women forgot self for service, thousands of treadle sewing machines clicked from coast to coast. They took cast-off clothes and repaired, restyled, recut them. They made new ones from flour sacks and torn sheets. They planted gardens in unused corner lots and "put up" tens of thousands of cans of food and cooked millions of meals. And on their knees they led the bereft and bereaved to God.

Despite grave burdens, Evangeline Booth remained the international-minded, crusading Commander-in-Chief, which meant much traveling and public speaking, besides administrative duties and a share in Salvation Army policy and government. The newspapers reported:

"It was as though a great actress, after thrilling her audience with some powerfully dramatic interpretation, should calmly walk off the stage to the managerial office and proceed to work out the business and technical details of the production in which she was starring."

She was widely acclaimed wherever she went—on the North American continent, in Europe, the Middle and Far East. Just as the depression hit, she visited Japan and was royally welcomed, received by Emperor Hirohito and invited to a garden party. As the Emperor approached, his subjects bowed low. Then there was a subdued gasp. The Emperor was breaking the tradition of looking straight ahead. He turned and saluted Evangeline Booth.

In 1932, Eva was asked to open the Democratic convention with prayer. She addressed God on behalf of the sweltering delegates. "Help us to remember," she said, in part, "that in this great throng this morning we appear before Thee as individuals, separate, and alone. Be Thou the Captain of our souls, then if poverty comes we shall not be so poor, and if sorrow comes we shall not be so sad, and if death comes, we shall not be afraid."

Herbert Hoover was nominated at the Republican convention but lost to Franklin Delano Roosevelt, whose promise of a "new deal," repeal of the Eighteenth amendment, and "continuous responsibility of government for human welfare" caught the imagination of the people.

As controversy continued to rage about prohibition, The Army continued its attack on the "bottle." But in December, 1933, prohibition was repealed and control of liquor traffic now reverted to the states. The Army was deeply disturbed and fearful, standing pat on its belief that the "bottle" was a nation, family, and personality wrecker. The stand-pat attitude caused distress among some good friends who agreed with The Army 100 per cent except on this one issue, though usually it was an amicable disagreement. James Speyer of New York, decided not to lead a drive for Army funds, the news got into the papers, and reporters gathered outside a closed door. Finally, Eva and Speyer appeared, and he told the reporters, "You see, she smiles."

"The incompatibility of belief," said the *Times,* "evidently is irremediable, but it is not often that two people with opinions so unlike agree so amicably to disagree."

As President Roosevelt enacted more recovery legislation through the Federal Emergency Relief Administration and through such agencies as the CCC and WPA, Salvationists carried on the simultaneous war against sin and poverty. Their uniforms grew frayed and shiny, their shoes were resoled until the uppers fell off. As always, they were not to draw their weekly allowance until current bills had been paid. The Army was carrying a staggering burden of depression relief now, but all ills were not caused by the depression and all good was not prevented by it.

The "Bishop of the Bowery," retired Lt. Colonel Wallace Winchell was still going strong as he made a personal attack on New York's Columbus Circle, a soap-box center. Spying out the land, he found "atheists, Communists, the hobo college, the House of David, a woman discoursing on sex, a physical culturist, and several missions." He was greeted with boos at this first speech. One gang yelled, "We'll all eat pie in the sweet bye and bye. . . ." He tried to shake hands with the opposition but they insulted him and started to mob him. Only the presence of police prevented trouble.

The next night, however, gang members were on guard "to keep The Army from the Circle." Flags and Salvationists alike were knocked down. The following night, singing women Salvationists quieted the mob, and two nights later the first convert was won. Among those participating were Billy Lawrence, a former Wall Street banker; Captain B. Aschenbrenner, former Communist leader; and A. B. McCans, a United States bank examiner.

The thirties were not without emergencies which demanded special action on the part of Salvationists. For instance, the Long Beach area of southern California suffered a violent earthquake in 1933, with considerable loss of life and damage to property. The Army set up relief activities in the city park, appealed for clothing and food supplies on the radio, and "by midnight all available Salvation Army forces rushed into service. Adjutant and Mrs. Ransom Gifford and the Los Angeles Evangeline Residence staff, began making 55,000 sandwiches, and preparing hundreds of gallons of coffee, which were rushed to devastated sections."

In an effort to show his appreciation in a practical way, Will Rogers, famed humorist and friend of The Army, decided, shortly after the quake, to make seven radio broadcasts and donate part of the proceeds to The Army. He telegraphed Eva:

"Here is how this rough and tumble broadcastin' thing come about: the Gulf Oil Company kept wantin' me to litter up the microphone with some Oklahome grammer. Now, Amos and Andy and others have never had any cause to be jealous of me in their industry, but I did want to make a donation to a couple of good causes that had done such fine work during our earthquake, but I didn't have the dough. . . .

"Mrs. Rogers . . . says, 'You got the wind to do it,' so she figures out how I could do it with just talk. . . . The only one I can see to lose is the Gulf Company, that is, if they don't sell enough gas to pay for the gas they bought from me. . . . Yours, Will Rogers."

Since Eva had begun her command in the United States, many new types of work had been established, others emphasized. The services of The Army now were many, and the need for personnel was acute. Nevertheless, pioneer work was still being done.

In 1934, a slight young mountain woman from Max Patch, North Carolina, was commissioned as an officer. Cecil Brown had met The Army while a student near Asheville and had a bold dream of carrying The Army banner back to her people in the mountainous Waynesville district. Opening fire in her home county, she used a broken-down trailer for a chapel and made visitation rounds on horseback.

She won and trained her immediate family first, then used them as aides. Although she considered evangelism of primary importance, she preached most effectively by exhibiting love in action: bathing new babies, sheltering children, reconciling married couples. She was intensely interested in the minds of the hill people and provided every educational aid she could. When facilities that her brothers constructed were habitable, she instituted a winter home for children who lived too far back in the hills to attend school.

So great was Cecil's ministry that a virile program resulted. When she retired in 1956, the Singing Convention, an annual weekend gathering which features gospel singing, drew 3,000 worshipers from throughout the hills. Socio-religious work had been established not only at Max Patch, but also at Shelton Laurel, Bonnie Hill, Little Creek, Sleepy Valley, and Timber Ridge; and a fleet of modern jeeps, a station wagon, and cars now substitute for Cecil's beloved horse. "The Shepherdess of the Hills" was awarded The Army's highest award, "The Order of the Founder." Also, a leading publisher asked permission to have a book written about her career. She declined, fearful her hill people might be misrepresented.

The Salvation Army High Council was called to choose the successor to retiring General Edward Higgins. On August 11, 1934, Eva set sail on the S.S. *Leviathan* for London, where she was chosen fourth General of the international Salvation Army. Once, long ago, at a meeting in London, William Booth had said tenderly of his little daughter, "I give her to the world." Now, it was a fact.

Cables and letters swamped International Headquarters. From President Roosevelt came this message: "In these troublous times, it is particularly important that the leadership of all good forces shall be for the amelioration of human suffering and for the preservation of the highest spiritual ideals. Through your efforts as Commander you have earned the gratitude and admiration of millions of your countrymen. I am confident that under your guidance The Salvation Army will go steadily forward in service to the unfortunate of every land."

In a covenant address to Army leaders after her election, Eva spoke with characteristic candor and drive: "I will seek to preach among you the truth as it is in Christ Jesus. Not with a faltering tongue, or unsound or questionable teaching, but I will preach it as the Apostles of old preached it—the one controlling principle of the soul; the one motive power. . . . I will be among you as 'one that serveth'. . . . You will ever find me in the front!"

Eva, accustomed to big receptions, nevertheless could not have foreseen her New York homecoming. As the *Leviathan* reached quarantine, The Salvation Army flag floated from her masthead, and Eva saw a flotilla of harbor boats, scalloped with flags, boasting banners which proclaimed: WELCOME HOME, GENERAL EVANGELINE BOOTH. Passengers shouted and blew horns; sirens whined. A city fireboat spouted a shimmering cascade. Aviatrix Ruth Nichols roared overhead, saluting and scattering roses on deck. An official city launch, "jammed with men of the press, photographers, sound cameramen, and the Staff Band steamed alongside." And Mayor Fiorello La Guardia, with 250 leading New York citizens, formed the reception committee.

Manhattan gave Eva its traditional hero's ticker-tape parade, led by the Sixteenth Infantry band and supported by four Salvation Army bands. At the City Hall, the proceedings were broadcast with Eva proclaiming, as always, her own and her father's life motto: "The world for Christ, and Christ for the world."

Many of her most devoted officers and soldiers, delighted as they were at the honor accorded her, wondered how The Army could get on in America without her. She was a part of them, a symbol of salvationism. In a sense, she was not their banner-bearer but their banner, flinging herself into the battering winds of disbelief and despair. Also, they sensed that she was lonely and that she would be lonelier still. In the last session of officers' councils she had passionately addressed her officers, "My children! My children in the Lord! My children under the flag!"

Surrounded by comrades and friends, she nonetheless faced the even more isolated path of top leadership.

"You seem like a woman who would have married," a reporter once commented.

A shadow crossed her strong features.

"I always liked men. But my only real love wanted me to give up The Army. So we parted. I have been devoted to millions of hearts, instead of one. I am not sorry, but I do remember."

Coupled with this is another incident, representative of many: During an East Coast trip, Eva had arrived in a town where her coming was front-page news. The press barraged her with questions. Finally, she was left alone to rest. As a woman reporter hurried down the corridor, Eva's door opened. She called and beckoned.

"Come back and chat a little," she invited. "You see, I get very lonely sometimes."

Eva was farewelled by the highest and the lowest. The *New York Times* stressed the fact of feminine leadership:

"Her election will act as a beacon to women the world over and will help them unite on a higher plane with a greater sense of responsibility for service to suffering mankind."

"Miss Eva" had been a brilliant leader for 30 years. How would the battle in the United States fare under the leadership of Commissioner Edward Justus Parker, National Secretary, the "boy from Elgin, Illinois"? The change over was far easier than some had expected. Parker was known and loved throughout the United States. He had risen in the ranks as a congenial, hard-working, imaginative, and dedicated officer. Positive by nature, he was cheerful and humble. His designated national powers were less than Eva's had been, however, and the territories became more autonomous, less able to operate as a unit. They were hampered by area decisions which, though seldom conflicting, lacked the punch of uniformity.

In the middle and late thirties, the New Deal came under a great deal of criticism but F.D.R. continued with the programs in which he believed. Industrial strife added additional emergency relief and family welfare burdens to those already existing for The Salvation Army, and often when riots occurred the local Captain was called upon to plead for nonviolence. Then too, Salvationists, like all citizens, began to feel uneasy about the onrushing tide of events in Europe. Hitler was on the march and antiwar sentiment became widespread in the United States. But for Salvationists there was no time either to fret or worry. There was work to be done.

Prison work was becoming more and more successful in terms of men rehabilitated. The program included regular interviews with prisoners, service to prisoners' families, job placement for ex-prisoners, parole sponsorship, and the placing of chaplains in many institutions. Services of worship were also conducted.

In Montgomery, Alabama, Adjutant and Mrs. Van Egmond conducted weekly meetings with 20 condemned men in Kilby Prison. Each man was given an Army song book to keep in his cell. "They all sing and their music is heard through all the prison," said the report.

There was an established corps in the Lansing, Kansas, state penitentiary, where a Negro "lifer" served as sergeant-major, "loving as fervently as he had hated." Guards and fellow prisoners were amazed at the change, and the sergeant-major became an undeniable power for good. At Lansing, as at many other prisons, the Brighter Day League, an Army sponsored program, augmented the corps program. Nondenominational, it exacted strict living from members. They promised that "from this day forward," they would read the Bible daily, pray night and morning, and would not indulge in liquor or drugs. A member must also be kind to his associates, obedient to officials and live the exemplary life of a good citizen in prison.

There was an increasing problem with juvenile delinquency. Perhaps children sensed growing adult uneasiness. Maybe they heard and saw too much. "Just kids," most people figured who were too busy trying to make an honest buck to fret. "It will blow over," some said. Others thought not.

In 1936, Major George H. Marshall, divisional commander for the Maryland Division, had been concerned for some time about boys roaming the streets. He wanted to institute a program which would "weave into the character and lives of boys that understanding and appreciation of God Almighty that alone can form a firm foundation for noble living." He thought Captain Doug Eldredge was just the man for the job.

A graduate of Tufts College, Eldredge, before becoming a Salvation Army officer, had been a boys' club executive in New England, specializing in camping, nature study, and Indian lore. He began his new assignment by forming small clubs in home basements, corps buildings, and borrowed halls, with an average of 15 meetings a week in five corps neighborhoods.*

Simultaneously, boys', girls', and co-ed clubs were springing up across the nation.

Camps, too, were blossoming elsewhere. Popular since the turn of the century, Army camps in the twenties attained recognition as important aids to good living and as therapy. In the thirties, almost all divisions throughout the country maintained a central camp from May to September, with many corps renting sites for shorter periods. Begun as a ministry to slum mothers and children, the camp system now gives total programmed encampment not only to large groups of mothers and children but also to the crippled, blind, mentally retarded, elderly, and a variety of youth groups.

Interest in the handicapped grew. For example, a weekly fellowship-education program for the blind was begun in March, 1937, by the Ohio State Department for the Blind, with classes in sewing, Braille, leather and other crafts, and typing. When the state was no longer able to supply teachers, it asked The Salvation Army to assume responsibility. Class members soon enjoyed not only educational activities but also recreation of all kinds, including annual cookouts, amusement park outings, and participation in bowling tournaments. Mansfield, Ohio's Blind Class, representative of many others of its kind, remains extremely active, meeting weekly at the corps building for lunch and the afternoon.

Also in 1937 The Army "opened fire" in Mexico through the efforts of Alejandro Guzman. A Mexican Methodist convert, he had organized a "Salvation Patrol" to reach the masses

---

* The club system in Baltimore boasts an advanced Indian Dance Club and a Clown Club, both authentic and expertly taught, besides regular club programs of athletics and crafts. In 1964, there were 2,500 club members in Baltimore. Affiliated with the clubs is spectacularly successful Camp Puh'tok, situated near Monktin, Maryland. Five-hundred boys attended the camp in 1964.

by barnstorming the *cantinas* in the slums of Mexico City. During a visit to the United States he met The Army, was impressed, and offered his forces. Supervised from the Southern Territory, U.S.A., the Mexican Division now has 22 corps and two outposts, 70 Mexican officers, 825 senior soldiers, and 647 junior soldiers, and operates homes, nurseries, schools, and a disaster service.

In Detroit, Michigan, a Bowery Corps especially for alcoholics was opened in 1939. Regular corps had previously been operating in the lowest districts of big cities, but the program was not directly slanted at the alcoholic. Now it was felt that, though God was the answer to any man's problem, some had become so ill in body, mind, or spirit—or all three—that the medical, psychological, and psychiatric professions should help to effect the rehabilitation "of the whole man."

Men's Social Service centers had long been working with alcoholic and other distressed men in a planned program, but they were not situated on the battlefield of skid row, and many men were not ready for their work program of picking up and reclaiming salvage as they themselves were reclaimed. The Harbor Light program, as it was called, consisted, in the beginning, of nightly worship services, a soup kitchen, beds for men who were sober and tried to stay so, a counseling service, and an employment bureau.

The divisional commander, Lt. Colonel James Murphy, a Scot who loved the men of the street, said at the dedication of the Detroit corps: "I hereby dedicate this great building to be the 'Church of the Homeless Outcast.' Come in every night if you can. Drunk or sober, ragged and lousy, destitute and hopeless, you belong here in your church on skid row."

Taking him at his word shortly afterward, Tom Crocker, a former Municipal Clerk of the Court, reeled inside, so drunk he half fell through the door. Henry F. Milans, famous convert of the first "Boozers' Convention," wrote of Crocker that "he was so filthy other bums near him took seats elsewhere or went out." He slept through the service but roused when an invitation to try God's way was given. Suddenly, he staggered down the aisle, sat on the floor and leaned his head on the penitent-form, too swollen from dropsy to kneel. "He pleaded with God to save him from sin," reported Milans, "and from eternal hell. God then and there delivered him from drugs and drink and every other sinful habit. He never touched either dope or liquor after that moment."

"Captain Tom," completely rehabilitated, became the miracle worker of Detroit's skid row, was given the rank of Captain, and was appointed first to assist at and then to command the Detroit Harbor Light Corps. Later transferred to the Harbor Light center on Chicago's skid row, Crocker had increasing success and did a great deal to organize the tremendously successful program that now exists. This includes the center at 654 W. Madison Street, the Harbor Light Residence, a "half-way" house for men eager to make the grade, an outpatient clinic, a medical clinic, an employment bureau, a thriving outpost on North Clark Street, and daily counseling of apprehended men at the Monroe Street court. In 1952, Chicago chose Tom Crocker as "Chicagoan of the Year" for his ministry among the forgotten men of skid row.

In 1937, Hitler decided that The Salvation Army could continue working in Germany but could not wear uniforms or collect money. Eva at that time wrote him a stiff letter:

"If we cannot wear uniforms," she said, "what in heaven's name are we to wear? If we cannot collect money, how can we get funds for our work? As I think you over, I have not decided whether you are a dunce or a devil. Let me remind you, sir, of the size and influence of The Salvation Army."

A fortnight later, there was an O.K. from *der führer.*

By the summer of 1939, world events could no longer be ignored, and when in September, Germany invaded Poland, Great Britain and France came to Poland's aid; it was war. Big war. Maybe not yet for the United States of America, but war for The Salvation Army, whose soldiers encircled the globe. The Army was literally on all sides. Interviewed about service difficulties during wartime, Eva said:

". . . A nation finds no difficulty in accepting the friendship of The Army for itself. But it seems strange in many quarters that this same friendship should be extended no less wholeheartedly to a rival nation, that there can be sincere service of the community by the same organization on both sides of a heavily guarded frontier. Yet it is only logic. Sin and suffering and hunger are the same whatever be the frontier. . . ."

Now, Eva determinedly continued to lead her worldwide forces, sensing that soon international communications would be shattered, travel limited, and personal contact cut off. The rank and file must be inspired and welded together as never before. Her "World for God!" campaign was inaugurated, and at a time when a trembling world began to dissolve in distrust, Salvationists waved their Blood-and-Fire flag in the face of war and sang lustily a song Eva had composed: "The World for God!"

She was told that the little princesses, Elizabeth and Margaret, were singing it in Buckingham Palace. Massed bands and songsters led soldiers throughout the world in its bold pronouncement. And Eva heard it sung by tiny leper girls in the Army's Poethenkuruz Leper Colony in southern India. Asked by reporter Dorothy Walworth, in an interview published in *Reader's Digest,* "You have had a great many honors. What was the greatest moment of all?" Eva told of these children:

". . . After the prayer they went up to the altar and stood

in their white dresses. Their faces and hands were badly scarred, but their voices were clear and true. When they came to the words in the hymn, 'With all my heart, I'll do my part,' they put their tiny scarred hands over their hearts. I was overcome."

Eva was 73 in 1939, retirement age. There was no colorful ceremony. The battle for Britain had begun, so she was whisked back to her adopted home, the United States. Her successor was General George L. Carpenter from the Canadian command. He was a good man—quiet, earnest, methodical, kindly—with a mind and heart illumined by faith. He had faith that under God, the worldwide Salvation Army now entering mortal combat would emerge still international in character—broken, bleeding, and disabled perhaps, but with every member country still a living, vital link.

Chapter Eleven
1940/1949

ON ALL
FRONTS

PRESENTING the combined United States Army and Navy award of Merit to The Salvation Army in May, 1946, Major General James A. Van Fleet praised The Army for its World War II service, "often with great sacrifice on the part of Salvation Army workers, to members of the armed forces in all parts of the world." The award stated:

"Mobilizing its nationwide resources, it dedicated itself, with high devotion, to the common purpose of victory to serving the spiritual, educational and welfare needs of the men and women in the armed forces and in war industries. Its contribution was of substantial aid in the successful prosecution of the war and in the preservation of the fundamental values of American democracy."

It was not an honor easily achieved.

When, in 1939, Poland was invaded by Germany and the possibility of world conflict was apparent, Salvationists immediately stepped up their attack on suffering of all kinds. In the early days of the push into Poland bundles of clothing and blankets were sent to refugees. As country after country became directly involved, The Salvation Army reported for duty. Though in many lands it followed the troops, with few exceptions it was already active in the nations affected by the war. Before hostilities, it spread practical Christianity in 103 languages in more than 97 countries and colonies.

Convened in November of 1940, the American Commissioners' Conference was primarily concerned with putting The Army on a wartime basis. During the summer of 1941, a National War Service Council was formed, with Commissioner Edward Parker, the national commander, as chairman. The immediate result was that in areas where problems due to excessive military population had arisen, Salvation Army officers worked to better conditions.

However, the needs of servicemen and defense workers had been in the thinking of many Salvationists for some time before. In October of 1939, Salvation Army leaders, especially those who remembered World War I days, were anxious to provide spiritual and recreational programs near camps and large factories. Seven religious and social welfare organizations had co-operated in World War I and greater participation was visualized now. After various preliminaries, instigated by The Salvation Army, six of the seven involved, the Travelers' Aid Society, Jewish Welfare Board, National Catholic Community Service, YMCA, YWCA, and The Salvation Army agreed to unite their war services. The Red Cross declined to join.

On January 31, 1941, the United Welfare Committee was formed and later incorporated as United Service Organizations for National Defense, Inc. The U.S.O. got into action immediately and began providing services on the home-front and in territorial areas. Units operated by member agencies had the atmosphere of gentlemen's clubs. Usually they consisted of a large lounge, with writing tables, books and magazines, a snack bar, a game room, handicraft shop, darkroom, and sometimes a gymnasium. The program included religious services, personal consultations and confidential aid, social events and entertainment, group activities and dramatics, educational classes and handicrafts, hospital visitation, distribution of literature, transportation, etc.

Often the clubhouses had to be put on wheels in order to reach men on detached guard duty in Hawaii and Alaska. Troops in transit were provided with a place to rest. In these mobile units there were easy chairs, showers, writing materials, and food. Though the primary service of the U.S.O. was to personnel of the armed forces, more than half of the units gave some kind of aid to servicemen's families, to war production workers and their families, and to men of the merchant marine.

When the U.S.O. was at its height, it employed 10,000 paid workers supplemented by 600,000 volunteers. The Salvation Army believed in the U.S.O., feeling that it embodied the motto at the training school for U.S. Navy chaplains: "Cooperation without Compromise," and would be effectual as a united spiritual, recreational, and welfare effort. Where this was effected, the U.S.O. and other service agencies were eminently successful. Where it was not, there was open criticism from service people. Referring to the spiritual motive of the U.S.O., John D. Rockefeller, Jr. said:

"I believe in the U.S.O. because it is based upon spiritual values. This war is fundamentally a death struggle between the material and spiritual forces in the world. . . . To our fighting forces we must bring spiritual power if they are to be invincible."

Reportedly, the "cup of cold water" was never enough. Only when it was given as a ministry did it work the miracle of encouragement and inspiration needed.

In World War I there had been difficulty in getting Salvation Army officers accepted as chaplains. In World War II they were welcomed with open arms. A great number of reports

were received at various headquarters which were similar to
the following received from a United States sailor in the South
Pacific theater of war:

"What do you know, Mom, last Sunday we were in Well-
ington Harbor, New Zealand, and I heard for the first time a
beautiful message and a fine service conducted by the U.S.A.
chaplain there. He's a Salvation Army officer, Mom, and if that
is what the Salvationists believe and how they minister to the
people, I can see now why you love to go. . . ."

The Salvation Army had a signal honor given it in the fall
of 1940 when Salvationist Colonel John Allan was appointed
by Secretary of War Henry L. Stimson to the five-man staff of
the Chief of Chaplains in Washington. He assumed his active
rank of Lt. Colonel which he held when he served with
the famed 77th Division in World War I. Colonel Allan had
received the Croix de Guerre for conspicuous bravery in that
war. Through the years he had been especially interested
in Bowery work, and his brilliant cornet playing had resulted
in a command performance before King George V of England.
Colonel Allan was one of many American Salvation Army
officers who now became U.S. chaplains, sharing in the life of
the fighting men.

A report on jungle warfare stated: "It has always been the
practice out here to put the chaplain in the front line, for he is
the visible symbol of the presence of the living God with the
fighting troops." Chaplains were also required to be on the
spot with all the answers. A good example of this was the time,
just before a major battle, when a G.I. rushed up to a chaplain
and demanded, "What do you know about God—quick!"

That Salvation Army chaplains adapted well to Uncle
Sam's forces was indicated by reports and letters written from
the front lines. Clarence Hall said of Salvation Army
chaplains:

"It's no secret to anybody that Salvation Army chaplains

have made an enviable record in this war. There's something about Salvation Army training that fits a man for the peculiar demands of the chaplaincy as perhaps no other church does. His readiness to mix and mingle with all kinds of men, a resilience of personality that enables him to fit easily and naturally into any kind of situation, the amiable informality with which he invests his worship services, and his trained competence in dealing with 'problem' people—these talents stand him in excellent stead the moment he switches from the uniform of General Booth to that of Uncle Sam."

Sometimes reports included reference to lay Salvationist servicemen who were pressed into service as spiritual leaders. Bill Hasney, a Salvationist from Waukegan, Illinois, joined the Coast Guard and was sent to Puerto Rico. There were no religious services because there were not enough men for a chaplain, so Hasney soon was leading worship services.

A report appeared in the *Chicago Tribune* sent by Sergeant John Rice of Los Angeles, who was serving with the 720th Railway Operating Battalion "somewhere behind the lines" in Europe. Sergeant Rice, a chaplain's assistant, noted that the chaplain was in the hospital and it looked as if the Christmas Eve service, already announced, would have to be skipped. The men were upset. Then someone said, "Why don't we ask the Major (U.S. Major William H. Roberts of Chicago) to pinch-hit?" Roberts, Executive Officer of the outfit and extremely popular with his men, was the Sergeant-Major of the Chicago Temple Salvation Army Corps. Rice said news of the special speaker "spread like wildfire":

"The next morning, glancing around the chapel, which had been converted from a captured German baggage car, I noticed faces that had never before blessed the inside of a church. . . . Around me was one of the toughest, cussin'est, sinnin'est gangs of men I've seen for some time, all with only one idea and purpose—worship. . . . Then the Major took over. He made a wonderful talk. . . . The meeting broke up and the men went about their work, but from the scraps of conversation I heard I was convinced they were different men inside."

Salvation Army services were distinctive, more informal than most, and often included musical numbers which the men seemed to enjoy. Many Salvation Army chaplains, like Captain Dick Holz, carried an instrument as part of their essential equipment. Writing from "somewhere in the Philippines," Holz thanked Salvationists for replacing a cornet (left behind on an LST), and concluded: "A cornet is a most valuable piece of equipment over here, especially in outdoor services. . . . Some Sundays I conduct six meetings. A few weeks ago we dedicated and named our Liberation Chapel. On Sundays it is a riot of color, with native flowers placed in bamboo vases about the wall and altar. Over our heads are hung three giant parachutes, one yellow, one blue and one red—quite symbolic of the Salvation Army colors. They were used in the first few days to drop supplies."

The 1945 Easter *War Cry* back cover, painted by A. R. Michaelson, showed a battlefield scene with a wounded G.I. being aided by a chaplain, while a German soldier held his fire in the background. The U.S. Chaplains' Corps had it enlarged, and it hangs in the Washington office of the Chief of Chaplains. There is now, as before, a Salvationist chaplain, Colonel Roy Morden, serving in the Headquarters 1, Corps.

On the home front, Salvationist women, augmented by thousands of volunteer helpers, gave generously of time, money, and energy to help United States service personnel. A great variety of services were given. Thousands upon thousands of surgical dressings were made; sewing, shaving, and writing kits were assembled. War relief boxes were packed and shipped. The women were generous blood donors, and their interest in the U.S.O. and Red Shield cooky jar was historic. In addition, their knitting needles whizzed as they made a variety of knitted sweaters, socks, helmets, armlets, trigger-finger gloves, and wristlets for servicemen. They also provided layettes for the new babies of servicemen's wives. They served suppers to the armed forces, gave volunteer service at canteens in induction centers and aided the League of Mercy in hospital visitation. In every corps the Home League also established a "Book of Remembrance" service which was conducted regularly for the comfort and encouragement of those who wished to meet for prayer and meditation. In a large book always kept near the penitent-form was a long list of the names of service people and their loved ones.

Philadelphia's vigorous wartime program under the direction of Major Samuel Hepburn, was representative of programs in many cities. Thirty canteens operated throughout the streets and countryside; a servicemen's center offered food, lodging, entertainment, and religious services; the Women's War Service Bureau, largely manned by volunteers, made sweaters, socks, afghans, and earmuffs, and did odd jobs for servicemen. Women Salvationists in Philadelphia visited the Valley Forge hospital once a week and still do. A particular feature of the hospital visitation was work with blind veterans. Major Hepburn's wife, Rose, took a particular interest in this and later became unofficial chaplain of the Blind Veterans' Association. The boys declared they could recognize her marching step in the corridor.

Rose Hepburn's "Home League of the Air," begun in 1940 and continued through the war years, attracted the interest of thousands of listeners who helped meet war and other emergency needs. Outstanding features of the radio programs were special rallies for Air League members and knitting festivals. With a motto of "Remember Pearl Harbor—Purl Harder!"

hundreds of women knitted articles for servicemen to the music of name bands.

Separate from the Home League but often distributing gifts it contributed, the League of Mercy entered veterans' hospitals across the country with spiritual and material aid. A visit from the League of Mercy usually meant a few personal words which might extend into a lengthy conversation, a small gift, a *War Cry,* and a prayer if the serviceman desired it. In 1944 the work received additional personal emphasis when the *War Cry* published addresses of many large veterans' hospitals, suggesting: "Have you a relative or friend in a military or naval hospital whom you would like to have visited by The Salvation Army? If so, notify the nearest Army corps or institution. . . ."

In addition to the 200 U.S.O. units it operated, the American "link in the world chain of 3,000 Salvation Army war activities" consisted of 219 Red Shield units, ranging from mobile canteens to spacious hotels. Red Shield services, internationally designated work with service people, included a great variety of efforts in the United States and abroad and were entirely separate from U.S.O. services and activities, and were financed completely from Salvation Army funds. The U.S.O. operations received support from the organization.

When the idea for a U.S.O. was first presented, many Army workers had already established Red Shield centers. Some of them were similar to U.S.O. centers but established in locations not designated for U.S.O.-S.A. work. Other Red Shield efforts provided canteen service for embarking and disembarking service personnel. Red Shield work in Hawaii and Alaska was in full swing long before the U.S.O. was formed.

When Pearl Harbor was bombed on December 7, 1941, even before the radio announcement of the attack began, a Salvation Army truck, coincidentally on the post, was used as an ambulance. At 9:30 A.M. evacuees were already being given shelter at Army centers, a boys' home and a girls' home. The aim, according to Brigadier Arthur Brewer, divisional commander, "was to do things that were desirable even though we were not instructed what to do."

Every available Army building, vehicle, and service was used. Workers cared for the wounded, fed soldiers at their posts, comforted the sorrowing, and calmed hysterical civilians.

Louise and Alva Holbrook, American Red Shield officers, had been ministering to servicemen for some time. When the attack began Mrs. Holbrook instinctively started preparing food "for a lot of people." Hungry men on duty soon followed their noses to her kitchen.

At two o'clock, Harry Okimura, food controller of Wahiawa, called on the Holbrooks. He wanted Louise Holbrook to set up a canteen to feed the police, nurses, territorial guard, military police on duty off the post, and all others who had been called into action so suddenly. They were without a place to eat because all restaurants were closed along with all other public facilities.

"But I have no supplies," said Mrs. Holbrook.

"I'll get you supplies."

"But I have no building to accommodate them."

"We'll get a building."

"But one person can't do it all."

"Mrs. Holbrook," said Okimura, "if you'll do this for us, we'll get you everything you need. You can't say 'No,' for I don't know another soul this side of Honolulu to ask."

In half an hour a canteen was set up in the new fire hall. By three o'clock, Louise Holbrook was standing at one end of a big table with her hands in a huge bowl of batter. Next to her Mrs. Raymond Squire, wife of the Methodist pastor, was rolling out doughnuts and three Korean Girl Scouts were frying them. Harry Okimura was making coffee, teachers from the local schools were cutting bread and making sandwiches, and little Chinese girls poured and served.

Men kept coming. The coffee supply ran out about 10 P.M. and Mrs. Holbrook used the grounds over again. When the supply of paper cups ran out, they were collected, washed, and reused. At 12 o'clock, a policeman complained, "Harry, this coffee is terrible. Can't you do something about it?" The grounds were boiled for the third time. At two in the morning the policeman smacked his lips and said, "Ah, this is more like it. You know, that stuff you gave us at midnight was pretty bad."

By morning more than 2,000 had been served.

The day after the Pearl Harbor attack, Congress declared war against Japan. And on December 11, Germany and Italy declared war on the United States. By 1942, the United States and The Salvation Army were completely on a war basis. U.S.O. clubs extended across the country; Red Shield canteens circled the world. The "Home away from Home" tried to serve in every way possible, from sewing on a new patch or button to comforting a soldier who had just gotten a "Dear John" letter.

By 1943, eight mobile canteens loaded with jugs of coffee and doughnuts were rolling in Hawaii. They covered a route which extended from Diamond Head to Pearl Harbor, traveled an average of 165 miles a night and passed out more than 1,000 cups of coffee, 1,500 doughnuts, 50 cans of cream, and 40 pounds of sugar.

Although some American Salvationists were temporarily appointed to Red Shield service in England, the major work of the international Salvation Army Red Shield service was done outside of the continental United States by Salvationists of the area involved. The American fighting men expressed appreciation generously for Army service in Africa, Alaska, Hawaii, the European and South Pacific theaters of war, as well as on the home front. They never thought of a British or French or Australian Salvation Army but only that the "Sallies" were on the job. William Booth's fervent desire that The Army be a single international force was proved undeniably advantageous during wartime.

Although England was set afire during the blitzkrieg, she would not give in. Army halls became centers for homeless air raid victims; camps sheltered thousands who had lost all. Salvationists, lay and officer, became air raid shelter chaplains, serving refreshments, praying, counseling. In all parts of the country they rushed to scenes of disaster as soon as the "All Clear" was given. Stories like this were routine:

"To one of our halls a little mother who had just given birth to a baby was brought by the ambulance and laid down in front of the penitent-form. From above beamed down the words, 'At the Cross there's room.' The young husband commented, 'When I was a kid, I hated religion because it was forced on me, but now—well, this is different.' "

When Salvationists arrived at the scene of a bombing in London within a few moments of the explosion, a grateful workman exclaimed, "Blimey, did you come down with the bomb?"

On May 11, 1941, major disaster struck the international Salvation Army when "101," the international headquarters building on Queen Victoria Street, was demolished by bombs. Ironically, nearby on the "puddled, hose-littered street" stood a mobile Salvation Army canteen, surrounded by grim-faced firemen.

G.I.'s embarking from the United States were always grateful to Salvationists for the smallest kindnesses. J. Tom Watson of Lakeland, Florida, was being sent overseas with a Navy detachment on the *Queen Elizabeth,* leaving on a "biting cold, snowy night." The men, Watson said, were "chilled to the bone carrying full overseas packs on our backs and tired, cold, and weary when we·reached the gangplank. Salvation Army lassies were there with doughnuts and coffee, and when the men disembarked near Glasgow, Scotland, there was The Army again."

Nicholas Horochivsky of Norwich, Connecticut, also wrote a representative letter, mentioning that in March, 1945, he embarked for Europe on "anything but a pleasure cruise," stripped down to essentials. Moneyless, he sat on the pier, like many others, waiting for further instructions:

"We must have all felt we belonged to a forgotten portion of humanity. Fortunately our thoughts were not shared by others in uniform—The Salvation Army. They did much to relieve our tensions and morose feelings. Hot coffee, doughnuts and entertaining books and games, were gratis."

Mr. Horochivsky also mentioned a little sewing kit, given him at his induction. "On October 13, 1963, the kit finished its 19th year of diligent service. To me the kit turned out to be a symbol of the wartime work of The Salvation Army, projected still further to satisfy the ambitions of peacetime activities. . . ."

When the American troops arrived in England, they found 60 Red Shield clubs, manned by British Salvationists, ready to serve them. A typical instance was that of a canteen where two workers served 1,000 daily at a large railway station platform. At another center five Salvationists served 5,000 Americans daily.

When leaving a British area the men would crowd into the Army hut the last night for an informal sing-song which included favorite hymns and always concluded with "God Bless America." For the most part British and Australian Salvationists aided American men on European battlefields.

One Yank wrote home from Italy: "The Sallies are in the front lines, and I do mean front lines. They are doing a fine job and it is all being accomplished under gunfire. . . . When I asked a soldier on the road if he could tell me where the Red

Shield was he replied, 'They run the whole town, sir. You can't miss 'em.' "

Lowell M. Jones of San Antonio, Texas, injured three times, wrote: "Every pagan and pious son of us is praising The Salvation Army in North Africa. It wasn't so much what they did. It was the way they did it. I'm telling you it means plenty to have a smile accompany a favor, when you're lying there feeling useless with the fighting still on.

"Plenty of efficient people come along and ask what you want, but inside you still feel like a droop until a Salvation Army guy comes along. He treats you like a human. He understands. Maybe he's only with you a couple minutes, but you find yourself asking him to write your girl that you're feeling fine, and all of a sudden you *are* in reality feeling fine. See what I mean?"

One of the first Red Shield units to arrive in North Africa was immediately attached to a bath unit, serving 10,000 men resting in vineyards. The men parading for baths received a cup of tea and had a sing-song while waiting their turn.

The Salvation Army invasion canteens used on the Normandy beachhead previously had seen action in Africa and Italy. They were six-ton, thirty horsepower models, with specially insulated bodies and facilities for serving 4,600 men before they needed to return to their base. Standard equipment included a small library, a radio set, a record player, and a sound film projector. Many of them also had folding racks for stretchers. Major Symester, a Red Shield canteen worker in Normandy, wrote: "When fellows walk several miles just because they have heard that the Salvation Army fellow is about, it makes one feel the job is worthwhile."

Red Shield work flourished in Rome, where within five days of arrival, Adjutant and Mrs. Johnston "opened a canteen just opposite the Vatican." Men on the drive through Italy kept saying to canteen lassies, "Are you real? Keep on talking.

Please don't stop." Some hadn't heard a woman speak English in three years.

The shield of red ringed the world.

A reporter commented of an Army canteen in Cairo, Egypt: "It's a great thrill to walk up the street and, in contrast to the evil all around, hear voices raised in gospel song."

Major General John L. Homer of the U.S. Army, after he returned from a 13 month tour of the island outpost of Iceland, said: "The only thing of a recreational nature that we found on our arrival—and it astonished us—was The Salvation Army. They were there from the start and their work in Iceland was positively superb. General Bonesteel has never ceased to remark about it."

In Alaska, the doughnut machine broke down, and canteen trips were cancelled. The Commanding Officer got on the phone: "They tell me you've called off the canteen trips because no doughnuts. Never mind the coffee. Send the canteens with someone to talk to."

Marvin J. Trad of Roy, Utah, was based at Fort Shafter, Honolulu, and picked for night patrol: "The day patrols weren't as lucky as we were. Why, yes, that God-sent Salvation Army. . . . The city was blacked out. . . . That's right, the truck, coffee, doughnuts, a little sweets and cigarettes. Two nice cute ladies. By the way, I just wondered if I ever noticed if they were pretty. But they just had to be. It wouldn't have made any difference anyhow. They were dolls. I'll bet they were plenty scared. Did they show it? Negative."

In the South Pacific theater The Army's welcome was always a cordial one. One Red Shield canteen arrived at dinner time "miles from anywhere." The driver apologized to the Commanding Officer for coming at such an awkward time, but the C.O. grinned and said, "I would have gone without my breakfast, dinner, and supper to see you today." Amplifiers flooded the camp with music, and the men rushed out, knives and forks in hand, "whooping when they saw the Red Shield."

A sailor in the South Pacific wrote: "The Salvos are wherever the men are. My ship was shot to bits, and I drifted four days before reaching land. . . . But along came a Salvation Army worker and carried me to his tent."

The *Jersey Journal* printed a letter from a local boy in New Guinea to his mother. Of The Salvation Army he said: "They are tops, and I don't mean maybe. If you can give, give to The Salvation Army. Those people turn up in the strangest places— foxholes, dense jungles, anywhere. Come hell or high water, The Salvation Army is there. . . . We were hungry as all heck, and dirty and tired to boot. We rounded the bend, and there, on the side of the road, was a battered old camouflaged truck. A Salvation Army guy stuck his head out and said, 'Hey, Yanks, how about a pot of coffee and some cookies?' And sure enough, he handed it out."

"The first thing I saw in Milne Bay," said a returned soldier, "was a Red Shield hut in the sun. I couldn't believe it."

One of MacArthur's wounded had this to say: "Maybe a glass of water isn't much, but when you've ridden a stretcher to the dressing station, bounced six miles in a jeep and it took three and a half hours to do the six miles, and you arrive at the temporary hospital to find 185 men there instead of the 25 it was built for, and you see a Salvation Army man come in and start giving a drink of water to every helpless, parched man of us. . . . Well, a drink of water is a miracle, sometimes."

One company in Hawaii had a record made of a singspiration conducted by World War II doughnut girls Olive McKeown and Luella Larder, officer daughters of pioneer American officers, and one of the men they had sung to reported later: "Even when things were hot on the Marshalls we thought of you and tried to sing those songs we sang with you and your accordion."

A sergeant wrote from Saipan: "Thanks for all you did for

us when we were in Honolulu. . . . It doesn't take a lot of money and glamor to make a G.I. happy. All we need is some down-to-earth kindness, and that costs less and means more."

Sometimes, the Salvation Army workers heard unusual stories, such as the one related by a young American sailor: "I met The Army in the middle of the Atlantic." His ship had been torpedoed and he had floated with three buddies for days. "But one member of the group undertook to cheer us up. He started to sing, 'God is with Us all the Time' and 'There's Power in the Blood.' We felt better whenever he sang and joined in as soon as we learned the words. He told us he heard the choruses from The Salvation Army on Saturday nights on the street corner. The Army reaches farther than it knows!"

When the wounded began to come home, they needed to know that people cared. Salvationists tried to help by offering little gifts, although what the men often wanted most was to talk about their grief and loneliness. The candy, the *War Cry,* the slippers, or toothpaste usually were keys to a man's confidence.

Sometimes, gratitude was out of all proportion to the gift. For instance, men on a Navy ship in San Diego were freezing, having just returned from the tropics. Charles G. Watts went ashore to The Army for help. Watts wrote: "Pandemonium broke loose when I put the quilts on the mess table. It was a mad scramble."

James E. Carrigan of Boston, wrote: "Salvationists have done the most for Navy morale. During World War II there were many times I said, 'Thank God for The Sallies.' Every sailor when he's broke, knows he can depend on The Salvation Army, America's outstanding HELP organization."

Coming home, G.I.'s were often detained. Clayton E. Sager, of California, Pennsylvania, was a member of the Navy Seabees, coming into San Pedro, California, on a troopship carrying many men who hadn't seen the States in three years.

They tied in but were quarantined for five days: "This is where The Army came in. You were always there when you were needed. Pads of paper and pencils were passed up to the decks of the ships. We wrote our telegrams on the papers and rolled them up and tossed them to the pier below. Salvation Army workers picked them up in little baskets and sent them for us at no cost. No one, unless in similar circumstances, can imagine the feeling of gratitude to you. . . ."

Perhaps John B. Ellery of Johnson City, Tennessee, a wounded veteran of seven years in the merchant marine, summed up articulately the aim of Salvationists. In a letter written in 1964, Ellery said, in part:

"Now, can you possibly understand what it meant to me to learn that wherever I might be, whatever my need, if I could find my way to a Salvation Army hut I would find friendship and assistance. It made no difference to anyone whether I was an enlisted man, a cadet or an officer.

"Well, The Salvation Army never asked me to prove my financial stability, never asked the names and addresses of my parents, never billed me for a bar of soap or a razor blade, never embarrassed me into sitting in a captive audience while someone preached at me. The only thing The Salvation Army asked me for was information about my needs. What did I want? How could I be helped?

"At a time when I was just one more man among millions of men, at a time when I had been wounded twice and knew that I would be sent back for more, at a time when I had been reduced to little more than a name, rank and serial number, I met someone who obviously liked me and was genuinely interested in me. Such things of the spirit are important to me. I think that they are important to most men. The Salvation Army understands this. Perhaps this is the answer. The Salvation Army understands. . . ."

Finally, the war was over, and The Salvation Army, with

the rest of the war-weary world, drew a deep, exhausted breath. General Carpenter had said his army would remain international. He now reported publicly:

"Tonight we think especially of God's goodness to The Salvation Army. That internationalism which is our great glory is exposed in a peculiar manner to destructive forces in time of world war. Yet I am able to report that, though we have been cut off from as many as 20 lands, our unity has not been imperiled. One after another the lands which have emerged from darkness have signalled their loyalty to God and to our flag."

Contact came from Germany as soon as hostilities ceased. German Salvation Army troops would march on with their world-flung comrades. In Japan, Salvationist Lieutenant Byron Cook, serving with the first United States occupation forces, visited Lt. Commissioner Masuzo Uyemura, leader of The Salvation Army in that country. By government direction, he had lived in retreat during the war years.

"It was quite a trip," said Cook, "but my efforts were as nothing when I saw Mrs. Uyemura smiling and waving as I walked up the path to their little cabin, high in the mountains. I knew the Commissioner immediately, for he had his coat open and his bright red guernsey shone out with the grand old words of The Army, BLOOD AND FIRE."

They chatted a long time, and the Commissioner sent his message to "My dear old comrades in the United States and elsewhere: I am so happy to send our warm greetings. . . . We have been shut out from the rest of the world these years. . . . We are very eager for the reconstruction of The Salvation Army in this country."

The national picture of The Army changed in 1944, when Commissioner Ernest Pugmire became National Commander at the retirement of Commissioner Edward Parker, the valiant "Eddie from Elgin." Handsome, courtly Ernest Pugmire, one of the few survivors of the *Empress of Ireland* tragedy in 1914, was described in the *War Cry* as "conscientious, of unruffled temper, astute in business and having the saving grace of humor."

International Salvation Army leadership also changed hands in 1946 when Albert Orsborn replaced the retiring, beloved warrior, George Carpenter, as General. Orsborn believed that The Army must remain "a permanent mission to the unconverted."

An American Salvationist also made news in 1946. Commissioner John Allan, former Bowery warrior, chaplain, and territorial commander of the Central Territory, was appointed to the second most important post in The Salvation Army— Chief-of-Staff. This was the first time an American was ever appointed to that position. Before his retirement in 1957, he became the only Salvationist to have visited every territory in the Army world and to have conducted spiritual campaigns on five continents.

During the post-war years, many important attacks on the American home front were being made simultaneously. To encourage spiritual vitality and train in spiritual warfare, the first National Brengle Institute, named for Commissioner Samuel Logan Brengle, the Army's "soldier-saint," was held for a three-week period in Chicago. Comprised of representative officers from each division in the United States, its purpose was "to emphasize the fundamental teaching of holiness." The institute was so elevating to officer delegates and to the people they influenced that it has been continued annually.

The expansion of the League of Mercy was amazing. For instance, in 1948, 17,586 patients in the Chicago area were visited at Christmastime. Members distributed gifts and provided music in 30 state, county, city, and veterans' hospitals.

Family welfare aid, for many years emphasizing material relief, now stressed counseling. A great number of youth centers were opened in an effort to combat the growing incidence of juvenile delinquency. Service Extension work grew rapidly and departments to direct operations were established. A program to ship clothing overseas to war refugees through Men's Social Service stores was instituted.

Pioneer work continued. Far to the north, the *William Booth*, a twin-diesel boat, launched in Alaskan waters in 1947 as a missionary craft, carried the message of salvation to those remote places where witchcraft still prevailed. Just before Christmas, 1947, Envoy Mary Peacock, a Georgian "sunk deeper in Christmas than a hog in a brier thicket," got a message that President Truman's daughter Margaret had received a request for Christmas aid from "some lady in Robertstown, Georgia" and wanted The Army to investigate. Mary Peacock took Christmas far up in the hills and soon was beloved through the Blue Ridge mountains of north Georgia. She won stern moonshiners to God. She took clothes to the sick, cooked meals, cleaned cabins. Once she cared for a newborn baby wrapped in a newspaper on a bench, while its parents lay dead drunk on the bed. She accompanied a hill boy to the electric chair. She started outposts "wherever her foot tracked." Mary Peacock now carries the Christ spirit to eleven Georgia counties.

Television was yet to be taken seriously by most Salvationists, but it was no uncommon occurrence to switch on a radio in even a fairly small town and hear a weekly Salvation Army broadcast. The programs usually followed the pattern of that used by Major Herbert Smith of Waterloo, Iowa:

"Good evening, radio friends. We count it a privilege to

come to you again from the Salvation Army citadel in Waterloo, Iowa. Through the facilities of Station KXEL we bring
you a program of song and music and a gospel message from
the eternal Word of God."

Prayer invariably played an important part in Army radio
projects, and many corps officers could tell similar stories to
that concerning the inception of the Waterloo program.

"This program needs your prayers," Herb Smith told his
soldiers, "and I believe if the Lord wants us to have it He will
send us enough money by the fifteenth of September to pay
for a full month's program in advance."

The money came—sent by total strangers. It amounted to
$153.00, three dollars more than were needed. He hurried down
to the radio station. "Hi, Major," said the manager. "Say, I
forgot to tell you that if the program is broadcast from your
building, it will cost three dollars more a month."

"Well, praise the Lord!" said Major Smith. "That's exactly how much He sent."

By 1949, many Americans were weary of crisis, they were
apprehensive and unsure of themselves. They longed for peace
of spirit but were growing distrustful of everyone, even of God.
Simple faith seemed a specter of the past. Possessions became
the rage. See the latest, buy the latest, get bored with the latest.

Salvation Army Men's Social Service centers (sleek new
name for industrial homes) were crowded again. Beneficiaries
were now called alcoholics, not drunkards, but they were as
drunk as ever. Some said the cause was disease, not sin, but
men and women were as ruined sick-drinking as sin-drinking.
Men's Social Service and skid row or Harbor Light programs
were enlarged.

Salvation Army corps, welfare, prison, and youth workers
now faced a hydraheaded monster of need: fathers who

Warner L. Sallman reproducing in pastels his head of Christ.

A

B

(A) *Contemporary kettle work;* (B) *Then Vice-President Lyndon B. Johnson greets Major Ernest Holz;* (C) *Jerome Hines, Metropolitan Opera star in the role of Christ in his original opera trilogy* I Am The Way; (D) *Mr. and Mrs. Meredith Willson with Commissioner Holland French and Colonel William Parkins.*

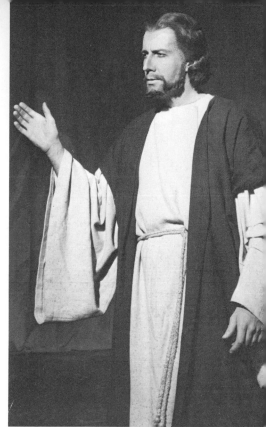

C

D

A

(A) *Salvationist greeted by young friend;* (B) *Scene at Salvation Army Day Nursery;* (C) *Baltimore, Maryland, day nursery.*

B

C

A

(A) *Orange, New Jersey, Bible day camp;* (B) *Chinese Corps work, San Francisco;* (C) *Beginner's music lesson, Western Territory;* (D) *Members of Wrangell, Alaska, Youth Corps.*

B

C

D

A

(A) *Booth Memorial Hospital, Flushing, New York;* (B) *Pittsburgh Golden Agers at Salvation Army club meeting;* (C) *Men's Social Service work, Atlanta, Georgia;* (D) *League of Mercy old age visitation;* (E) *League of Mercy hospital visitation.*

B

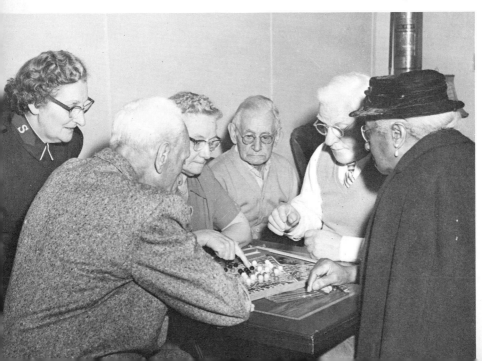

C

D

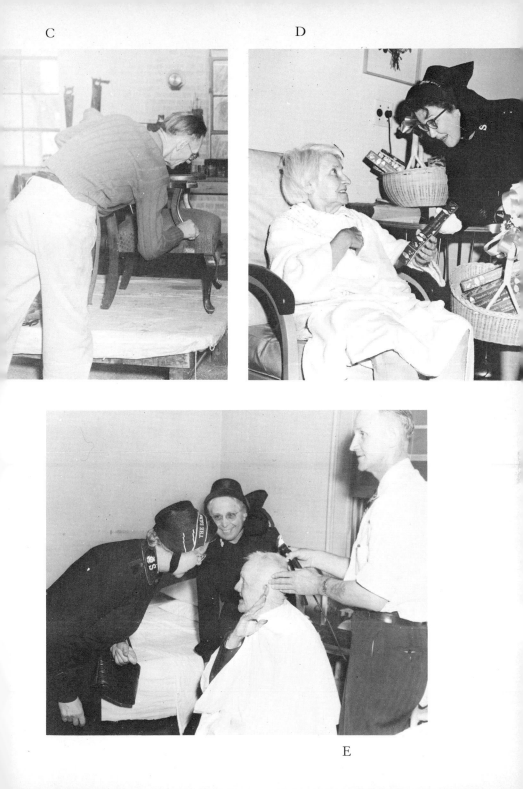

E

Varying modes of transporation and collection used by the Salvation Army, 1906–1964.

C

(A) *Special services to firemen;* (B) *Mobile canteen at scene of fire in Savannah, Georgia;* (C) *Emergency service.*

A

(A), (B), (C) *Emergency service at scene of Alaskan earthquake, 1964;* (D) *Salvation Army officer helping a Texas family in wake of hurricane Karla, 1961.*

B

D

C

A

(A) *Correctional services "Toy Lift" efforts;* (B) *Prize-winning Salvation Army Rose Bowl Float, 1965.*

B

couldn't settle down, couldn't forget war brutality; mothers who gave up the struggle in divorce, drink, psychosis, or degeneracy; distressed children who had no one to care enough about them, whose elders were too busy worrying about themselves; hospitalized veterans; golden-agers; unmarried, pregnant girls; rural distress in non-corps areas, disasters, and other emergencies. Americans developed neuroses like boils. *Cardiac* became the most used word. The need for expansion of services and changes in methods was, in many instances, crucial.

A new generation of fear—the feared and the fearing—stepped on the verdant American scene.

Chapter Twelve

1950 / 1965

FLEXIBILITY AND FIXED PURPOSE

A NEW era began for The Salvation Army in the 1950's. Although William Booth's spirit still directed his battalions, the immediate family had been reduced to Evangeline, Lucy, and Catherine. Now, more than ever before, every soldier *was* The Salvation Army. The name, the uniform, the symbol, evoked good will from the public. Everybody knew The Army. A man could trust The Army. For Salvationists, only a sense of divine purpose, of divine presence, made bearing the burden and responsibility of public trust possible. But the responsibility grew heavier, humanly speaking, as pioneers fell on the battlefield.

On her eightieth birthday, asked if she foresaw a better world, Eva replied, "We are already in a better world." She had never grown disheartened in her fight against evil, want, and despair. On July 7, 1950, Evangeline Cory Booth, 84 years old, laid down her sword. Besides Eva, many other Army leaders retired or were promoted to Glory.

Within 13 years, the rank of National Commander in the United States was held by Ernest Pugmire (1944–1953), Donald McMillan (1953–1957), Norman Marshall (1957–1963), and the present Commissioner Holland French, an articulate, aggressive commander who has challenged his troops. He has emphasized the selection and training of candidates for officer-

ship. During the Centenary year, he was the first Salvationist to address the men of Annapolis and the personnel assigned
to duty at the Pentagon.

The international command changed twice: Wilfred
Kitching (1954–1963), and the present General Frederick
Coutts, who has exhibited his eagerness to re-express Christianity in terms relevant to the modern world. This is evident in
his enthusiasm for clear, concise writing. He feels that drama
and modern music are effective tools for propagating the
gospel.

During the fifties and on into the sixties people in the
United States incessantly knocked on The Army's door and
jingled its phones. The times demanded frequent shifts in
emphasis and expansion of programs.

In 1960 a national report on The Army's major efforts
included these paragraphs:

"Certainly through the years our methods have changed,
but the motivation has remained the same. The old-type 'rescue
homes' for unmarried mothers have been replaced by modern
maternity homes and hospitals which help the girl to cope
with her problems and, at the same time, seek to educate society concerning the social maladjustments implicit in the
problem.

"The early-day 'Boozers' Parade' and 'Drunkard's Drama'
have no place in the up-to-date treatment which seeks to combat the toll of alcoholism.

"From The Army's primitive musical aggregations have
evolved a network of music camps,* institutes, bandmasters'
training courses, and well-trained bands which not only en-
hance Salvation Army worship services but also carry a spir-

---

* The four territories now have well organized music camp programs, and many divisions throughout the states also have encampments. In 1963, 5,679 young people attended 47 music encampments in
the United States.

244 / BORN TO BATTLE

itual message through the ministry of music to churches, hospitals, schools, and civic gatherings.

"Old methods of fund raising in rural areas have been supplanted by today's Service Extension program, with permanently functioning local committees which provide funds to administer health, welfare, and recreational services in communities where there is no regular established Army unit in operation.*

"The early limited youth program has given way to planned vacation Bible schools, released time religious education in co-operation with public schools, summer camps, youth leaders' training institutes, weekend conferences for teen-agers, boys' and girls' clubs, and community center programs.†

"In the place of the publicly presented Christmas basket there is today's Christmas check for the family, with the head of the household working out with a Salvationist adviser the manner in which it can be spent to bring maximum pleasure to all in the family.

"The Army has been able to develop this multi-faceted program because of the incredible flexibility and mobility of the organization in meeting need wherever it exists."

———

The new expanded programs required The Army to raise its standards of service and train leaders more effectively. The officers' training course was extended from one year to two of in-residence study plus a summer of preceptorial training in field work. The in-residence curriculum now includes training

———

* Today there are 6,523 Service Extension units in the United States and many more are planned for.

† At present there are 260 clubs with a membership of 55,444 and a total attendance for the year of 6,635,547.

in social welfare, community services and business administration, a practical field experience in adjacent corps and social
service institutions, orientation in all possible areas of Army
service and, of course, studies in spiritual ministry. Specialists
are encouraged to enter Army officership and opportunities are
given for advanced education after an officer is commissioned.

Another internal need which The Army met was the development of a literature and body of knowledge which enabled the organization to handle problems of many kinds more
effectively. Manuals of operation for every major field of service
performed by The Army were published. Officer-delegates
were appointed to many conventions and conferences of national bodies, and to commissions for self-study on evangelism,
religious education, and current national problems.

The Army continued to move into areas new to its personnel. Among the innovations of this period were the prison
"Toy Lift," the publication of *El Grito de Guerra,* a Spanish
language *War Cry* for Mexico, a women's magazine published
in braille, and the opening of Army work in Puerto Rico.

The "Toy Lift" was begun in the fifties by Captain Raymond Cameron, corps officer in Green Bay, Wisconsin. Cameron, with little but a sense of concern, devised the idea of taking sample toys to prisons for personal selection by inmates
for their children.

Salvation Army aid and cheer to inmates and their families were nothing new. But the Toy Lift was new—a personal
gift from prisoner to child. Salvationists now carry with them
Christmas decorations and a record player when they set up
shop inside "the gate." After selection is made from the sam-
ples, tags are written by the father or mother and stapled to
the original order. Inmates are given a carbon so they will have
something tangible to look at. Identification with The Army
is kept to a minimum. The task is a big one. For example, in
1964 the Wisconsin Division bought, wrapped, and mailed

1,796 toys to inmates' children from "Daddy" or "Mother." Many officials report that at no other time do they see their prisoners "so mellow and softhearted" as when The Army visits with Christmas toys.

The first braille edition of *Centralite,* a magazine for Home League women, was published to meet the need inherent in the fast-growing ministry to the blind. It was conceived as a natural extension of interest by Mrs. Commissioner Samuel Hepburn, the indomitable "Rose" of wartime Philadelphia.

One of the most active departments of The Army in the fifties, and even more so today, was the League of Mercy. Its ministry is one of small things: crepe paper blossoms, baby-food jars decorated and filled with bath salts, bars of soap tied in nylon net to look like fish, beanbag clowns for trays, gumdrop dogs and cats. Nevertheless, it's one of the most rewarding ministries in The Army as the following stories indicate.

About 10 o'clock one Christmas Eve in Natchez, Mississippi, Captain William Gratham was visited by an elderly man whose granddaughter was in the hospital, seriously ill, and not responding to treatment.

"But tonight," said the grandfather, "when the nurse brought her supper tray there was a little rag doll on it. Her eyes lit up and she ate her first real meal in weeks." The rag doll, with many others, had been made and distributed by the League of Mercy.

Work with the mentally disturbed is often extremely rewarding. In the wards of a state mental institution, League of Mercy women caroled at Christmastime. In one, the leader hesitated. "That poor woman over in the corner. She hasn't moved. Let's sing one more for her."

"You're wasting your time," said the attendant. "Others will listen and enjoy, but Greta's a vegetable. She hasn't spoken in 12 years."

"One more," the leader persisted.

To the music of a piano accordion the women sang "Silent Night."

"Quick! She's saying something." The attendant rushed over, and they bent down. In German, Greta was singing softly: "Silent night, holy night, All is calm, all is bright. . . ."

Although Disaster and Emergency service have always been part of Salvation Army ministry, only after World War II did special mobile facilities become a permanent part of its rolling ammunition, when wartime canteens were converted to peacetime use. Previously, cars and trucks of every make-shift variety had been employed. Now, every division* and most corps own a mobile canteen, ready at any time to be commanded by its corps and divisional officers and staffed by trained volunteers.

In addition, many Men's Social Service institutions have canteens and often augment them with their fleet of pickup trucks. For example, in Chicago at the Central institution two canteens are ready for dispatch 24 hours a day. As reports on a fire come in over short-wave radio, the canteens can reach the scene almost as soon as the fire trucks.

In times of drastic emergency, these canteens and trucks across the nation can be pooled, thus bringing dozens or hundreds of workers to a disaster area. This is an evident value of William Booth's determination to head a commanded army,

---

* A division consists of approximately 26 corps. There are 43 divisions in the United States.

not a commiserating committee. The help and generosity of laity, advisory board members, and other friends, have made it possible for The Salvation Army to function as an effective disaster service.

In 1955, when the northeastern states were hit by the worst floods in modern history, a large emergency food kitchen was rushed from New York City to Waterbury, Connecticut, where Lt. Colonel Roy Barber, working in conjunction with Civil Defense authorities, secured enough food to serve an average of 2,000 hot meals per day, plus light refreshments to relief crews at all times. Equipment and personnel were dispatched from southeastern to northern Pennsylvania, which was even harder hit. Thirty officers left camp meetings in Old Orchard, Maine, to assist at key points.

On Monday evening, December 21, 1964, CBS-TV broadcast a documentary program entitled, "Christmas in Appalachia," depicting incredible poverty in the southern mountains. Response by generous Americans was instant and almost overwhelming. Since the company had no facilities to handle contributions, officials turned to George S. Knight, member of the New York Salvation Army Advisory Board, for Salvation Army assistance, and The Army took over as distribution agent.

Major Andy Miller and CBS officials immediately went on closed circuit television to inform outlets across the nation of the plan. Offers of help coming to CBS switchboards were referred to The Army. Lt. Colonel Roy Barber, representing The Army nationally, flew to Appalachia to join forces with Brigadier Walter Swyers, divisional commander for the Kentucky-Tennessee Division. A Citizens' Co-ordinating Committee was organized, all Salvationist personnel were alerted, and by Christmas Eve, tons of "tangible Christmas joy" were distributed.

The Missing Persons Bureau is another service being conducted with increasing effectiveness. A worldwide tracing and locating service begun by William Booth in 1888, Missing Persons work is conducted from territorial centers and largely carried on through correspondence, advertisements in the *War Cry* and foreign language newspapers, and personal investigations.

Cases vary greatly. Husbands desert wives; and wives, husbands. Some people suffer a complete loss of memory. Some commit crimes. Disgraced girls are ashamed to go home. Some families simply lose track of one another. Of 3,715 requests for service in the United States in 1963, 1,395 people were located.

Radio efforts have been expanded and some television appearances have been made, although costs of production make the latter largely prohibitive. The generosity of network and local stations, both television and radio, account for most of the excellent "airings" of Salvation Army programs. However, three efforts became a significant part of the ministry in the fifties and have remained so.

In 1955 Salvationist Lloyd Docter of the Western Territory wrote the first script of "Heartbeat Theater," a radio program dramatizing The Army's present ministry. Listener response was so favorable that the program is now heard throughout the United States, Canada, and over 97 stations in the Armed Forces Overseas Radio system.

"The Living Word," a 15-minute television series, now in its ninth year of production, was conceived by Major Arnold Brown of Canada and begun in the States in 1957.

Another brainchild of Lloyd Docter was a transcribed Christmas program, "Army of Stars," featuring San Francisco

Opera Company artists. Begun in 1948, it was so popular that records have since been made annually. In 1964 the program was broadcast over 994 United States and 108 Canadian stations. The American Broadcasting Company's standby orchestra is used for recording sessions and the recording, a combination of Christmas, sacred, and operatic music punctuated by good wishes from The Army, is offered without charge to radio stations.

Artists have included Ezio Pinza, Kirsten Flagstad, Lily Pons, Jan Peerce, and members of the Azusa College Chorale. Host commentator for 1964 was actor Ronald Reagan. Announcing the 1964 release, William Pabst, General Manager of KYVU, San Francisco-Oakland station, said: "The programs are truly worthy of preferred programming."

During the late fifties and early sixties, Army youth councils and congresses, and both leadership and music camps attracted thousands of teen-agers. This increasing emphasis on youth fits William Booth's vision. On his eightieth birthday, he had said:

". . . It is in the clatter of young feet that we hear the tramp of the coming worlds. It is from the arsenals of the playground, the schoolroom, and the nursery, that we alone hope to replenish our resources and march our armies to contend for God and truth, when we ourselves are marshalled above."

Army youth were and still are eager for challenge. They want more discussion and more inclusion in adult warfare. Many, though by no means all, of these young people grew up in the ranks. They know the best of Salvationism and the worst. They are getting good educations, being thrust into a world of frenzied fun, bombs, modernism, declining morals, and spiritual apathy. They know that nothing but an aggressive presentation of an experiential gospel stated in contemporary terms can interest a fretting world. They try a variety of methods.

Not too long ago, Chicago teen-agers marched on skid row and Rush Street (night club district), where listeners clapped for more. Afterward an article appeared in the neighborhood variety paper, *Near North News:* "One of the best bands in the area is The Salvation Army group that works at Rush and Oak outside the BIG. The gals swing mean tambourines as the band blows like crazy. . . ."

The Western Territory inaugurated "Adventures for Christ," a program in which college Salvation Army students conduct Daily Vacation Bible School and recreation programs in northern Alaskan villages for children whose parents work almost around-the-clock in fish canneries.

In five Tennessee and Virginia mountain cities, open-air meetings were held by teen-agers, during which many people confessed spiritual needs and several decided to let God direct their lives.

Other young people decided upon *War Cry* distribution for their special ministry. For instance, two students in an Eastern college visited nearby taverns regularly on Saturday nights, selling the *War Cry* and conversing about God. On Sundays they visited those contacted on the night before. This ministry reached many troubled people.

Sometimes there were dramatic results. Five Salvationist college students got jobs in Atlantic City, New Jersey, and nightly, throughout the summer, conducted meetings on the boardwalk. A number of conversions resulted. One young man "with a Greenwich Village slant on life" listened condescendingly at first, but came back night after night. Finally, he approached cornetist Tom Gabrielsen, said, "Well I gave my heart to Jesus," and handed him a poem, "Beatnik Salvation," which read in part:

I was cruising the woodwork without any cares,
When my eyeballs latched on to some Psalm-singing squares;
I just hit this burg and didn't know a chick
So I stuck around and listened to their pitch.
It hit me kinda funny as I looked at them down there,
'Cause they were standing on a platform just like them—square.
Now listen to me, man, and listen to me good;
I never been a pusher, and I never been a hood.
I always thought that I was a pretty level cat,
But what they were putting out with made me feel like a rat.
The warrior cats should cut a record or two;
Imagine #1 on the Hit Parade, "Jesus loves you."
Then we all sang, and that included me,
"Rock of Ages," and "I come to Thee"
Then the redhead told how for me Jesus died;
Man, in 25 years, that's the first time I cried.
And there and then for all to see
I really let loose with my decree.
Tell Him you're with Him all the way;
That's all you gotta do, that's all you gotta say.
It doesn't matter who you be,
He even digs the likes of me.
Man, I'm gonna be saved, and man, I'm gladdio;
Man, He's got me—He's my Daddio!

This was one indication among many that The Army has a
ministry with "the new minority."

———————

The Army has always had a special interest in minority
groups which usually contain great numbers of needy people.
In the early days in the United States, The Army's evangelistic
ministry included work with Scandinavian, German, and Italian immigrants, and Negroes in the larger northern cities. The

latter, when not enlisted in large groups, were easiest to integrate. They seemed to exult in the lighthearted worship of Salvationists. In some places where there were large Negro communities, such as New York, Cleveland, and Washington, Negro corps were established during the pioneer days, and segregated because of locale. Integrated welfare, community center, club, camp, and institutional care have always been accepted in northern and western states although Chinese and Japanese work was segregated in California.

Scandanavians, Germans, and Italians were harder to integrate because they wanted exclusiveness and were separated by language and culture. Not until 1950 was Scandinavian work first combined with American work in some areas of this country, and the final amalgamation was accomplished in 1964.

The situation with the American Indian and the southern Negro has always been a complicated one, and although welfare and youth-serving activities have been, and are, virile, corps efforts so far have had little success. Research reveals that the need for qualified personnel to direct this ministry is the key requisite.

The Indian, traditionally independent and with a strong, ritualized faith of his own, did not easily submit to the rigid requirements of soldier and officership, although outstanding converts were made in some places. But the plight of the Indian is distressing and, through extended Service Unit programs, The Salvation Army has been able to bring some assistance to this group. However, much more is required in this area. As the Service Extension program develops, a more concerted effort is planned.

Initially, the southern Negro, still under restraints of a postwar era, and often committed with deep devotion to the religion of his former master, was not eager to bind himself to soldiership in a religious army in which strict adherence to

254 / BORN TO BATTLE

rules and regulations was required. Consequently, almost no
Negro leadership was developed over the years.

The Army has always had deep concerns about meeting
the particular needs of the Negro in the deep South, but its
ministry has been limited. It has few corps there and until
recently, welfare, community center, and children's club work
has been segregated. To defy existing laws would be to risk
the ruin of the entire program, affecting thousands of people
of all races. And although The Army defied the law in its fight
for free speech in the early days, at that time members could
harm no one but themselves.

After the Supreme Court decision on segregation in 1954,
The Army could and did move speedily forward. Community
centers and institutions have been integrated and Negro members have been added to a number of local boards. But problems do arise. For instance, wide press coverage was given to
the 1964 "Turkeys for Mississippi" incident when a group of
northerners headed by Dick Gregory raised the money for
20,000 Christmas turkeys to be given to the poor in Mississippi.
Offered to The Army for distribution, the gift was refused by
local Mississippi Advisory Board members. With the approval
of the National Commander, the southern territorial commander, Lt.-Commissioner Paul Carlson, issued this statement:
"The Salvation Army anywhere in my command will accept
gifts from anyone to alleviate suffering. We will meet the need
at the point of need without regard to race or creed." The
turkeys were then distributed by The Army in conformity
with its policy.

A relatively recent Spanish-speaking minority group, the
Puerto Ricans, have presented a new challenge to The Army,
mainly in the industrial cities of the North and Midwest. In
Chicago many attempts over the past years were made to reach
this group with a spiritual ministry. But little was accomplished
until Raul Guererro, a Salvationist tailor from Chile, began

personal visitation in homes. This was the beginning of an outstandingly successful work. It is interesting to note that although adults in the program continue to want services in Spanish, the children are thoroughly integrated into the corps.

What characterizes the salvation soldier of postwar years? Certainly, it is not similarity in social background or education. There have been soldiers like Tom Crocker, who had sunk to the depths before rehabilitation, and urbane brothers-in-arms like Frank Staiger, sergeant-major of the Port Huron, Michigan, corps for 20 years and outpost director for 32 years. Staiger was drafted as mayor when a nonpolitical person was needed "to steer the floundering city government to a safe port," city officials stated. It was usual for the mayor's constituency to see him rush home after work and reappear in Salvation Army uniform to lead a street meeting. Whatever his background, the most important requisite for soldiership is still a man's acceptance of his responsibility to serve God and his fellowmen.

Although it is common to hear, "I got my start in The Salvation Army" from musicians, athletes, ministers, and business and professional people, many were also won *to* Army service in this period. Some joined as soldiers, some as adherents, advisory board and auxiliary members, and many as regularly participating friends.

Josephine Bapst of Aurora, Illinois, was one who became a full-fledged member, commissioned in 1957 as Home League Secretary. When Jo's husband Harold, a surveyor, lay dying of cancer, she was struck by a newspaper ad which read: "If you are in need of counseling and prayer, call The Salvation Army. Phone 7-7265."

Distraught, she called and the Bapsts were visited regularly by Captain Alfred Muter. They both found spiritual peace and not long before Harold died, the Army flags were brought to their home so that they might be commissioned as soldiers in the usual manner. Neither had ever visited the Army hall or attended a meeting.

In San Pedro, California, the death of an Army convert with quite another background was considered copy by all local papers. The Long Beach *Independent* headed its feature story: "TAKE SIN STREET TO HEAVEN'S GATE."

"If anyone from Beacon Street ever goes to Heaven, they'll find Indian Mae there—ready to lend a helping hand. Beacon Street, avenue of ill repute throughout the ports of the world, opened its black heart and shed a few alcohol-flavored tears yesterday for Indian Mae, Salvation Army worker and ex-bar girl on this gaudy waterfront 'street of sin.' "

Five years before, Indian Mae had "traded the bottle for the bonnet," when she was told by a Salvationist in jail, "Jesus loves you." "Me?" Indian Mae repeated again and again. "Me?"

After her conversion she'd spent her time and every cent of her money helping her old buddies in every possible way and telling them that God loved them. Although she loved the Army fellowship, she continued to live on Beacon Street. "These are my people," she said. "They need me."

For her funeral, "the winos, the derelicts, and the drifters of the hard-bitten seven-block street of bars and pawnshops dug to the bottom of their pockets," according to the Los Angeles *Herald Express,* "to buy a casket, flowers, grave, and marker for their Mae."

Wreaths were numerous and their inscriptions bore such sentiments as "To Mae from Big Helen," and "From the girls in San Pedro Jail. We won't forget you, Mae." One was from the men of the police force. Among the pallbearers, "as tough-looking a crew as could be found on any waterfront," was Shanghai Red, a saloon owner who had often befriended Mae in the old days. The funeral procession wound slowly along

Beacon Street, where "tavernkeepers, barmaids, storekeepers, pawnbrokers, newsboys, and sailors stood in reverent silence."

In the sewing room of the jail, The Salvation Army placed a print of Warner Sallman's "Christ with Outstretched Hands," in honor of Mae.

———————

From widely diverse fields, friends of The Army contribute time and talent. Meredith Willson, well-known music composer, radio and television personality, became interested in The Army in the early fifties when he wrote the music for "Thou Bethlehem" an Army Christmas presentation played for many years over a coast-to-coast network. He was inspired to write a song about Salvationists while attending commissioning exercises for cadets of the San Francisco School for Officers' Training, and was especially impressed by the declaration of faith, which states, in part:

". . . Do you regard it as your duty to feed the hungry, clothe the naked, love the unlovable and befriend those who have no friends?"

The song, "Banners and Bonnets," set to an arrangement featuring cornets, flags, and the bass drum, is used in special Army festivals.

And it's not unusual for some individuals to find a special ministry on the Army battlefield. In 1951 Major Olive McKeown, New York Bowery corps commander (World War II doughnut girl of Hawaii service) was asked to speak about Army activities in Manhattan's Christ Church. She took a convert with her. In that service was a "poor" churchgoer, six-foot-six Metropolitan Opera basso, young Jerome Hines.

"This man stirred me," Jerry Hines said later, "and I vowed I would some day sing for The Salvation Army."

His promise was forgotten in the duties of a professional career, but when in London for a few days the following fall he heard an Army band; he remembered his promise and went to a Men's Social Service Center of The Army, asking, "May I sing for the men?"

He sang operatic airs but also "Onward, Christian Soldiers," in a way that made homeless, tormented men think maybe life was a battle, not a bottle, and maybe there was still a chance to win.

When Hines returned to New York he called Olive Mc-Keown and asked to sing. He has been singing for the men ever since. His petite Italian wife, Lucia Evangelistica, often sings too. Hines has presented scenes from his opera trilogy on the life of Christ at the Army's New York Temple.

"My God, as I know Him," Jerry Hines testifies, "led me to the Bowery and the men who have fallen so far they have no faith left."

———

One of the postwar problems for The Salvation Army and still very much a problem today is the difficulty of following William Booth's directive, "Go to the people." Commissioner Holland French is very much aware of this problem and has said: "We must reach more people. We must be careful not to become too rigid in our program or settled in some localities because of ever moving populations, urban developments, etc. We must continue to go where the people are who need us. We need a renaissance of home visitation to reach the heart of human need in the family and household setting.

"We need also to seriously study our ever-growing administrative set-up which demands more and more people doing more and more things with more and more paper for not many more people. Our study should lead into an efficient medium of reaching more people with the Gospel and Christian service at the *point of need*.

"We need to forget our traditionalism in the interest of

what is best for distressed, disheartened, discouraged, disinherited, disgruntled, disheveled people. We must be careful we do not draw away from the hearts of the lowly."

The basic unit of all Salvation Army warfare and the key to its federation of services is the corps. Under the direction of an officer who administers both religious and welfare activities, the corps is the center for a varied program which includes evangelistic campaigns, regular religious services, pastoral counseling, institutional and family visitation, character-building activities for youth, and such social welfare programs as are dictated by the needs of the community.

Today's corps officers are the persons who must face up to the problems cited by their National Commander—problems created by the extremely mobile modern era. Where great numbers of people had in the past been glad to enter Army buildings, fewer come to worship now. It has been increasingly difficult to attract a listening audience on busy street corners. What approach is best to reach these people of depressed urban areas, of varied ethnic and racial backgrounds, of varied needs?

The situation that Captain Robert Voeller met when, in 1958, he was appointed to the Milwaukee, Wisconsin, West corps shows one Salvationist's approach—in this case, a highly successful one. Captain Voeller found that the corps building, located in a district where there had been a large population shift, was small and run-down. Integration was a problem. What could he do to make The Army again an important part of the neighborhood? He visited homes, walked streets, and talked to everyone he met. He observed that children were getting into trouble because they had no suitable after-school activities, so he started daily craft classes. These became so successful that he had to limit periods to 45 minutes in order to accommodate everyone interested.

Today, there are 400 in the classes, clubs, and music groups, and Voeller has a thriving corps, particularly strong in its youth-serving program. Many young people who once caused trouble for the neighborhood police have become responsible leaders of their peers, both in school and at The Army, and some now intend to become Army officers. The police give credit to The Army but admit they don't know how the miracle came about.

According to Bob Voeller, the answer is God—and what he calls interested availability. This means he is on the job seven days a week, always approachable. Recently, school officials, with whom he works in a drop-out program, asked him to make himself unavailable in the mornings. "You see, our youngsters are coming to school late. Too many want to stop by and say good morning to the Captain."

Bob Voeller, like hundreds of other officers throughout the country, found that he got amazing results with children and teen-agers when he kept them purposefully busy, following William Booth's injunction: "Don't coddle them, mind! Put them to work."

Yet purposeful activity is not necessarily the answer in many areas, and The Army must continue to change and adapt its methods until the answer to fit the particular need is found. It will never abandon inner city warfare. It was begun as an urban fighting force against sin and suffering, and it will continue in this role.

One of the major areas today contributing to this whole urban problem is the growth of narcotics addiction. In New York City, especially, The Army is making successful inroads in some phases of combating it. The Army provides counseling, housing, employment, and arrangements for hospitalization when necessary, and when the request is voluntary. Through the Correctional Services of The Army, many women drug addicts and alcoholics learn of the organization's interest.

In the foreseeable future, The Army plans to open a residential treatment center for women drug addicts who will be assigned to its care by the court or other agencies, or who themselves volunteer for care directly to The Army. A property has been designated for this purpose in New York City.

The Army is also stepping up its program of service for alcoholic women, another major problem of the times. Much is being done, and has always been done, for alcoholic men by The Army, but there is at present no prescribed program for women. Their plight is tragic and their numbers swell alarmingly. Some find their way to corps and emergency centers, but the majority do most of their drinking at home and resist the idea of institutional care. Plans are in the making to set up personal, group, and family counseling, and group discussions with the emphasis on spiritual aid. And in the large cities, a combined institutional care-work opportunity program is being planned. Programs will be publicized more widely in Army and secular publications in order to more effectively reach the group at which they are aimed.

Another field of interest is education. This is not new, nor is it of foremost concern, as The Army is as yet limited in the number of qualified personnel to deal with the special types of problems that arise. But along with other welfare and church groups, The Army is moving into this area on a limited basis as the needs arise.

After-school classes in remedial reading are proving successful in some instances and there are plans for a Salvation Army Book Brigade which will tie into this program. There is also a program for the retarded, still in the developmental stage, which will be expanded in the future. An important part of this is the use of Salvation Army facilities—referral services and special activities and classes, including Sunday School classes. Sometimes it is felt wiser not to separate the mildly retarded but to include them in existing corps activities. Projected for the future are classes on retardation in the officers' training schools, a manual adapting already available material for special classes, and the establishment of a team skilled in the care of the retarded to be sent to areas where special problems along these lines exist.

Other programs in which The Army is already active, and which it hopes to augment and expand as effectively as possible, is work with the blind and handicapped, a variety of classes conducted at the Men's Social Service Centers, accredited elementary and high school programs now in operation in many homes and hospitals for unwed mothers, and released school time, a religious education service to unchurched children.

"The vitality and adaptability of The Army in the presence of new opportunities is one of the happy auguries for the future," Bramwell Booth once said prophetically. As needs change and services are broadened in scope and application, some may be dropped entirely. The Army position has never been that of peaceful coexistence in an overcrowded field but gradual withdrawal to another field of action toward which little or no attention is directed.

The Men's Social Service and Harbor Light Centers, for example, both aid homeless and alcoholic men, but they offer programs that do not duplicate each other. On the other hand Army medical clinics have all but disappeared in this country because governmental agencies, at all levels, meet this need. In another area, emergency and long-term family welfare were first administered in the United States almost exclusively by The Salvation Army. Gradually, a great number of voluntary agencies entered this field and in the past thirty years, governmental public aid has become the most dominant. There will not be a hurried de-emphasization in this area, but The Army is placing more emphasis on temporary care which includes "around-the-clock" emergency service. Disaster services are also being extended and more mobile canteens employed.

Another new projected service is the "Living Room," an adaptation of William Booth's "Reading Room," established in Christian Mission days for those who did not possess adequate homes or who were lonely and wanted companionship. "Living Rooms," located in corps centers or storefront rooms, will attempt to provide a homelike atmosphere where a person may read, watch television, play games, drink coffee, or talk to the Salvationist host. Evangeline Booth had proposed such home spots as part of her "big punch for prohibition," explaining that if the neighborhood saloon was eradicated, she wanted to replace it with a convivial place of relaxation where soft drinks could be served.

In the effort to interest and convict with new approaches, it is planned that secular locations such as rinks, halls, and theaters will be used more and more for meetings. Wider use of the informal discussion and the substitution of religion-centered drama for sermons may be tried to reach those people who are no longer attracted or challenged by formal worship. Radio and television (as budgets permit), timbrel brigades, choric speech and pantomime groups, already in use, will continue to be stressed. But, of course, open-air evangelism will continue to be of primary importance to all Salvationists. The "Church of the Street" must remain, for William Booth's open-air cathedral still is the best place to encounter mankind.

In 1964, General Coutts said in the *War Cry:*

"Every effort made by The Salvation Army is directed to helping a man work out the complete salvation of his entire personality through the power of God. I therefore ask our many friends not to attempt to divide our activities into "social" and "religious." These are false opposites. In effect, they are one—two sides of the same sheet of paper, two conjoined aspects of the one and indivisible work of grace."

There can never be any separation of the religious and welfare work of The Army, for if The Army should lose its spiritual emphasis, it would be destroyed. Although some local fund-raising groups have desired to do just this, separate the "religious" and "social," the unity of The Army's work is such that most groups of this kind support the total program without question. To the Salvationists, the only reason for the cup of cold water, the shelter, the clothes, the doughnuts, the counsel, is to glorify God and lead men closer to Him. To the often asked question, "How much of your work is religious and how much welfare?" the answer is and must always be, "It's 100 per cent religious."

During 1961, one Salvationist opened her door to a tall, lank young man, obviously ill at ease.

"You won't remember me," he said, "but I'm Sammy West. I used to live at the corner with my mother and sister."

She invited him in, remembering a broken home, a troubled mother, and lonely children who had played with her own. She learned he had dropped out of high school, joined a gang, and later had been sent to a correctional school.

"I heard you on the radio at Christmas," he said, "and remembered you from when I was a little kid. You see, there's this big void inside. I've got to find some meaning, some purpose, in life. I thought maybe you could help me. I thought maybe God is the answer."

For the Salvationist, God *is* the answer. And today, for the Sammy Wests of the United States and of the world, The Salvation Army is striving to meet the demand for effectively handling problems created and intensified by unsettled times. It is reviewing and revising old methods of attack and devising new ones. But its power for action still lies in old weapons:

prayer, faith, love, and hard work. And it is still eager to enlist both members and friends in practical concern for the needy.

William and Catherine Booth did not start their ministry as co-founders of The Salvation Army but as two people dedicated to God. The Army, they believed, was *His* Army. They marched on through deprivation, desertion, world conflicts, theological disputes, and materialism. They traveled light. Their gear was the Scriptures. Their banner was love. Their war cry was "the world for God!" They were scorned and ridiculed, battered and imprisoned, but they believed their troops would march around the world, singing, advancing, and triumphing.

In this period of swift social change, The Salvation Army may be battered about and it may make mistakes and sometimes falter, but it will continue to fight in the most practical way possible until William Booth's original plan for implementing the gospel becomes fact: "God hath made of one blood all nations of men for to dwell on all the face of the earth." (Acts 17:26)

Among American Salvationists there is hope of the kind their beloved Evangeline Booth had, who, in love with God and America, met onslaughts with imaginative daring. Confronted on one occasion with the criticism that she gave her soldiers too large an ideal, too difficult a task, with "flashing eye and emphatic tone" she exclaimed in words appropriate for today, "Can *anything* be too hard for Americans or too difficult for America?"

General William Booth had believed in America and had been concerned that the country be true "not only to her great traditions, but also to her momentous destiny." Then Evangeline concluded:

"O America, how vast is your opportunity for making a lasting mark for good on the entire human race! What will you do with this mighty, magic force? If you are permitted to realize your ambition to lead the world, whither will you lead it?

"Where else can you lead this poor blind, stumbling world of ours but to the mighty, just and holy God . . . to self-sacrificing service to mankind?

"I invite you to make our common Christianity an ungainsayable reality, and thus wipe out the reproach fast gathering over us, that it is nothing more than an exploded tradition, a fashionable association, or a lifeless ceremony. Then when a wondering world asks, 'In what country can I find the faith described in the Bible and set forth in the life of Jesus Christ?' the answer will be 'America!' "

Trumpets sound, troops line up, ammunition is readied. The Blood-and-Fire flag is raised.

Born to battle, The Salvation Army marches on.

TENETS OF DOCTRINE

1. We believe that the Scriptures of the Old and New Testaments were given by inspiration of God, and that they only constitute the Divine rule of Christian faith and practice.

2. We believe that there is only one God, who is infinitely perfect, the Creator, Preserver and Governor of all things, and who is the only proper object of religious worship.

3. We believe that there are Three Persons in the Godhead—the Father, the Son and the Holy Ghost—undivided in essence and co-equal in power and glory.

4. We believe that in the person of Jesus Christ the Divine and human natures are united, so that He is truly and properly God and truly and properly man.

5. We believe that our first parents were created in a state of innocency, but by their disobedience they lost their purity and happiness; and that in consequence of their fall, all men have become sinners, totally depraved, and as such are justly exposed to the wrath of God.

6. We believe that the Lord Jesus Christ has, by His suffering and death, made an atonement for the whole world, so that whosoever will may be saved.

7. We believe that repentance toward God, faith in our Lord Jesus Christ, and regeneration by the Holy Spirit are necessary to salvation.

8. We believe that we are justified by grace, through faith in our Lord Jesus Christ, and that he that believeth hath the witness in himself.

9. We believe that continuance in a state of salvation depends upon continued obedient faith in Christ.

10. We believe that it is the privilege of all believers to be "wholly sanctified," and that their "whole spirit and soul and body" may "be preserved blameless unto the coming of our Lord Jesus Christ" (I Thessalonians 5:23).

11. We believe in the immortality of the soul, in the resurrection of the body, in the general judgment at the end of the world, in the eternal happiness of the righteous and in the endless punishment of the wicked.

INDEX

SALLIE CHESHAM, a Salvation Army officer, is a staff member of the Central Territory Editorial Department, Chicago, and teacher of Salvation Army history at the Central Territory School for Officers' Training. She has written more than 250 feature articles, stories, booklets, brochures, plays and pageants, including *Creators All,* the Army's report to the 1960 President's White House Conference on Youth; *It Isn't So,* interpretive booklet concerning The Army; *Plus and Minus,* The Salvation Army's 1964 report on juvenile delinquency; and a centennial pageant with a cast of 200. Besides the United States, her writings have also been published in Britain, Canada, Finland, Holland, Sweden, Switzerland, and Africa. A third generation Salvationist, Sallie was born in Detroit, Michigan, and spent her childhood in Michigan, Ohio, and Florida, later studying journalism at Northwestern University. Her husband, Brigadier Howard Chesham, is head of the Central Territory Audit and Statistical Department, son David is a junior at Princeton University, and daughter Julie, a sophomore at Northwestern University.

PRINTED IN THE U.S.A.